IMPROBABLE WOMEN

Contemporary Issues in the Middle East
Mehran Kamrava and Carol Fadda-Conrey, *Series Advisers*

IMPROBABLE

FIVE WHO EXPLORED THE MIDDLE EAST

WOMEN

WILLIAM WOODS COTTERMAN

SYRACUSE UNIVERSITY PRESS

LIBRARY OF CONGRESS CATALOGING-IN-PUBLICATION DATA
Cotterman, William W.
Improbable women : five who explored the Middle East /
William Woods Cotterman. — First edition.
pages cm
Includes bibliographical references and index.
ISBN 978-0-8156-1023-6 (pbk. : alk. paper) 1. Women travelers—Middle East—
Biography. 2. Middle East—History—19th century. 3. Middle East—
History—20th century. 4. Zenobia, Queen of Palmyra. I. Title.
G490.C64 2013
915.604'1509252—dc23   2013025934

To my wife, Kennethe;

my daughters Elizabeth, Kennethe, and Dana;

my granddaughters Jennifer, Lauren, Sarah, Emily, Lily, and

Alena; and my great-granddaughters Harper, Alexa,

and Violet—improbable women all.

WILLIAM WOODS COTTERMAN, PhD, worked in many countries in the Middle East during the past fifty years and lived in the area for three years. First full-time chairman of the Computer Information Systems Department at Georgia State University, he wrote six books and a number of articles on information systems–related subjects. In 1973, he took a leave of absence to work in Kuwait on an input-output analysis of the economy that led eventually to the establishment of Kuwait's national accounts. Subsequent assignments in the Middle East came from the United States Information Agency, United Nations Development Programme, National Science Foundation, and American University in Beirut Services Corporation, in addition to private companies. President Carter appointed him to a Committee on White House Information Systems to analyze and make recommendations on the use of computers and information technology within the Executive Office of the president.

Bill lives in Norcross, Georgia, with his wife, Kennethe. He is now a professor and chair emeritus of computer information systems at Georgia State University. He continues to study Arabic and remains an ardent traveler: most recently as the only passenger on the motor vessel *Hanjin Boston* on a five-week voyage from Long Beach, California, to Korea, China, Taiwan, and back. In the course of the voyage they sailed through a typhoon in the East China Sea.

CONTENTS

PART FOUR

ISABEL ARUNDELL BURTON: 1831–1896

PART FIVE

GERTRUDE MARGARET LOWTHIAN BELL: 1868–1926

PART SIX

FREYA MADELINE STARK: 1893–1993

Maps and Figures

Maps

Figures

ACKNOWLEDGMENTS

Few are able to say that their book was written entirely on their own. I am not one of those. First, I must thank Syracuse University Press and its able staff, in particular Deanna H. McCay, Kelly Lynne Balenske, Fred Wellner, Mary Selden Evans, Kay Steinmetz, and Lisa Kuerbis, who were both kind and professional. I learned a great deal from each one of the anonymous readers who evaluated the manuscript. I learned also from Barbara Nichols; Carol Lee Lorenzo; Patricie Burgess; Gillian Cooper, Public Affairs, British Consulate-General Atlanta; Captain J. D. W. Husband, RN, Estate Office, Chevening Estate; Timothy Shroder, Burton Pynsent. Special thanks to the following libraries: Maidstone Public/Reference Library, Centre for Kentish Studies; Dr. Lesley Gordon, Special Collections, The Robinson Library, University of Newcastle upon Tyne; Dr. James G. Crow and Averil Robson, Department of Archaeology Library, University of Newcastle upon Tyne; The British Library; and Georgia State University Library, especially the Interlibrary Loan Department. For the maps, I am indebted to Jack Reed and Jai Singh, Department of Geosciences, Georgia State University. My thanks to Sir John Bell for his kind welcome to Rounton Grange and to Kennethe for help and support over many years.

INTRODUCTION

On October 8, 1973, the Israeli Inner Cabinet, in desperate moments of what Israelis now call the Yom Kippur War, decided to arm their nuclear weapons, and on October 9, the General Staff recommended taking "extreme measures" against the Arabs.[1] The war began with an attack by the Egyptians and the Syrians, a body blow that forced the Israelis into their first defensive war, a war that Arabs now call the October War. In Kuwait at the time, I was on assignment as an economist and assistant project manager for Thomas H. Miner & Associates, Inc., a Chicago consulting firm.

Though at least a thousand miles from the battles, tension was high in Kuwait. The night the war began, Thomas H. Miner's manager for the Arabian Gulf, his wife, and I had dinner in the rooftop restaurant of the Sheraton Hotel in Kuwait City, and afterward, late in the evening, we encountered military roadblocks at major intersections. Kuwait soon sent a brigade to participate in the war, but in retrospect it seems that Kuwait's greater concern may have been Iraq and its claim that Kuwait was an Iraqi province. The previous June, Iraq had launched an attack across the Kuwait border, killed one Kuwaiti, and withdrew. It did not require paranoia to imagine Iraq's using the cover of the October/Yom Kippur War to invade Kuwait again.

A month earlier, beginning our descent into Kuwait aboard an Air India 747, we found that the starlit expanse of desert we had expected was an ocean of black, illuminated at scattered points by blossoms of burning natural gas, then a wasted by-product of oil extraction:

eerie, writhing columns of flame. We stepped to the top of the mobile stairs at one in the morning to find a 97-degree temperature and air heavy with the mingled odors of jet fuel and burning gas.

In the months that followed, the war began, evacuation plans were made and then canceled, and we completed a survey of every business with four or more employees. Everyday events were initially strange and slowly became routine, while language overheard shifted from an undifferentiated flow of sound to a series of words, some understood.

Six months after landing in Kuwait, I boarded a 747 bound for Greece with a newly discovered set of interests: the Middle East, its history, its deserts, the Arabs, their culture and their language. Besides the oil wells and modern buildings of Kuwait City, I had found pastel sand dunes, nightingales (in Iran), mysterious *souqs* (markets or bazaars), mosques of gleaming marble, and a fascinating people that I had only begun to know.

During the next twenty-five years, I flew to the Middle East two or three times each year and lived there for almost three years. Somewhere along the way I became aware of extraordinary women travelers who had explored the Middle East in the nineteenth and twentieth centuries, times as unsettled as the present. These strong-willed women had no jets, no five-star hotels, and few embassies to get them out of scrapes; yet they would sail to the Middle East and think nothing of buying camels, hiring a cook and camel drivers, and setting off into the desert. Through the years I made a point of learning about these women, and threads of information began to weave themselves into the fabric of stories.

Many women had made the difficult journey to the Middle East in the nineteenth and early twentieth centuries, and after reading about them, I reduced the list to six that I found most compelling. They lived in times when women were deemed inferior to men in nearly all regards, when their roles were narrowly restricted to bearing children and raising families. These women defied the conventions of their day. Then I discovered that five of the women shared an intriguing connection.

These forceful ladies were fascinated by Zenobia of Palmyra, the legendary warrior queen who reigned and fought in Syria seventeen hundred years ago. Each of the five had made a pilgrimage to Palmyra and the ruins of her city-state in homage to Zenobia, perhaps in recognition of the mystery of their own spirits, so much like hers.

During the last eighteen years, I have traced this exclusive sorority of six (including Zenobia) in libraries in England and the United States. In hopes of understanding them on a more personal level, we traveled to their old haunts in England, Canada, France, and Andorra, and relied on my earlier travels to Italy, Turkey, Lebanon, Israel, Jordan, Egypt, Kuwait, Saudi Arabia, Iran, Greece, and India for at least some appreciation of their journeys. My wife and I visited birthplaces, homes, routes, and destinations that provided the backdrop to these women's adventures. As research and my previous and current travel carried me along the paths they had graced, my initial fascination evolved into admiration, awe, and finally affection.

ZENOBIA OF PALMYRA, 241–275?

Born in the Syrian Desert at the far eastern reaches of the Roman Empire, Zenobia came to power as the regent of Palmyra after her husband, the king, was murdered, leaving title to their son, a boy too young to rule. Cultured and educated, Zenobia spoke four languages, rode horses, hunted as well as any man, and employed a prominent philosopher as her adviser. Zenobia's husband had been loyal to Rome, but three years after his death she launched a military campaign that would wrest the eastern third of the Roman Empire from the control of the emperor. Emperor Aurelian eventually headed east to confront her and, in a series of bloody battles, pushed the queen and her forces back to Palmyra and captured her.

Defeat did not diminish her appeal as a paragon for other strong, adventurous women. Centuries after her death, her admirers braved dangers of the Syrian desert to experience the lingering glow of her spirit. Even today, her magnetism exerts its pull on travelers from every country.

LADY HESTER LUCY STANHOPE, 1776–1839

The first Western woman to seek out Zenobia's fabled city was Lady Hester Lucy Stanhope, who arrived in 1813 at the head of a colorful caravan that included a phalanx of bedouin chieftains and a long train of camels and horses bearing servants and supplies. Only a handful of Western men had ever risked the hazardous journey to Palmyra through a desert inhabited by warring tribes of bedouin, bandits, and animals both domesticated and wild. The Middle East was then part of the Ottoman Empire, governed for hundreds of years by sultans in Istanbul. The sultans discouraged incursions by infidels into their Muslim world and did little to keep order outside the major cities.

Hester was up to the challenge. Though she was the granddaughter of William Pitt the Elder and niece of Prime Minister William Pitt the Younger, she bore little resemblance to a conventional British lady. Today, her intellect, resolute will, and leadership skills might incline her toward a career in politics or the military; but in the early 1800s, with no opportunity to attain a position of power, she created an astonishing life outside the confines of her country and class. Her forty-year odyssey in the Middle East became the source of legend.

LADY JANE DIGBY EL MESRAB, 1807–1881

Jane Elizabeth Digby, a slender, ethereally beautiful noblewoman, was as fascinated with men as they were with her. After an early marriage ended in a scandalous divorce and cut her off forever from London society, Lady Jane moved to Europe, where she began an all-for-love odyssey that would carry her through three more husbands and at least six lovers including King Ludwig of Bavaria.

In 1853, at the age of forty-six, Jane moved to Syria. There she hired Abdul Medjuel El Mesrab and his tribe of bedouin to guide her to Palmyra. Medjuel promptly fell in love. Graciously, she took on the role of a bedouin wife in a union that scandalized both London and Damascus. An accomplished horsewoman and an expert shot, she charged into battle at her husband's side. Their marriage lasted until her death at age seventy-four.

Pretty and passionate, this woman whose love affairs were the basis for several romantic novels lived her life entirely on her own terms.

ISABEL ARUNDELL BURTON, 1831–1896

Isabel Arundell Burton was propelled to the Middle East by a great notion that had captured her imagination in adolescence, that was reinforced by a Romany fortune-teller's prediction, and that played out in a series of remarkable coincidences that shaped her life. At school she remarked, "I was enthusiastic about gypsies, Bedawin Arabs, and everything Eastern and mystic, and especially about a wild and lawless life."[2] Soon afterward, the Romany woman cast her horoscope and predicted that she would marry a man named Burton (coincidentally the name of the woman was Hagar Burton). When she was twenty, she came face to face with the object of her dreams and whispered to her sister as he walked past, "That man will marry me."[3]

"That man" was Richard Francis Burton, adventurer, explorer, linguist, and writer. She dedicated herself to her erratic genius husband, acting as his secretary, business manager, agent, and apologist. In 1867, she was finally able to secure for him the post they wanted most: consul to Damascus. In those twilight years of Ottoman rule, the Syrian desert was more dangerous than ever, but nothing could keep her from setting off with Richard to see Zenobia's city. After his death, she fought to ensure his place in history.

GERTRUDE MARGARET LOWTHIAN BELL, 1868–1926

Born to great wealth, Gertrude Bell was among the few young women of her day to graduate from Oxford University. After finishing with honors, she visited Teheran, where her uncle served as British ambassador to Persia, and immediately fell in love with the East. During the next several years she circled the globe twice and became a celebrated mountaineer. In 1899, she made her way to Syria and the ruins of Palmyra.

Political and social unrest were rife in the decaying Ottoman Empire but Gertrude became proficient at confounding authorities who tried to restrict her movements. She searched the deserts of Syria and Mesopotamia for ancient ruins, conducted archaeological surveys, drew maps, took photographs, and moved so easily among the sheikhs that they called her "daughter of the desert."[4] When World War I broke out, she was recruited into British Intelligence, becoming Oriental Secretary to the British High Commission in Mesopotamia. In 1921, she drew the lines on the map that became the boundaries of Iraq and then drafted its constitution.

DAME FREYA MADELINE STARK, 1893–1993

On her ninth birthday, Freya Stark received a copy of *The Arabian Nights*. Those fabulous tales of the strange and wondrous kindled a flame of enthusiasm for the Arab world that would blaze for more than ninety years. The child of a divorced mother who lived modestly, Freya suffered a serious accident at thirteen when skin and hair were torn away from the right side of her head, leaving her with a long recuperation and scars she would conceal with her signature hats throughout her life. Not until she was thirty-four did a small inheritance finally free her to travel, and she headed to Syria, the first of many journeys to the Middle East.

Freya began her Eastern travels after World War I, when the English and French were still carving their territories from the defeated Ottoman Empire. Political tensions ran high. She charmed her way past officious territorial governors and hostile tribal chiefs to visit remote, forbidding areas: the places that interested her most. Fighting off frequent illness, she wrote travel articles and books to pay her way.

When World War II began, she served Britain as a member of the Foreign Service, serving with such distinction that she was knighted.

IN THE YEARS between Hester Stanhope's first trip to Syria in 1813 and Freya Stark's final journey to Turkey in 1977, important political, social, and cultural changes occurred that would fuel the fires of today's Middle Eastern conflicts. The adventures of each woman illuminate different periods and aspects of the complex history of the area.

What motivated these women to leave comfortable lives for the hardships and danger of inhospitable lands, and what was it in their characters that allowed them to do so, ignoring the roles that gender had allotted them? At least part of the answer lies in a romantic mystique associated with the Middle East in the minds of Westerners during the nineteenth and early twentieth centuries when little was known about those lands. We will examine that mystique.

———•◦•———

Depending upon whether you read English or American sources, the geopolitical term "Middle East" was coined either by U.S. naval historian Alfred T. Mahan in an 1894 letter or by British intelligence officer General Sir Thomas Gordon in a 1900 article, "The Problem of the Middle East." Perhaps it was in use verbally even earlier among the handful of policymakers who were beginning to recognize the strategic importance of the area in southwestern Asia and northeastern Africa that lay between the Near East and the Far East: thus, the Middle East. Even today, there is some disagreement about which countries are included. Commonly, the blanket term "Middle East" covers the Asian countries of Bahrain, Cyprus, Iran, Iraq, Israel, Jordan, Kuwait, Lebanon, Oman, Qatar, Saudi Arabia, Syria, Turkey, the United Arab Emirates, and Yemen plus the North African country of Egypt. Culturally, one might include the Muslim countries of Algeria, Tunisia, Morocco, Libya, Sudan, Afghanistan, and Pakistan.

Parts two through six of this book each begin with a "World" chapter. My objective in these introductory chapters is to give you an idea of the historical and social context in which each woman lived her life. The chapters are not intended to describe events that are directly connected to the subject's lives. Rather, the World chapters try to provide this context with vignettes: short pieces that I hope will enhance your appreciation of each woman's story. The process is cumulative in that each World chapter provides background not only for the woman named, but also for those who will follow. The first chapter in part two takes on the admittedly hopeless task of providing a rickety bridge over the 1,500 years that separate Queen Zenobia from Lady Hester Lucy Stanhope. Even so, the events included provide background to Lady Hester's life and to the lives of the other women. The beginning of Islam, the Crusades, the beginning of the Ottoman Empire, and trade between East and West help one to appreciate the setting of Hester's great adventure, while the French Revolution, Napoleon's expedition to Egypt, and the British Empire provide background to the first segment of her life in England.

It is probably no surprise that the English spelling of Arabic words presents a problem. Because they are in different alphabets, there are no exact transliterations from Arabic to English. Some spellings are more accepted in the West than others, and I have attempted in this book to stick with those. When T. E. Lawrence wrote *Seven Pillars of Wisdom*, he deliberately varied the spellings throughout the book just to annoy his editor. In deference to readers as well as editors, I have tried to be consistent.

Map 1. Western Europe. Courtesy of Georgia State University–Geospatial Laboratories.

Map 2. Eastern Europe. Courtesy of Georgia State University–Geospatial
Laboratories.

Map 3. Middle East. Courtesy of Georgia State University–Geospatial
Laboratories.

PART ONE

AUGUSTA ZENOBIA
241–275(?)

Zenobia is perhaps the only female whose superior genius broke through the servile indolence imposed on her sex by the climate and manners of Asia.

> —EDWARD GIBBON, *The Decline and Fall of the Roman Empire*

Figure 1. Herbert G. Schmalz, Britain, 1856–1935. *Zenobia's Last Look on Palmyra*. 1888, London. Oil on canvas, 183.4 x 153.6 cm. South Australian Government Grant 1890. Reproduced with permission from the Art Gallery of South Australia, Adelaide.

1

THAT WOMAN IN PALMYRA

Zenobia! Zenobia! Zenobia!" Her name throbbed through the city.

Astride her white Nubian mare, she stared into the distance far beyond pounding war drums and the crowd chanting her name. Tendrils of smoke rose from temples where priests and priestesses sent incense into the early light of dawn, petitioning for her victory and safe return, a momentous day for Palmyra, the day Zenobia would march to meet her destiny.

At her side under the Triumphal Arch, generals reined restless warhorses, their ceremonial armor glistening in the sun's first rays. Behind them a phalanx of Palmyra's famed archers, the finest in the world, awaited her command. At last Zenobia shouted the signal to advance in a voice that would call to future generations.

Trumpets blared as she paraded her honor guard down the colonnade, cheered at every step by tens of thousands who had come to see their young warrior queen. Resplendent in polished armor and a golden helmet, a purple fillet with gems hanging along the lower edge, and a large shell-shaped jewel, a cochlis, positioned above her brow, Zenobia seemed indomitable.[1] She was a beautiful and radiant woman; the world had not seen such a queen for centuries.

At the Damascus gate, legions of archers, cavalrymen, and infantrymen fell in behind, following her into the silent desert in columns that stretched for miles, every man equipped, trained, and ready. In their wake came camels and donkey wagons bearing weapons and supplies, the most important caravan ever to leave Palmyra.

3

DESERT PEOPLES have been traders for millennia, middlemen specializing in the movement and exchange of goods. They coalesced into villages and towns at critical points on caravan routes, at road intersections and near wells or springs, servicing the caravans and providing for the exchange and transshipment of goods. Some caravan masters traveled back and forth from Palmyra to Mediterranean ports, picking up and delivering goods to ships from Greece, Rome, and lands to the west. Others plied the routes south to Damascus or eastward toward riverfront docks along the mighty Euphrates where barges unloaded cargoes of foodstuffs from the fertile lands it watered.

A large caravan might have a thousand animals bearing the burdens of trade between East and West, with sturdy white donkeys from Palestine loaded with supplies and heavier loads piled on one-humped dromedaries of Arabia. Silk from China, cotton from India, precious stones from Ceylon and Burma, pearls from Mesopotamia and Bahrain, incense and myrrh from Arabia Felix, copper, gold, silver, ivory, scents, cosmetics, spices, rare woods, wild creatures, eunuchs, and slaves were borne one plodding step after another over hundreds of miles of desert. In Zenobia's era, the destination for much of this commerce was Rome, the heart of the Roman Empire, where citizens had an insatiable appetite for the best the world had to offer.

Records show that a town has existed at Palmyra from the second millennium BCE and perhaps thousands of years earlier. The Arameans, a Semitic people who settled in Syria, are credited with building the village of Tadmor and giving it the Aramaic language. (There is general agreement that Aramaic was the language spoken by Jesus; it was still spoken in Zenobia's day and is spoken in the Syrian villages Ma'loula, Bakh'a, and Jubb'adin today.) Its reliable water supply and strategic location made Tadmor (Palmyra) a popular stopover, and it grew into the largest caravan center of its time with many of the features of a seaport: shops, warehouses, banks, currency exchanges, scribes, translators, physicians, food stalls, taverns, bakeries, butchers, and brothels. Palmyra's columns are Corinthian, like those in the Roman Forum, with rows of acanthus leaves at the top once covered with bronze. The statues were painted, as were the homes of well-to-do citizens. After a long trek through the desert, hearts of caravanners must have lifted at the sight of glistening white marble columns topped with bronze and brilliantly colored statues and buildings waiting at the end of their journey. The paint faded over the ages, leaving the ruins in the monochromatic beige and off-white tones we see today.

In Aramaic, "Tadmor" means date palm, an acknowledgment of the half-million date-bearing trees that once surrounded the springs. After Alexander the Great conquered Syria, the city came to be known as Palmyra, the city of palms.

Palmyrenes prospered by catering to the commercial, physical, and spiritual needs of those who passed through their city's gates, and Palmyra was at the peak of its wealth and prestige when Zenobia reigned at the side of her husband, King Odenath, in the latter half of the third century CE. Today's ruins barely hint at the grandeur of Zenobia's city of some 200,000 souls.

She left her mark on history, but we know little about her early years except that she was born about 241 CE. Her name was Bat Zabbai in Aramaic, al Zabba in Arabic, while Zenobia was the name used by Latin and Greek writers. Zenobia claimed that she was descended from Cleopatra's family, the Ptolemys, the great Greek dynasty that ruled Egypt.[2] Possibly her mother was a Ptolemy, but other historians believe that Zenobia's ancestors were Nabatean Arabs, the tribe that built the great cities of Petra in Jordan and Medain Saleh in the Kingdom of Saudi Arabia.[3]

Trebillius Pollio claimed in the chronicles of the Roman emperors, *Historia Augusta*, that she was not a native of Palmyra, but other historians believe that she was the daughter of the Palmyrene general Julius Aurelius Zenobios. Having a general for a father would explain her mastery of the arts of war. He and his soldiers would have taught their eager pupil to ride as well as any man and far better than most; few could best her in a foot race, and her skill with bow and arrow would have qualified for the first rank among his archers, the most acclaimed in the world. General Zenobios must have been an enlightened man, surely demanding, but taking pride in his daughter.

She enjoyed accompanying him on his military campaigns, a common practice in a day when campaigns took months or even years. Families straggled behind the army with the prostitutes, laborers, merchants, and other camp followers, but Zenobia's father would have brought her to the head of the column where she could absorb lessons of strategy, logistics, and the command of men.

Zenobia's beauty matched her athletic prowess. Pollio tells us, "Her face was dark and of a swarthy hue, her eyes were black and powerful beyond the usual wont, her spirit divinely great, and her beauty incredible. So white were her teeth that many thought she had pearls in place of teeth. Her voice was clear and like that of a man."[4]

Her parents hired the most accomplished teachers of history and philosophy to challenge her keen intellect. In addition to Aramaic, her native language, she learned Arabic, Latin, and Greek. From storytellers and teachers, she heard tales of women who had risen to power in the ancient world. Cleopatra was of course her favorite heroine. Semiramis, the legendary queen of Babylon, who conquered neighboring states after allegedly killing her husband, King Ninos, intrigued her as well. That most of Semiramis's story is probably an invention of Greek historians would not have made it less exciting to young Zenobia. She also wondered at stories of Tomyris, said to be responsible for the death of Cyrus the Great and of Artemisia, who took over when her husband, a Greek king, died in 500 BCE, and who then led her navy against her husband's country. Then there was Boudica, queen of the Iceni in Britain in 60 CE, just two centuries before Zenobia's time, and an especially fascinating study as Boudica had led the Iceni and other tribes in revolt against the occupying Romans. The Romans had refused to honor a treaty they had reached with Boudica's husband before his death and had flogged her and raped her daughters for her effrontery in trying to continue to rule: a serious miscalculation. Before the Romans suppressed the revolt, she burned three major Roman towns, Londinium (London), Verulamium (St. Albans), and Camulodunum (Colchester). These initial victories must have left a lasting impression on young Zenobia's mind: The Romans could be challenged—and by a woman.

When she reached the age of fifteen, it was time for marriage. Odenathus, the king of Palmyra and perhaps a friend of her father's, made her his second wife in a ceremony celebrated throughout all of Roman Syria with days of feasts and dancing. In 198 CE, his grandfather, Odenathus I, had helped Emperor Septimius Severus beat back the Parthians, capture their capital, and send an enormous trove of treasure back to Rome. To show his gratitude for loyal service, Septimius Severus declared Palmyra a Roman colony and rewarded Odenathus I with full Roman citizenship, bestowing on him the honor of appending the imperial name to his own, making him Septimius Odenathus. Zenobia's husband inherited the aristocratic name and status it conveyed. Upon their marriage, she became Septimia Zenobia.

Zenobia took pleasure in the company of her husband, galloping at his side as he drilled the troops on desert maneuvers. She delighted in long hunts in forests near Emesa (now Homs), the caravan city eighty miles west of Palmyra. There they enjoyed cool summer air, sparkling streams filled with fish, and an abundance of lions and leopards to chase down for sport. According to Pollio, Zenobia was a more daring hunter than her husband, and legend holds that she saved Odenathus from a tiger by hurling her spear into the beast's heart as it leaped straight at him.

Less to her liking was the marriage bed. She was described as very chaste, engaging in intercourse for the purpose of conception only. She would receive Odenathus once a month, and then wait to see whether she was pregnant. If not, she would allow him a single return engagement the following month. Despite these restrictions, she managed to present her husband with two sons: Timolaus, who may have died in childhood, and Vaballath, whose name means "gift of Allath," the Arab goddess of wisdom. Herodianus, a son of Odenathus, was her stepson.

In 268, Odenathus took Herodianus and a cousin, Maeonius, to Emesa on a hunting trip. During the hunt, Maeonius offended Odenathus by hurling both the first and second spears, a privilege reserved for the king. Odenathus reacted, perhaps too quickly, by having him confined for a short time. At a birthday celebration not long after, Maeonius and his friends assassinated both Odenathus and Herodianus. Maeonius was found dead after the fray, and suspicion remains that Zenobia arranged the murder of her husband and his heir in order to position Vaballath as inheritor of the throne, but there is no solid evidence either way.

Since Vaballath was too young to rule, Zenobia appealed to Emperor Gallienus, Valerian's son and successor, to recognize Vaballath as king of Palmyra and herself as his regent. Gallienus granted her request, but soon afterward Roman commanders murdered this unpopular emperor. In March 268, Marcus Aurelius Claudius was named emperor by the generals. One of his first acts in office was to set aside Gallienus's decree authorizing Vaballath and his mother to rule Palmyra. Claudius's other swift decision was to name the rough-hewn soldier Aurelian as commander in chief of the armies of Rome. Zenobia must have reacted with shock at the news that Rome no longer considered Vaballath the boy-king of Palmyra, but it was Aurelian's appointment that was to have more serious consequences for her in the long run.

With Odenathus's fortune at her disposal, she lived in a sumptuous palace with columned porticoes, colorful mosaic floors, and frescoed walls, its lush gardens filled with bubbling marble fountains. Like Cleopatra, Zenobia luxuriated in dazzling gems, tableware of purest gold, magnificent carpets of fine wool, and garments of lustrous Chinese silk. She wore fragrances blended in the city's famed perfumeries from exotic flower essences imported from the East. Ornately decorated saddles and armor were fashioned to her exact measurements by Palmyrene craftsmen in workshops near the Damascus Gate.

She assembled a salon of scholars and intellectuals, among them the renowned Platonic philosopher Longinus, who came from

Athens and remained at her court for the rest of his life. He tutored Vaballath and assisted Zenobia in her studies of Roman and Greek authors. She is said to have written a history of Egypt, perhaps with Longinus's guidance, but the manuscript has never been found.

Amid the luxury, wars and rumors of wars filled the days of Zenobia's life. Rome had fought off Parthian incursions successfully for decades, and Palmyra was a staging point for their expeditions, with Palmyrene troops fighting alongside Roman legions. While chroniclers of the time left much to the imagination concerning personal lives, they scrupulously described battles and political affairs. We know that during the third century, the once-invincible Roman Empire was disintegrating rapidly, and legionnaires were creating emperors at will.

The Pax Romana, two hundred years of peace, had been maintained through an aggressive policy that demanded large and costly armies on every frontier. Italy had for years imported more than it had exported and its once-prosperous economy was collapsing. Though there were threats on all sides, this eastern portion of the empire was still relatively secure. Well-guarded caravans continued plying the trade routes without pause.

WITHIN THREE YEARS of Odenathus's death, Zenobia led her troops out through the Damascus Gate. She had decided to reclaim the power she believed Claudius had stolen from her and to expand her territory into the empire's domain. First on her list was Antioch, a city twice as large as Palmyra with half a million people—not counting women, children, or slaves. As the Palmyrenes rode north through the desert, fighters from surrounding villages joined their ranks until the force totaled almost seventy thousand. The young queen dismounted frequently to march along with her foot soldiers in full armor, reinforcing the admiration and fealty of the men.

The city fell without putting up great resistance, indicating that Zenobia had significant support for her cause among the Antiochians. The people of Rome were infuriated when she installed herself and her troops in this splendid city, and their ire grew to explosive dimensions when she ordered the Antioch mints to issue coinage with her picture on one side and Vaballath's on the other. This unforgivable defiance of the emperor caused mobs to demonstrate against her in the streets of Rome.

Two empires watched with a shiver of anticipation. Emperor Claudius and General Aurelian decided that other enemies of Rome were the higher priority. Aurelian turned away from the threat of Zenobia with some regret, but he had another woman to deal with first. Earlier, the Roman provinces of Gaul, Britain, and Hispania had taken advantage of a gap in leadership to break away from the empire and set up their own independent realm known as the Gallic Empire. Gallienus had been unable to quell the rebellion, which was then left to Claudius and Aurelian to resolve. The so-called Gallic emperor, Victorinus, had ruled for only a short time. A young man and a notorious womanizer, he was murdered by jealous husbands. His mother, Victoria, assumed power, with the treasury needed to maintain control. She appointed the next two puppet emperors, whom she ruled from behind the scenes, going so far as to assume the imperial title of Augusta and to have coins minted in her own name. Worse, she dubbed herself "Mother of the Camps," a title reserved for Roman empresses.[5]

Earlier, on news of the death of Odenathus, Aurelian had been quoted as saying that if he had his way, he would quickly bring "that woman in Palmyra" to heel.[6] Now that he was moving against Victoria first, one suspects that Zenobia was still on his mind.

When spies informed Zenobia that Aurelian was marching in the opposite direction, she knew she had time to stake a larger claim on Roman territory. Taking Antioch had made her more confident that she could advance through the Eastern Empire without encountering strong resistance. She decided to expand her domain to the south and immediately sent her general Zabdas with a legion of Palmyrene troops to attack Lower Egypt, the northern half of the country along the Mediterranean coast. Great trade advantages would accrue to Palmyra if they could take the Nile Delta and the port city of Alexandria, the Roman capital of Egypt. It was a risky move, as Rome depended on grain supplies from Egypt and Zenobia knew that the emperor would retaliate. Was she obsessed with following in Cleopatra's footsteps? Or was she motivated by economic considerations, willing to take the risks involved in order to expand business opportunities for Palmyra's powerful merchants and thus ensure their loyalty to her?

Zabdas quickly won a decisive victory. Egyptian coins were struck in the name of Zenobia and Vaballath to indicate their rule over the country. Before marching back to Zenobia's side in Antioch, Zabdas established a garrison of five thousand men to maintain control over Egypt, a reasonable number considering that North Africa from Egypt to the Atlantic was policed by a single legion of Romans, about six thousand men. Claudius, however, would not surrender Egypt without a fight. He sent more forces, and by the end of 271 the Palmyrenes were routed.

During the Egyptian campaign, a shift took place in the empire that would soon threaten Zenobia's ambitions. After a reign of only twenty-eight months, Claudius died of the plague and Aurelian was declared emperor. Lucius Domitius Aurelianus, born to peasant parents in Illyria in the northwest Balkan Peninsula, had risen through the ranks to become general in the Danube army of the Roman Empire. His exploits gained him such favorable public attention that Gallienus, the emperor prior to Claudius, had recommended him as his successor. And now Aurelian's time had come. He would prove to be a formidable foe for Zenobia.

With Antioch as her base, Zenobia launched a campaign to the north. She goaded her troops to move quickly through the Cilician Gates, a treacherous pass over six-thousand-foot mountains that formed the boundary between Syria and Asia Minor (Turkey). Again facing sparse resistance, she gained control of Asia Minor as far north as what is now Ankara, and at that point she controlled approximately the eastern third of the Roman Empire. Having come this far, one more important goal lay within her grasp, which perhaps was her long-range objective from the start: the Hellespont, the straits between the Bosporus and the Sea of Marmara that separate the continents of Asia and Europe. Controlling the strait's narrowest passage near present-day Istanbul would give Zenobia extraordinary advantages. She would be able to tax vessels that passed through the shipping lanes and keep her troops supplied by trading for provisions with ship captains. The surrounding hills offered armies the perfect place to defend their position. She knew that Aurelian would attempt to reclaim Rome's eastern territories soon, but if she could command that strategic location, she might stop him in his tracks and solidify her victory over all of Roman Asia.

Aurelian must have been on her mind constantly, and she was well aware that he knew of her every move. It was only a matter of time before he came after her. But time might work to her advantage. With her mounted archers and fast-moving cavalry, she might be able to secure the Hellespont before Aurelian arrived, as his large number of foot soldiers meant his progress would be slow.

Believing that the prize was worth the gamble, she marched her troops past Ankara toward the city of Nicaea near the Sea of Marmara only to discover that the city's walls, recently fortified by the Romans, were too strong for her forces to overcome without a lengthy campaign. Her spies brought her news that Aurelian had finally suppressed the uprisings on the northern frontier and had turned his forces eastward. Time had run out. She was forced to retrace her path to Antioch where she believed she could turn him back.

Aurelian marched unopposed until he reached the city of Tyana in southeast Turkey, the last city before the Cilician Gates. There he would reprovision from the city's store of food, as the surrounding countryside had been scoured by the two passages of the Palmyrene army. The gates of Tyana were closed and armed men stood on the walls, their arrows and spears aimed at Aurelian's troops. The governor informed Aurelian that Zenobia had ordered him to refuse supplies to the Romans or allow them entry to the city. The infuriated Aurelian swore, "In this town, I will not leave even a dog alive." Knowing the emperor's reputation for brutality, the inhabitants had ample reason to worry.

After a short siege, the city was betrayed by one of its citizens, and Aurelian marched in. In an uncharacteristic act of clemency, Aurelian decided not to slaughter the population, but fulfilled his pledge by killing all of the dogs along with Heraclammon, the man who had betrayed the city. Aurelian's leniency left Tyana loyal to him, and he soon marched out in pursuit of Zenobia. He led his army through the Cilician Gates toward Antioch, where he hoped to finally put that irritating woman in her place.

Zenobia arrayed her army in front of Antioch. Zosimus tells us that Aurelian soon realized that the Palmyrene cavalry surpassed his own in horsemanship, but they were encumbered with heavy armor. The wily commander set his cavalry on the far side of the Orontes River, ordering them not to engage the fresh Palmyrene cavalry immediately, but to take their charge and pretend to flee until they saw that the pursuers were abandoning the chase, exhausted by the midsummer heat and the weight of their heavy armor. The strategy worked. As the Palmyrenes tired, Roman troops wheeled their horses and charged, trampling Palmyrenes as they fell from their mounts. The survivors fled to Antioch.

Zenobia rallied her troops and stood again at Antioch but lost. She tried at Emesa and lost again. She escaped and led those who survived to Palmyra, eighty miles away, with Aurelian at her heels. Brigands of the Syrian desert, loyal to Palmyra, beset Aurelian's forces, inflicting heavy casualties, and the delay gave Zenobia time to have Palmyra's outer walls reinforced. In a last-ditch attempt to keep their city safe, frantic citizens pulled granite blocks from their buildings and dragged them to the wall where engineers worked them into the fortifications.

Aurelian arrived and laid siege, although Pat Southern in *Empress Zenobia: Palmyra's Rebel Queen* suggests that the action may have been more of a blockade than a siege.[7] As the assault went on day after day, the situation in Palmyra became increasingly bleak; the city's strong walls held against Roman battering rams, and the people made a valiant effort to hold off their attackers, climbing ladders to throw boiling oil into the faces of Roman soldiers, shooting arrows, and launching stones over the walls. Aurelian urged the Palmyrenes to lay down their arms, but they fought on. He was receiving shipments of food and supplies from cities he'd retaken on his way through Syria, but he prevented caravans from entering the city. When defectors from Palmyra informed him that conditions within the walls were desperate, he sent a letter to Zenobia demanding her surrender.[8]

> From Aurelian Emperor of the Roman world and recoverer of the East, to Zenobia and all others who are bound to her by alliance in war. You should have done of your own free will what I now command in my letter. For I bid you surrender, promising that your lives shall be spared, and with the condition that you, Zenobia, together with your children shall dwell wherever I, acting in accordance with the wish of the most noble Senate, shall appoint a place. Your jewels, your gold, your silver, your silks, your horses, your camels, you shall . . . hand over to the Roman treasury. As for the people of Palmyra, their rights shall be preserved.[9]

Zenobia's counselors might have advised her to take Aurelian's offer and be done with it. Officials of the city and leading merchants and caravan owners whose businesses were in ruins must have urged their queen to end the battle.

Zenobia would have none of it, and she sent a reply:

> From Zenobia, Queen of the East, to Aurelian Augustus. None save yourself has ever demanded by letter what you now demand. Whatever must be accomplished in matters of war must be done by valour alone. You demand my surrender as though you were not aware that Cleopatra preferred to die a Queen rather than remain alive, however high her rank. We shall not lack reinforcements from Persia, which we are even now expecting. On our side are the Saracens, on our side, too, the Armenians. The brigands of Syria have defeated your army, Aurelian. What more need be said? If those forces, then, which we are expecting from every

side, shall arrive, you will, of a surety, lay aside that arrogance with which you now command my surrender, as though victorious on every side.[10]

It was a brave response, but the game was nearly over. Desperate for assistance, Zenobia resolved to slip through the siege, make her way to Ctesiphon, and persuade Shapur to come to their aid. Perhaps she thought that having another chance to defeat a Roman emperor with their combined troops would be enough to draw Shapur into an alliance with Palmyra. Since she and Odenathus had defeated Shapur twice, her attempt to lure Shapur to her aid certainly qualified as a hard sell. She and her escort made it to the Euphrates, and while they waited for a boat to ferry them across, a party of Romans caught up with them and took her prisoner.

Aurelian took Zenobia with him to Rome. Reputedly laden with her fabulous jewelry that now belonged to Rome and bound by chains of pure gold, she became a centerpiece of his triumphal procession into the city. It is said that like other heads of state conquered by the Romans, she was offered a chance to pledge fealty to Rome and live out her days in relative comfort. Though some scholars argue that she was executed or died on the way to Rome, many agree that she took up Aurelian's offer and spent the rest of her life in a villa in Tivoli, east of Rome. The site of the villa has never been located nor has the fate of Vaballath been determined.[11] There is also speculation that the haughty Zenobia chose Cleopatra's path and pressed an asp to her breast.

Palmyra's heyday was past, and in the centuries following Zenobia's defeat, caravan trade drifted away to other cities. Blocks tumbled from the ancient façades and sand drifted over the remnants. Eventually, Arab villagers built hovels within the walls of the monumental Temple of Bel. Except for their voices and the cries of their livestock, silence settled over the once glorious city. Zenobia became a mythic figure whose life was recorded by few historians, but storytellers retold her story through generations and her legend lived on.

Each of the women discussed in this book made it a point to visit the ruins of this city no matter what the danger, and each experienced it in her own fashion.

Lady Hester Stanhope, the first Western woman to see Palmyra, hazarded the trip in 1813 when the surrounding Syrian desert was fraught with warring tribes and bandits, holding few, hard to find, and unreliable water sources. Conditions were equally dangerous a generation later when Lady Jane Digby rode in, protected by the hired Arab sheikh who had fallen in love with her along the way. Not long after, against the insistent advice of their friends, Isabel Burton ventured with her husband, Richard, the British consul in Damascus, into the lawless wastelands. In 1900, when explorer Gertrude Bell attempted the journey, Western travelers were still a rarity and still at great risk from bandits and hostile tribes, many descended from those who had threatened Hester Stanhope almost a century earlier. Even in 1935, on the brink of the Second World War, British adventurer and writer Freya Stark faced risks when she came to see the ruins of Zenobia's world.

The women had pitched tents among the fallen marble and gathered their impressions. Both Jane Digby El Mesrab and Isabel Burton had written of the ruins' unearthly beauty. On her honeymoon, Jane had bathed for her husband, naked in the moonlight, pale among silver-lit date palms, with a background of shadowy columns pointing to the stars. Palmyra so touched her romantic soul that she returned dozens of times and became an expert on local history. For Isabel, Palmyra was a dream come true, allowing her to experience the danger, the adventure, and the romance she had craved in her youth. She vividly recalled that at the campfire their soldiers and muleteers "danced a sword dance with wild cries to musical accompaniments and weird songs."[12] To the west outside Palmyra's walls rose tower tombs several stories tall that resembled abandoned apartment buildings. Gertrude Bell had been particularly taken with them, writing to a friend, "As we drew near Palmyra, the hills were covered with the strangest buildings, great stone towers, four stories high, some more ruined and some less. . . . They are the famous Palmyrene Tower tombs. . . . I wonder if the wide world presents a more singular landscape."[13] Freya Stark noted that the white ruins exuded a rosy glow.

A colonnade is the dominant feature of Palmyra's ruined landscape, consisting of a thirty-six-foot-wide avenue flanked by 325 Corinthian columns, many of which have toppled to the ground. Colonnaded avenues can be found in other cities of this era, but none as grand as Palmyra's. The Great Colonnade was erected for the most part during Roman times, in the second century CE, though the original columns may have been erected earlier, during the Greek occupation of Syria. It runs generally in the direction of the city's expansion and begins near the remarkable Temple of Bel, which predates the city. With the Funerary Temple in the west and the Temple of Bel in the east, the pulse of the city flowed from the spiritual beginning of life in the east to the sunset of death in the west. It is likely that this overarching symbolism was intentional, and Palmyra is a numinous place where visitors may find a sense of mystery.

A great triple arch known as the Triumphal Arch marks the end of the colonnade. Here in 1813, Arabs who lived in the ruins crowned Hester Stanhope with a garland of flowers. One biographer recorded her extraordinary excitement at being considered "the next Zenobia" by these uneducated folk, who surely had learned of the great Palmyrene queen from storytellers.

The Temple of Bel is an enormous stone structure built on a tell: the accumulated debris of past temples. High walls surrounded the temple complex as if to protect its privacy from unanointed eyes, and within, four hundred Corinthian columns once surrounded a huge, ten-acre courtyard paved with large stone slabs. In the seventh century, long after Zenobia, Muslim warriors claimed Palmyra and destroyed ancient buildings, using their stone blocks to build a mosque on the temple ruins. A community of rough Arab huts grew within the temple walls and remained until the 1930s, when archeologists demolished the mosque and huts to reveal the original temple in all its glory, roughly as Zenobia had seen it. But Zenobia's later pilgrims had arrived during its Muslim manifestation. Gertrude Bell described "the immense Temple of Baal; the modern town is built inside it and its rows of columns rise out of a mass of mud roofs. And beyond all is the desert, sand and white stretches of salt and sand again, with the dust clouds whirling over it. . . . It looks like the white skeleton of a town."[14] And this was the stage that awaited the entrance of Lady Hester Lucy Stanhope.

PART TWO

LADY HESTER LUCY STANHOPE
1776–1839

A European woman will come and live on Mount Lebanon at
a certain epoch. She will build a house there and obtain power
and influence greater than a Sultan's.
>   —DUCHESS OF CLEVELAND, *The Life and
>   Letters of Lady Hester Stanhope*

Figure 2. Robert Jacob Hamerton, printed by Charles Joseph Hullmandel, published by Richard Bentley, *Lady Hester Lucy Stanhope*. Lithograph, 1830s. © National Portrait Gallery, London.

2

HESTER'S WORLD

End of the Roman Empire—Islam—
Crusades—Ottoman Empire—Trade from East
to West—French Revolution—Napoleon's
Invasion of Egypt—The Grand Tour

While Zenobia slipped into the mists of time, Aurelian, who led her into Rome in golden chains, came to a conclusive end. In 275 CE his personal secretary, Eros, began to fear that Aurelian was planning to have him killed, and in a preemptive move prepared a fake "hit list" containing the names of army officers and saw to it that the list was circulated among the troops. A group of the listed officers assassinated Aurelian, and when they learned of Eros's treachery, killed him as well. Within a century, the empire had become unwieldy and began to crack with an administrative separation into Eastern and Western Empires with the Eastern capitol at Constantinople. Two centuries after Zenobia's defeat, the Western Roman Empire itself left the stage, ending a remarkable thousand-year run that had begun with the founding of the Roman Republic. The Eastern Empire continued into the fifteenth century, when the Ottoman Turks captured Constantinople.

About a century after Rome lost its empire and power shifted to Constantinople, a tribe known as the Quraysh settled in the town of Mecca not far from the western coast of the Arabian Peninsula. The Quraysh were pagans, as were the majority of the people in Arabia. They worshipped many gods and believed that rituals could be devised to influence those gods. There were a few Jewish tribes, mostly in the north near the town of Yathrib, now known as Medina, and there were very few Christians.

The valley of Mecca was already holy and a place of pilgrimage. The Ka'aba, a cube-shaped granite structure with a sacred black stone embedded in its eastern corner, was ancient even then and was dedicated to the Nabatean god Hubal, a god that Zenobia was likely to have worshipped. Somewhere around 570 CE a man named Muhammad was born in Mecca. A contemplative man, he tended to wander alone among the rocks, hills, and cliffs of the sere landscape, and at some point he had a supernatural experience in which he was visited and commanded by the angel Gabriel. Later generations described this as "The Night of Destiny." There were additional visitations and visions in which he received text as if by dictation; after his death this text became the Quran. His role as a messenger of God, a prophet, put him in conflict with the powerful pagan families of Mecca, and in 622 he left Mecca and traveled to Yathrib (Medina), two hundred miles north. This journey is known as the *hijra*, or flight, and the Prophet Muhammad's eventual return to Mecca is the basis for the modern pilgrimage known as the hajj, one of the five "Pillars of Islam." (The other four are *shahada*, profession of faith; *salah*, prayers; *zakat*, giving of alms; and *sawm*, fasting during the Islamic month of Ramadan.) The year of the hijra, 622, has come to be considered the beginning of the Muslim Era, which was followed by an astonishing expansion by conquest. Vast armies of mounted warriors led by fluttering green banners and trailed by clouds of dust rode out in all directions to extend the rule of Islam east to the Aral Sea and west to the Atlantic Ocean in less than one hundred years.

The wave of Arab conquest crested about 750 CE and began to recede. Berbers supplanted Arabs in North Africa; Persians and Kurds dominated east of the Euphrates. In the eleventh century when William the Conqueror led his Normans to victory in England and was crowned William I, the Muslim Seljuk Turks emerged from Central Asia, invaded the Byzantine Empire, and seized the area that is now Turkey. The Byzantine emperor Alexius Comnenus I asked the Roman pope for help. This was no small step given that the Greek Orthodox Church had broken with Rome years before. Though no friend of the Byzantine Empire, Pope Urban II gave a speech in 1095 asking all Christians to join in a war to help their brothers and sisters in the east and to retake the Holy Sepulcher in Jerusalem from "the wicked race." Thus the Crusades were born.

Thousands of people responded to the call with mass enthusiasm but with neither plan nor organization. Pope Urban had given them two objectives: to rescue their brothers in the East and to liberate Jerusalem. Muslims were the enemies of Christ and so, for many, were the Jews. The seeds sprinkled through this era continue to sprout weeds to this day. The first Crusade, surprisingly, was successful. Against the odds, in 1099 they did conquer Jerusalem and begin to build a Christian state in Palestine. Thus began a bloody cycle of stroke/counterstroke between East and West that has been repeated till today—almost one thousand years later. Seven crusades followed, though none matched the success of the first, and Muslim states responded by becoming stronger.

Out of the Turkic peoples that had invaded Asia Minor emerged a man named Osman, who in 1300 founded an empire that would become known as Osmanli or Ottoman and would continue for over six hundred years. The course of the empire was one of struggle or *jihad* against the Byzantines, Europeans, and other Muslim states. By 1493, the Ottomans occupied Constantinople, renamed it Istanbul, and made it their capital. This was the end of the Byzantine Empire, but the Ottomans gave the Greek patriarch authority over all Orthodox Christians in the Ottoman Empire.

The empire reached its peak in the mid-sixteenth century, extending from what is now Hungary through Greece and Turkey, the area around the Black Sea, Syria, Iraq, Lebanon, Palestine, Egypt, the Mediterranean coast of Africa, including part of Spain, and the eastern coast of Arabia as far as Aden. While this marked the zenith of the empire, the decline was far from precipitous. It would be 356 years before the Ottoman Empire ceased to exist, and this conclusion would be reached during the lifetimes of Gertrude Bell and Freya Stark, the last of our improbable women.

WHILE THESE CENTURIES were torn and tossed by political and religious waves, there was an ongoing smooth and powerful under-current of trade. Political upheaval is much easier to bear if the foods, flavors, and luxuries to which one has grown accustomed continue to flow to the local marketplace, and the obligation of religious gathering is more bearable when body odor is masked by the use of scented balms and incense. Of course, if one is wealthy and important, it is satisfying to make that known with gold and precious gems. So trade continued in the centuries after Zenobia. In the years immediately following, the dimension of trade was still primarily east and west: China and India shipping west with the trade routes converging on the shores of the Levant, routes from Persia and Aleppo to the Syrian coast, and routes up the Red Sea to Alexandria. All of these routes finally joined at Venice. Only a trickle of goods headed north into the benighted lands of northern Europe, as this was the early medieval period known as the Dark Ages, when feudal lords governed their own lands and a traveler's safety depended upon their whims.

As Europe matured politically, power became centralized in kingdoms and empires, and in the fifteenth century north-south trade eased as several nations began to look for goods from the East. As early as 1530, English merchants were living in the Levant, and with trade came consular representation. English trade prospered.

When Hester Stanhope arrived in Constantinople on November 3, 1810, the Ottoman Empire was no longer a military power. Its continued existence depended more upon maneuvering among the Great Powers than on any of the factors under control of the empire itself. The next century would include an elaborate dance by England, France, the Austrian Empire, and Russia to determine if and what each might share in the remains of the empire. The reigning sultan, Mahmud II, was a reformer several cuts above his recent predecessors. Preoccupied with the struggle to avoid dismemberment of his empire, he was unable to craft the reforms that would reinforce the empire's structure and fight the turmoil within. Thus Hester would have to deal with the sultan and his overall powers as well as with the regional pashas who were usurping power.

IN EUROPE, the big news was the French Revolution and the eruption of what many considered to be dangerous ideas of freedom and equality. The spread of these ideas was feared in England and set up perilous divisions of opinion in English society. Hester's father was an outspoken admirer of the revolution, while her uncle William Pitt (the Younger), soon to be prime minister for the second time, was a staunch opponent of the spread of French revolutionary thinking. A major preoccupation of Pitt and his government would be the military threat posed by France, and the tensions of this conflict would shape the course of Hester's great journey.

In 1798, the East received a startling "wake-up call" when Napoleon invaded Egypt. Napoleon's motives have never been completely clear although the British were convinced that it was a move to interdict England's routes to India and perhaps the opening move in a grand plan that would lead to India itself. Napoleon, in his diaries, said that it was for "glory," and it is at least plausible that he was attempting to emulate the achievements of Alexander the Great. Whatever the motive, Napoleon committed 34,000 troops aboard 400 transports guarded by 55 men-of-war to the invasion, and the immediate result was the defeat of the Mameluke rulers of Egypt and their permanent removal from the stage. The transport ships sailed away, leaving the troops in Egypt and the French fleet guarding the coast at Aboukir Bay. Within days, a British fleet under the command of Admiral Horatio Nelson attacked the French at Aboukir Bay, and only two of the French ships escaped, leaving Napoleon and his army stranded in Egypt.

The real success of Napoleon's invasion was not the ultimately temporary military victories, but the presence of some one thousand French civilians including artists, poets, botanists, zoologists, surveyors, and economists, whose findings were documented in the twenty-two-volume *Descriptions de l'Egypte*, the beginning of Egyptology and the definitive work for centuries. Napoleon eventually escaped from Egypt and returned to France, leaving his troops stranded. They succumbed to disease and eventually surrendered to the British. Yet what should have been a humiliating defeat was redeemed by the new revelation of the Orient. The impact on French and English art and culture was massive and would last for centuries.

Empire became the "idea du jour" of the great powers, and England was well along in the process of building hers but still a century from its peak. Her navy was her strong card, but the French had a powerful navy of their own. The issue was partially resolved by Nelson's victory at Aboukir Bay and concluded seven years later on October 21, 1805, when Nelson met a combined French and Spanish fleet at Cape Trafalgar and inflicted a crushing defeat—though it cost him his life. Napoleon's naval power was gone, and although he remained a threat on land, invasion of England was no longer a possibility.

Closer to home, continental travel by the aristocratic class began in the sixteenth century, and by the eighteenth century such travel became known as the "Grand Tour" and had become a fairly common experience in the upper classes. The experience was seen as educational: an exposure to the culture, fashions, art, and classical treasures available in Europe. For many of the young gentlemen, the education was somewhat broader and involved excessive drinking, licentiousness, and general exploration of debauchery in the relative safety of distance from home. By the late eighteenth century, women who could afford the cost were availing themselves of this educational opportunity as well, although possibly with more decorum than their brothers. Women's travel beyond the continent was not as common but was not unheard of. In general, the changing attitude toward travel and the growth in travel seem to have paralleled the growth of the empire. After all, as the citizen of an empire, it was almost a patriotic duty.

So Hester Stanhope was far from the first Englishman or Englishwoman to travel to the continent and beyond, but the way she traveled became radically different and would set a standard for a whole new genre of women's travel. Before that, she would follow other paths, including that of "first lady" of England.

3

FORGED IN CONFLICT

More than 1,500 years after Zenobia left the scene, Lady Hester Lucy Stanhope marched in, greeted by great fanfare. No European woman had ever attempted the perilous journey to Palmyra; the British consul urged her to abandon the venture, and the pasha in Damascus warned her that the desert was dangerous even for Arabs, as local tribes were at war and a force of fierce Wahabi warriors was rumored to be approaching. Lady Hester ignored the warnings and assembled a caravan at the city of Homs, whose residents had never seen a European woman and were eager to remedy that deficiency. As her expedition set off to the desert, cheering throngs gathered along the road, held in check by Janissaries the pasha had sent to protect her until she departed from the city; beyond the gates, he could not guarantee her safety.[1]

Six feet tall, fair-skinned, and regal, Lady Hester presented a striking picture leading her expedition astride her powerful mare; dressed as a bedouin chief in an ankle-length belted shirt, high yellow boots, and a white cloak clasped with a golden brooch at the right shoulder, she wore on her head the traditional Arab scarf, or *kefiyya*, held in place by a fine braid of horsehair rope around her forehead. Behind her rode her hired bodyguards: a phalanx of bedouin sheikhs in black-and-white-striped cloaks carrying lances topped with black ostrich feathers. In the wake of the horses, forty camels laden with provisions plodded along, their arrogant heads high. Next came twenty horses bearing cooks, tent-pitchers, dragomen (interpreters), servants, a stud-groom, a water carrier, and her secretary. Her faithful physician and her young lover were consigned to bringing up the rear, literally eating dust as the caravan made its way into the desert.

As they neared Palmyra several days later, a tower of blowing sand in the distance heralded a force of two hundred Palmyrenes riding out to welcome the woman they believed to be the daughter of the English king. Greeting her with shouts, thudding drums, and weapons fire, near-naked riders displayed their riding skills with mad dashes and skidding stops.[2]

When they entered the gates and made their grand march down the ruined colonnade, the fifteen hundred bedouin residents cheered with great enthusiasm. Arab girls bearing garlands of flowers posed in graceful positions on the pedestals jutting out from the columns that once had held statues of Palmyrene dignitaries. They leapt to the ground as Hester passed, dancing beside the caravan as it proceeded to the Triumphal Arch at the end of the colonnade. There, a girl suspended from the arch held a wreath over Lady Hester's head and proclaimed her "Queen of the Desert."

The unlikely desert queen, a British noblewoman from a prestigious family that included members of Parliament, a secretary of state, and a prime minister, had not intended to become a new Zenobia when she left England three years earlier, but the role suited her unique temperament and talents. Extraordinary childhood experiences had equipped her to set aside the stifling conventions of the early nineteenth century and to rule, if not a country, at least her own domain.

She believed that destiny had guided her circuitous path from the fashionable drawing rooms of England to the woven camel-hair tents of the East, and here she built a life that ranks her among the world's notable adventurers. Yet she grew up at a time when girls were raised like hothouse flowers to develop into ladies devoted to social and family obligations. But while she was sheltered in many ways, she was also exposed to radical ideas and had unusual access to power. Lady Hester Lucy Stanhope responded to the pressures of complex and opposing influences in ways other women of her time would not have dreamed or dared.

CHEVENING, one of Britain's great estates both in 1776 and today, is a 105-room Georgian mansion located on 3,500 acres of beautifully tended fields and forests twenty miles from Piccadilly Circus. North, across the fields in front of the house and beyond the quail runs, the road struggles to the top of a ridge on the estate where one can see Canary Wharf, a skyscraper in the Docklands of London. From the front gate the view to the east includes a tree-shaded church and a small village that originally housed those who worked on or supported the estate.

Here, on March 12, 1776, Lady Hester Mahon, wife of Charles Stanhope, Lord Mahon, gave birth to the couple's first child, Hester Lucy Stanhope. Lady Mahon's father, William Pitt, First Earl of Chatham, was England's secretary of state. Her favorite brother, William, would become prime minister of England.

Hester's young father, Lord Mahon, soon to become the Third Earl of Stanhope, was tall and gaunt with a hooked nose, an angular face, and a growing reputation as an eccentric. His background was aristocratic but his agile mind swirled in new directions and his political beliefs were far ahead of his time. The year Hester was born, America declared her independence from England and the French Revolution was beginning to take shape. Liberty was in the air, much to the consternation of most of England's ruling class. Lord Mahon held unorthodox opinions. He had lived in Switzerland for fourteen years with his family, where he was exposed to the radical ideas of Rousseau and Voltaire and believed that all men are born free and equal and that religious intolerance is unacceptable. In significant defiance of the styles of the day, he refused to powder his hair and shocked London society by appearing at an audience with the king in his natural black locks. Many thought that this was a political statement, but Charles simply observed that powder gave him a headache.

Lady Hester's maternal grandfather, William Pitt the Elder, had captured public imagination with his thundering voice and eloquent speeches. He was revered for guiding the country to victory over France and Prussia in the Seven Years War. On his watch, Britain was established as a major world power, and the Industrial Revolution, which would assure Britain's world dominance for the next century, was well under way. Though Lady Hester would not have remembered her illustrious grandfather, who died when she was two, his reputation colored and influenced her life.

In 1778, the year that her grandfather died, Hester's sister Grizelda was born. Then, in 1780, one month before Hester's fourth birthday, her sister Lucy came into the world. The family with its stair-step girls was shattered when Lady Mahon died on July 18, 1780, of complications from childbirth.

Inconsolable, Charles Stanhope roamed aimlessly over the estate paying scant attention to his three small daughters, whom he felt were responsible for the death of his wife. Charles's mother, Grizelda Stanhope, stepped in to take charge of her granddaughters and the retinue of servants attending them. This engulfing loss molded Hester's life. Perhaps as a way to avoid similar pain, she began to develop an indifference to women and outright scorn for most who ventured too close.

Charles Stanhope was elected to Parliament in 1780 and submerged himself in his work, largely ignoring his daughters. Then, nine months after his wife's death, he married Louisa Grenville, his first wife's cousin, whose own granddaughter described her as "a worthy and well-meaning woman; but, as I remember her, stiff and frigid, with a chilling, conventional manner."[3] Louisa produced three half-brothers to add to the Stanhope sisters: Philip in 1781, Charles in 1785, and James in 1788. After a brief struggle with motherhood, she abandoned the children to nurses and servants and concentrated on her social life.

Hester gradually assumed the role of surrogate mother and authority figure to her sisters and half-brothers, striving to care for and protect them, and perhaps supply the emotional support they did not receive from their parents. They responded by treating her with affection and a certain respect. In her memoirs, she noted, "I, even when I was only a girl, obtained and exercised, I can't tell how, a sort of command over [my sisters and half-brothers]."[4] Her experience as the responsible oldest child brought forth adult qualities of leadership.

She enjoyed wielding power but also was moved by stories of sorrow, distress, and oppression and often used her gifts in the service of others. Her brothers, in particular, would be early beneficiaries of her kindness, as would many others throughout her life. Her niece, the Duchess of Cleveland, wrote in *The Life and Letters of Lady Hester Stanhope*, "Above all, she had a kind and tenderly compassionate heart."[5] She also mentioned Hester's imperious and impetuous temper and her inflexible will. From the beginning, she had boundless self-confidence and believed herself born to command.[6]

When she was about seven years old, Count d'Adhemar, the French ambassador, visited Chevening. The count's elegant French manners and his finely dressed footmen made a deep impression on Hester. At the first opportunity, when she was sent to the seaside town of Hastings with her governess, she found a boat near the shore, cast off the line, and bobbed off alone toward France. Her frantic governess persuaded a fisherman to retrieve the premature traveler.

Hester's relationship with her remote, tyrannical father was complex. Learning how to deal with him provided lessons that would prove valuable in dealing with despotic, inflexible men later in life. She wrote, "I could always govern my father better than anybody, because I could bear his oddities with more patience, and could joke him into things plain sense and argument would have failed in."[7] With natural energy and intelligence that equaled his, she took on some of his characteristics over the years, gaining a reputation for being as eccentric and demanding as he was.

Whatever his other characteristics, he was intellectually stimulating. He is credited with inventing a model steamship predating Fulton's, a calculating machine that preceded Babbage's, and the first printing press made entirely of iron, which speeded up the printing process severalfold.[8] In following years he became more absorbed with the ideas of liberty emanating from the French Revolution and began to call himself Citizen Stanhope. His sympathy for French thinking earned him scorn and suspicion in England and put him in direct opposition to the position of his recent in-laws, the Pitts.

King George II asked Hester's uncle, William Pitt, to become prime minister in 1793 at a time when threats from France were escalating. Pitt was twenty-four, the youngest prime minister in England's history. Though she was still a teenager, Hester must have celebrated his new prominence along with the rest of the family. Pitt and Charles Stanhope had been colleagues and friends in Parliament, sharing many liberal views, but with responsibility for the government on his shoulders, Pitt necessarily became more cautious, and their interests began to diverge, putting a strain on their friendship and family relationship.

In 1790, when Hester was fourteen, Stanhope removed the coat of arms from the gates of Chevening and renamed the palatial manor Democracy Hall. He prohibited finery, forcing his offspring to wear plain, coarse garments. He thought that education was not good for children, particularly girls, but that manual labor was beneficial. This signaled the end of the siblings' schooling and they were pressed into menial jobs. Philip was apprenticed to a blacksmith and Charles to a shoemaker, and Hester was sometimes sent to tend turkeys on the common.

The earl's treatment of his children might have been an effective introduction to the plight of the poor, but it also had a great and critical impact on their development. They were subjected to gossip among their peers and ridicule in the newspapers. Hester developed a thick psychological skin, adding another layer to her already complex personality.

In 1794, Charles Stanhope was defeated 61 to 1 on his motion that Britain would not interfere in the internal affairs of France. His colleagues satirically commemorated this "Minority of One"[9] by creating the Stanhope Medal, with his likeness on one side and on the other the inscription "Stanhope the Friend of Trial by Jury, Liberty of the Press, Parliamentary Reform, Annual Parliaments, Habeas Corpus Act, Abolition of Sinecures, and of a speedy peace with France."[10] One of these medals is now on display at Chevening. By today's standards, the inscription sounds like a testimonial.

He did manage to pay some personal attention to Hester's intellectual pursuits. He took her aside from time to time to discuss "philosophy," and in these discussions would gently (by his standards) correct her logic. Private time with him made her quite sure that she was his favorite. Much to her delight, he permitted the girls to hunt, riding after game as opposed to shooting, and she became an accomplished horsewoman.

While we know something about her skills and abilities, there are no physical descriptions of Hester during her teenage years. According to Sir Tresham Lever in *The House of Pitt*, by the time she was twenty she was "Tall, stately, aristocratic, with dazzling complexion and expressive features, her blue, flashing eyes, now lightening up at some pleasing fancy, now darting scorn at some poor trifler, she recalled the hauteur of her terrible grandsire . . . [she] compelled attention at any circle."[11] In her memoirs, Hester in describing herself said, "If you were to take every feature of my face, and put them, one by one on the table, there is not a single one would bear examination. The only thing is that, put together and lighted up, they look well enough. It is homogeneous ugliness and nothing more."[12] How attractive she might have been is almost irrelevant given her compelling personality and presence. Her grandmother described Hester's voice as unmusical and somewhat masculine, an opinion corroborated by various other writers who had known her personally. Both her grandfather and uncle were admired for their strong voices, and she may have inherited a female version of the resonant Pitt vocal cords. With her family's wealth and connections, she was a high-quality entry in the social lists.

Lord Mahon did not oppose the arrangement of suitable marriages for his daughters, but events where they might meet appropriate suitors had to conform to his ideology. In 1796, his neighbor Lord Romney invited the gentry, including King George III and prime minister William Pitt, to the social event of the season in the form of a military review. Lord Mahon objected to his daughters' attending because he disapproved of all military display. Twenty-year-old Hester took the matter into her own hands. She wrote, "I was obliged to play a trick on my father to get there. I pretended, the day before, that I wanted to pay a visit to the Miss Crumps . . . and then went from their house to Lord Romney's. Though all the gentry of Kent were there, my father never knew."[13]

During the review, the king invited her to dine with him at his table. "Oh, what wry faces there were among his courtiers? Mr. Pitt was very much pleased at the reception I met with. The King took great notice of me, and I believe, always after liked me personally."[14] When he and the queen were leaving, the king was moved to take her with them. As the queen got into the carriage, he said to her, "My dear, Lady Hester is going to ride bodkin [squeezed between] with us: I am going to take her away from Democracy Hall." The queen saved the day, saying that because Lady Hester did not have her maid with her, it would be inconvenient for her to go at such short notice.[15]

Although Charles Stanhope denied education and displays of wealth to his children, they lived in a cultural climate in which it was impossible not to learn about England's worldwide adventures, which filled the newspapers and social conversations. Hester lived in a circle in which lavish goods from the far corners of the British Empire were commonplace. In the mid-eighteenth century, Robert Wood and James Dawkins, intrepid English travelers disguised as Arab traders, had stumbled upon Palmyra and had drawn precise pictures of the ancient city. Their book, *The Ruins of Palmyra*, filled with detailed engravings, helped fuel the neoclassical architectural movement that swept the country. Palmyra ceilings and Palmyra cornices became fashionable in the stately homes of Britain. As Mr. Wood went on to be undersecretary to William Pitt the Elder, Palmyra was surely discussed in the Stanhope and Pitt households. There were other opportunities to learn about Zenobia in books, notably Gibbon's *The Decline and Fall of the Roman Empire*.

Public interest in travel was great but only the boldest traders had traveled to the forbidding lands of the Ottoman Empire, which spread from Tripoli on the coast of North Africa below Sicily to the Persian Gulf, the Caspian Sea, and the countries around the Black Sea. Then, in June 1798, when Napoleon invaded Egypt and his fleet was destroyed by Admiral Lord Nelson, leaving England with control of the Mediterranean, word of Nelson's decisive victory reached London in October, and the city erupted in jubilant celebration. Interest in the mysterious Muslim world grew, especially after an alliance of English and Ottoman troops defeated Napoleon's army in Egypt in 1799.

In 1800, during these lively days of empire, Lady Hester at last left the restrictive atmosphere of Chevening, taking advantage of an invitation from her maternal grandmother to move in with her at Burton-Pynsent, Somerset. Mounted on her favorite black mare, Hester sped to the estate, eager to begin a new life with her beloved "Grandmama,"[16] who adored her spirited granddaughter. This was the strongest bond that Hester experienced with a female throughout her life.

By the time Hester moved from Chevening at the age of twenty-four, both of her sisters had married—Lucy to a country surgeon in 1796 when she was sixteen and Grizelda to an army officer in 1800. Grizelda had left home in 1796 and moved into a cottage at Walmer Castle, lent her by her uncle William Pitt the Younger, who was, like the rest of his family, uneasy about the future of the Stanhope girls. The Stanhope boys, more distantly related to the Pitts, were still captive at Chevening, but the newly independent Hester would soon remedy that.

Her oldest half-brother, Philip Henry, was desperate with the circumstances at Chevening. Their father refused to send him either to school or to college and made no other preparations for his future. The third earl's motives seem entirely selfish. He had to keep Philip, his legal heir, close by in order to gain the power to dispose of his title and the estate. French nobles and clergy had renounced their privileges in 1789 out of fear; Stanhope wished to renounce his on principle. However, under British law, he could not give up his title without the approval of his heir at age twenty-one.

In a fortuitous move, Philip confided his despair to his sister, who committed herself to his escape. With the cooperation of wealthy, influential acquaintances, she arranged for money, letters of credit, a passport, letters of recommendation, and admission under an assumed name to Erlangen University in Germany. With her grateful brother well on his way to Germany, Hester wrote to her father's lawyer telling him that Philip was now safely abroad under a false name and that while she would never reveal his location, she would see to it that letters were forwarded to him.

Other than her father, the only family members unaware of the planned escape were her Grandmother Stanhope, so completely devoted to her son that she would accept no action so treasonous to his wishes, and her two younger stepbrothers who remained at Chevening. Hester kept Charles and James ignorant of the affair so that they would be completely above suspicion. Her father had a less violent reaction than she had expected, although he never forgave her and she never again lived at Chevening.

Her doting Grandmama encouraged Hester to plan a Grand Tour of the continent, a trip popular with moneyed young men of the day and not a few young ladies. Before she left, she spent a few days with her uncle at Walmer Castle on the southeast coast of England. Though he was out of office at the time, he was still surrounded by colleagues and friends who held important military and political positions. Lady Hester found her stay at Walmer much to her liking. She wrote that she was "enchanted with everything here. I have never seen the face of a woman until today. Charming!—nothing but pleasant men."[17]

4

FIRST LADY

In September 1802, Hester set off on her European tour. She planned to see her brother Philip and fully experience the continent so often discussed by her family and friends. By this time, tours followed organized coach routes and offered the options of purchasing or hiring carriages, some fitted with elliptical spring suspensions that minimized shocks from rutted roads. Cross-channel service was regular but subject to the whims of weather, and some road segments, such as the Mount Cenis pass from Switzerland to Italy, might become impassable so that carriages had to be disassembled and carried by pack animals. Most important, one had to precisely schedule one's trip to avoid periods of conflict between French and English forces.

Hester traveled with a carefully arranged set of chaperones—a couple unlikely to interfere with her activities. It is interesting that Hester with her disregard of convention still felt it inadvisable to tackle Europe on her own. Of course, her solution was eminently effective in that she had the appearance of chaperones with little of the constraint.

After a joyous reunion with Philip, the reality of a younger brother growing into his own independence beyond her control seems to have strained their relationship. Nevertheless they traveled together, and when they reached the mountains between France and Italy they had to hire mules and muleteers to take them across. The rigors of the journey brought them closer together and the relationship was largely repaired by the time they parted, although the affair foreshadowed the future state of their relationship.

Hester wintered in Italy among English travelers and expatriates of her own class who feted and entertained her, giving her an experience of Europe not unlike her life in England. In May 1803, the party made its way back to England through Germany, and when she arrived, anticipating a fond reunion with her Grandmama, she learned that Lady Chatham had died in April. She had lost someone who loved her dearly and she had lost a home; her uncle was soon to gain a hostess.

Pitt, the son of William Pitt the Elder, entered politics in 1780 at age twenty-one. He became the reform leader and established his first ministry in 1783 at age twenty-four, the youngest prime minister in England's history. This ministry lasted until 1801. In the second ministry, 1804–6, he led Britain during the Napoleonic wars.

It was in 1803 that Hester returned from Europe to find herself without a home. Hester's mother had been Pitt's favorite sister, and though at this point he did not get on well with her father, he had always been supportive of Hester and her siblings. Still, it was a major step for a forty-four-year-old confirmed bachelor to adapt his life and habits to a headstrong twenty-seven-year-old woman. Some years before, when asked what would happen to Hester after Lady Chatham died, he replied that "[u]nder no circumstances could I offer her a home in my own house."[1] Yet, when the occasion arose, he did not hesitate and welcomed Hester to Walmer Castle.

It became an excellent arrangement for both of them. Pitt appeared to regard her almost as a daughter, whose presence brightened his life. Hester gained a replacement for a father who had all but disowned her and began a period that ranked among the happiest of her life. In the last years of her life, she loved to recall this time when she was in charge of the prime minister's household and hostess at his table. She was clearly in her element with "three or four men staying in the house" and dinner for "eight or ten almost every other day. Military and naval characters are welcome here; women are not . . . You may guess, then, what a pretty fuss they make with me" (53) was Hester's happy summary. It had also been a formative experience. Like Charles Stanhope, Pitt was a brilliant, accomplished man, and he offered Hester a very different view of the world.

Among the men she met was Sir John Moore, one of Pitt's favorite generals. He had begun his distinguished army career at fifteen, when he served in England's fight against American independence, and later distinguished himself as a ranking officer in the battle against Napoleon's army in Egypt in 1801. The Ottoman ruler, Sultan Selim III, had officially declared war on France, and English troops fought alongside Ottoman troops to defeat the French. Moore's experiences in the Egyptian campaign must have abetted Hester's interest in the mystery-shrouded Muslim world, and the strategic importance of the area surely generated discussion at Pitt's table, adding to her knowledge.

Hester was a charming and engaging woman, but she never sat for a portrait. She acknowledged that she was never good looking, and a number of writers agreed that she was not beautiful. At the same time, there is general agreement that she was eminently attractive. Her niece, the Duchess of Cleveland, described her as "A daughter of the gods, divinely tall, with a very fine figure, and the air and gait of a queen; she had a skin of dazzling fairness, bright eyes—blue in reality, though often described as black, as they darkened and flashed in the excitement of the moment—and a wonderful play of expression" (48).

A fellow officer of her brother Charles, age "near nineteen," found her captivating: "so rapid and decided was her conversation, so full of humor and keen observation, and withal so friendly and instructive, that it was quite impossible not to fall at once into her direction, and become her slave, whether for laughter or seriousness" (61).

Quick-witted, with a talent for satire and mimicry, she enlivened the prime minister's household. The unregulated use of these talents also gained her a share of awkward moments as well as outright enemies. She managed to offend leading politicians of the day as well as members of Pitt's own cabinet such as Lord Castlereagh, whom she insulted by calling him "His Monotonous Lordship" (61). When she achieved some new indiscretion, Pitt would remonstrate with a rather mild, "Hester, Hester, be careful. What are you saying?" (55).

More frequently, he would laugh and enjoy the antics of his irrepressible niece.

Walmer Castle was a focal point of this happy period in Hester's life. On the southeast coast of England, Walmer Castle looks toward France, a short twenty-five miles away, and in the early nineteenth century when Hester lived there with Pitt, there was great concern over a possible invasion by France. Napoleon had used both uneasy peace and armed conflict to expand his empire. With Britain, he effected a partial blockade by closing continental ports to British trade, and began building and training a possible invasion force. Pitt, in addition to his other responsibilities, was warden of the Cinque Ports—five ports in southeast England nearest France—and responsible for the defenses along the coast.

Today, Walmer Castle is still the official residence of the warden of the Cinque Ports, and a nice thing about castles is that they do not change much over the centuries, at least externally. From the top of the east tower, freshly painted black cannon still point menacingly over the beach toward the bright, empty horizon of the English Channel. Incongruously, a wood and canvas deck chair sits beside a pyramid of cannonballs. The relatively low walls of three of the castle's four towers set in the moat give the whole assemblage a squat, hulking look when viewed from the adjacent gardens, lush with marigolds, ageratum, and purple salvia, and walks lined with daylilies.

The gardens were planned and begun by Hester, and among her responsibilities was their ongoing care. In a chalk quarry two or three hundred yards behind the castle, at the far end of the gardens, lie the overgrown and tangled remains of a garden of exotic plants and steep, shaded paths that she created and called the Glen. The dark tangle of green, now closed off by a fence, seems mysterious and somehow suited to the life of the enigmatic Hester.

Inside the castle, the drawing room and dining room are much the same as in her day. Dining room chairs that belonged to Pitt are still arranged around a banquet table. His living quarters were in the tower of the castle now used by the current warden, but the actual location of Hester's quarters is unknown, although they were probably those nearest the dining room later occupied by Queen Victoria and her consort.

To fulfill his responsibility for defense of the coast, Pitt raised and commanded a regiment of his own and made Hester the nominal commander of the 15th Light Dragoons and the Berkshire Militia. Hester took her duties quite seriously and would ride miles in order to review her troops, a process that involved sitting motionless on her horse for hours as the troops passed in review. Hester was among the few young women of her time to have two regiments and a regimental band at her disposal. On at least one occasion, she called on the troops of "her" regiments to help her plant and tend the gardens.

Looking out over the Channel with Hester one day, Pitt told her, "I have plenty of good diplomatists, but they are none of them military men; and I have plenty of good officers, but not one of them is worth sixpence in the cabinet. If you were a man, Hester, I would send you on the Continent with 60,000 men and give you a carte blanche; and I am sure that not one of my plans would fail, and not one soldier would go with his shoes unblacked."[2]

With 70,000 troops, Zenobia conquered one-third of the Roman Empire; one can only imagine what Hester might have done with 60,000. She might have wondered the same thing as she stood in the ruins of Palmyra a few years later.

SOMETIME DURING HER YEARS WITH PITT, Hester was asked to visit a famous fortune-teller named Brothers whom Pitt had ordered imprisoned. From his cell, Brothers had begged to be allowed to see Lady Hester, and eventually she went to the prison fully expecting to be asked to intercede. Instead, Brothers predicted that she would "one day go to Jerusalem, and lead back the chosen people; that on her arrival in the Holy Land, mighty changes would take place in the world, and that she would pass seven years in the desert."[3] Strange prophecies for a woman who was immersed in one of the happiest periods of her life, influential, admired, and feted by the top tiers of society. She shrugged it off for a time and turned her attention to matters at hand.

While Pitt's unofficial first lady, Hester began the first of her serious love affairs. The object of her affection was the politician Lord Granville Leveson-Gower, a spoiled dandy, and a Don Juan of his generation. Lord Granville was in love with the Countess of Bessborough, a married woman twelve years older and an ancestor of the late Princess Diana. It appears that Granville was using Hester as a pathway to Pitt, perhaps with the added enticement that as an old maid of twenty-eight she might be persuaded to overlook the accepted limits on sexual behavior. Hester, for all her nonstandard behavior, expected the affair to lead to marriage. Subtlety might have eventually won the somewhat effeminate young man for Hester, but subtlety was not her strength. She made no secret of her attraction and actively pursued the relationship. This shocked and perhaps frightened Granville and provided London with a topic for lively discussion. The situation was resolved when Pitt, tiring of the embarrassment, appointed Granville ambassador to Petersburg.

Before he left for Russia, Granville told Hester that he would never marry her, and Hester took the news badly. She made no attempt to cover her distress and continued to titillate the London gossips, this time with the depth of her misery. One misery erased another when Pitt died at age forty-six. Near the end, Hester slipped into the dying man's room against orders of the doctor. Until that point she had been unable to shed a tear, but when Pitt recognized her and thanked her, the gates opened and tears fell. After she left, her brother James went in. Pitt continued to speak of her, several times repeating, "Dear Soul! I know she loves me. Where is Hester? Is Hester gone?"[4] A major pillar in her life, her uncle, her friend and supporter, was crumbling. Hester's heady days as first lady of the British Empire came to a sad, untimely end.

Pitt had been an honest man, but his debts far exceeded his assets. Parliament paid his debts and honored his last wishes expressed to the bishop of Lincoln by granting a pension of £1,200 per year to Hester and £600 per year to each of her sisters.

She took a house on Montague Square, a new yet wealthy area of London, intending to provide a home for her brothers Charles and James. She tried to resume her life in London, but the abrupt descent from her previous status was difficult to accept. Hester had been dislodged from her position as "princess" and was instantly an outsider. Many of her friends proved inconstant. Enemies she had made now closed their doors to her, some celebrating her downfall. Nevertheless, during this time Hester found her second and life-turning romance.

In 1807, upon his return from a campaign in Sicily where he was opposing Napoleon's expansion in the Mediterranean, her friend Sir John Moore stopped at Montague Square to pay his respects. The general was a man of great physical beauty and Hester was a woman in need of an admirer. She had, however, learned from the affair with Leveson-Gower, and this time she was discreet. In her memoirs, Hester describes a discussion with her brothers in which they were comparing the physical beauty of various men. Charles asked her if Sir John were not the more handsome of the two and when she replied that he was certainly handsome, Charles said, "Oh! But Hester, if you were only to see him when he is bathing, his body is as perfect as his face."[5] Hester noted that she never even smiled though she was amused at the naiveté of his remark.

Hester was sufficiently discreet that there is little written about the seriousness of this affair. The slim written evidence in Moore's letters supports the idea of friendship rather than romance. Hester, on the other hand, told friends that they were to be engaged when he returned from his next assignment in Spain. Years later, she referred to him as the man she was to have married, and to the end of her life she kept sleeve-links containing his hair. Perhaps the general was also being discreet.

Hester involved herself in procuring a new appointment for General Moore, agreeing with him that he was being treated unfairly by the government. When she pulled several strings that she had gathered during her time with Pitt, Sir John was appointed commander of the forces in Spain. When he left, he took Hester's brother Charles with him as his youngest major and aide-de-camp. Her brother James followed later as a second aide-de-camp.

On the afternoon of January 16, 1809, near the port of Coruna, Spain, the French attacked. The battle seesawed, then the British rallied with an attack by the regiment commanded by Charles Napier and Charles Stanhope. "Well done my majors!" shouted Sir John.[6] But his majors were down. Charles Napier was wounded and a prisoner, Charles Stanhope was dead. Later the same day, Sir John was mortally wounded. They carried him back to Coruna and he lived long enough to see James Stanhope. "Stanhope," the general said weakly, "Stanhope, remember me to your sister."[7] After that he never spoke again and died a short time later. A mutual friend brought Hester a bloodstained glove he had worn in battle. She kept it to the end of her life.

The devastation of losing her brother and her lover was more unbearable because she had been instrumental in placing them in harm's way. During her mourning, Hester found London intolerable, and she decided to return to a small farmhouse named Glen Irfon in Wales, where she had spent a pleasant holiday the previous year.

OUTSIDE THE VILLAGE of Cilmary, Glen Irfon is still a working farm, and the simple gray, slate-fronted farmhouse that housed Hester is still standing. Even today, the farm would provide the peace and quiet that Hester was seeking.

She stayed at Glen Irfon from May to October, occupying herself by dabbling in dairy operation, practicing medicine with the villagers as her willing test subjects, and entertaining the vicar's family. It must also have been a time of intense self-assessment, for at thirty-three her options were closing. Given her penchant for feuding, her options were undoubtedly closing faster than most. Would she remain in Wales for the rest of her life? Return to London one day? With her future clouded with uncertainty, the Brothers prophecy must have seemed sheer fantasy.

Then, toward the end of her stay at Glen Irfon, her brother James, recently returned from Spain, came to visit with a friend, Nassau Sutton, who was recovering from an illness. During this visit, the idea of an extended journey took shape. James, who was going to rejoin his regiment, offered to accompany her abroad and Nassau Sutton happily agreed to join them.

Hester wrote to her first cousin, General Richard Grenville, who was also First Admiral of the Fleet, and suggested that "[i]f after Mr. P has added during his Administration, 600 ships (line of B and frigate) to the Naval force of this country, a relation or even friend of his cannot be accommodated with a passage in one of them it is rather hard, and if they do not chuse to do the thing handsomely they may let it alone. . . ."[8] The admiral decided to do it "handsomely" for Mr. Pitt's niece, offering Hester and her party passage on the *Jason*, a frigate scheduled to escort a convoy of merchant ships bound for Gibraltar.

On the advice of a surgeon friend, Hester employed a young doctor named Charles Lewis Meryon to accompany her. A small man, Meryon was full of courage and a degree of loyalty that is hard to fathom. This faithful man ended up spending thirty years of his life in her service, most of it under difficult and often dangerous conditions. He also became her biographer and was the author of the three-volume *Memoirs of the Lady Hester Stanhope* and the three-volume *Travels of Lady Hester Stanhope*, major sources of information on her life.

She left Portsmouth on February 10, 1810, accompanied by James and his friend Nassau Sutton; her maid and companion Mrs. Elizabeth Williams, who had accompanied her to Glen Irfon the year before and who would continue to serve her for years; a manservant; and Dr. Meryon. After a few hours with the smell of pitch and the creaking of masts and yards, the ship was becalmed, taking seven days to reach Lands End at England's southwestern extremity. Just past Land's End, they ran into a severe Atlantic storm, and all of the party except Hester and James took to their beds. James had been a midshipman serving at sea, while Hester was simply partial to sailors, and her spirits rose with the storm.

The gray silhouette of Cornwall diminishing in the *Jason*'s wake was the last glimpse of England that Hester would ever see.

5

ON DEALING WITH BRUTAL MEN

The towering mass of Gibraltar formed a gateway to Hester's new life. She and James were received by the governor-general, whose quarters still exist, and they were besieged with offers of hospitality. The experience was similar to that of her Grand Tour, but the social life of Gibraltar was a pale shadow of London and Rome, and her bruised emotions left her ill-suited to official banquets and polite conversation.

Her interest level picked up somewhat with the arrival of the yacht of Howe Peter Browne, the marquis of Sligo, a wealthy, unrestrained young Irishman famous, in part, for owning a brig that had been converted to a pleasure yacht. He was soon to achieve more fame by inducing two British sailors to go absent without leave and join his crew. Since Britain was at war, the navy viewed this absence rather seriously. Lord Sligo did not, however, and when questioned by a court of inquiry, lied about the matter, unaware of the trouble that was facing him. He and his traveling companion, Michael Bruce, congratulated themselves on the wonderful joke they had played on the royal navy. At the age of twenty-two, they were simply wandering the Mediterranean enjoying salt breezes and other pleasures. Because they were also acquaintances of James, they were drawn naturally into Hester's party.

Bruce, son of a wealthy merchant member of the East India Company and fourteen years her junior, was entranced by Hester, by both her charms and her past. There is some disagreement over when admiration ripened into romance: some writers argue for subsequent ports, while at least one believes it happened "among the shadowed walks of the convent garden" on Gibraltar.[1] Nassau Sutton, the previous prime admirer, suddenly took permanent leave of the party and traveled to Minorca.

The party began to break up, with James recalled to his regiment, Michael Bruce off on business to Palermo, and Lord Sligo setting sail for friendlier waters. Curiously, more than one hundred years later, this irresponsible young man's great-granddaughter would marry the Seventh Earl of Stanhope. Hester accepted passage on the frigate *Cerberus* to Malta with Dr. Meryon, Mrs. Williams, and a manservant.

On Easter, April 21, 1810, *Cerberus* maneuvered into the harbor at La Valetta, Malta. Hester was still a well-known personality, especially in the outposts of the empire, and on her arrival she was met and warmly welcomed by the governor, General Hildebrand Oakes. She declined the general's offer of accommodation to accept an invitation from Mr. Fernandez, the deputy commissary general whose wife was Elizabeth Williams's sister. The sisters had been educated by the generosity of Mr. Pitt. This, however, was not the driving reason for her choice of accommodation, as Michael Bruce arrived shortly thereafter to take up residence with the Fernandezs as well. Later in her stay, St. Antonio, one of the governor's houses, became available.

> A 250-yard avenue of orange trees led into the courtyard of the palace. It was a large irregular building, made from the soft island stone. Vines grew in profusion over the walls, square belfry-like towers dominated the palace. Inside the rooms were cool and dark. The floors, also of stone, were free of carpets. The garden was magnificent, full of orange, pomegranate and lemon trees. The walks were lined with ten-feet-high myrtle trees and oleanders.[2]

This may have been the most idyllic period in Hester's life. The governor, who subsequently became her close friend and confidant, entertained the large expatriate English community continuously, so Hester and her party dined at the Governor's Palace nightly. She was passionately involved with a man whose only claim to status was a commercially successful father. But this time the passion and infatuation were returned. She openly became his mistress.

Michael Bruce wanted to become a politician, and this ambition accounted for some of his fascination with Hester. Hester concluded that he had the potential to become a great politician and decided that she would tutor him. The lovers were facing a problem, however, and that was Patrick Craufurd Bruce, Michael's father.

Compared with Hester's father, Earl Stanhope, Craufurd, for that was how he was known, was no problem at all. A rich, successful businessman of Scottish descent, member of the House of Commons, senior partner of a banking house and a commercial house in Bombay and London, he was generous and devoted to his family. The sole support for Michael in his, until now, aimless wandering, he would have to be guided somehow to a positive understanding of his oldest son's liaison with a woman fourteen years his elder. The cause was aided somewhat by the fact that Craufurd himself had eloped with Michael's mother when Craufurd was thirty-seven and she was eighteen. Hester took charge and attacked the problem forthrightly with a letter that informed Craufurd that his son was beautiful, talented, and possessed of a great statesmanlike mind, and "while loving him to distraction,"[3] she knew that she must eventually give him up and pass him along to some fortunate woman; she gave her promise that she would do exactly that. In the meantime, as his companion she would do her best to polish his rough edges. She then includes a warning not to mistake the tone of humility she has taken in the letter because she is actually a very proud woman and cares little what the world may think of her.

Craufurd's reaction to this letter and that of his son, which was sent simultaneously, was positive, and this surprised me until I realized that in his mind Hester was an alternative to Lord Sligo, who found nothing wrong in suborning British sailors in time of war. His feelings about the relationship did fluctuate over the years, as did Hester's and Michael's anxiety levels as they waited for and dealt with his subsequent correspondence and financial support.

After four months on Malta, the heat had become intolerable, and Hester was ready to move on. Napoleon was in firm control of Europe and the Ottoman Empire was the only area still friendly to British travelers. Once again, Hester and her party embarked on a frigate—this time the *Belle Poule* bound for Zante, an island west of the Peloponnese.

The trip from Malta to Constantinople was relatively uneventful. They did encounter Lord Byron, a friend of Lord Sligo, in Piraeus, and he spent a great deal of time with the party in Athens. He was no more impressed with Hester than she was with him. "[T]hat dangerous thing—a female wit!" Lord Byron said of Hester.[4] "I saw nothing but a well-bred man like many other. . . . As for poetry, it is easy enough to write verses; and as for the thoughts, who knows where he got them? Many a one picks up some old book that nobody knows anything about, and gets his ideas out of it,"[5] said Hester.

CONSTANTINOPLE, now Istanbul, is still a gateway to the Orient and, to the Western eye, exotic with cavelike bazaars, palaces, and a grand cathedral turned mosque. The major difference in Hester's eyes would certainly be the roaring, exhaust-belching herd of cars streaming through the lanes and thoroughfares, threatening humans and animals alike. Yet one would imagine that Hester would quickly overcome the initial shock and commandeer this new resource to suit her purposes.

By the time Hester arrived in 1810, the Ottoman Empire was well into its decline. Coveted by the great powers, it was one of the prizes in a gigantic game of strategic maneuver, while partially protected by the standoff between those powers. The central authority of the government was weakened by strong local pashas, insubordinate officials, and the poverty and misery of the people.

It was in Constantinople that Hester began to form an emotional attachment to the East. Until now, her travels had been such that she was rarely out of the English expatriate community, that part of the community of her own rank and status. Culturally, it was as though she were traveling in a narrow vein of English upper-class culture threaded through the Mediterranean. This situation was now changed because British presence in Constantinople was small, the embassy consisting of one young man.

Hester set out to become acquainted with the Turks. Her initial entrée was owing to the demand for the services of Dr. Meryon, but eventually the Turkish families desired to meet Hester socially. For her part, Hester was charmed. Uncharacteristically, she liked and admired the Turkish women as well as the men, and on occasion she would retire with them to bathe and relax. With the men she was equally at ease. She wrote to Stratford Canning, minister of the British Embassy, "When did four Turks, and one the brother of a Captain Pacha, visit and dine with a Christian woman? I wore my sword with such an air that it has made a conquest of them all."[6] On another occasion, she was invited by the captain pasha to visit a ship of the Turkish fleet, the *Sultan Selim*, on the condition that she did not wear women's clothing. So Hester wore "a pair of overalls, a military greatcoat, and cocked hat,"[7] explored the ship thoroughly, and declared it magnificent. She found the captain pasha to be equally impressive, but on the day of her visit he had been cutting off heads; nevertheless, he was "just as composed as at another time."[8]

She saw Sultan Mahmoud one time while on horseback on a street of Stamboul, the oldest Turkish section of Constantinople. She had the audacity to ride through the streets of the city unveiled, and when she encountered the procession accompanying the sultan on his way to Friday prayers, she failed to bow her head, but rather sat proud and erect and watched calmly as his majesty passed. Though it was her only glimpse of the sultan, she was loyal to him throughout her life. In this gender-divided society Hester was able to break the bonds of custom, in part because she was a foreigner and also because she tended to create confusion about her gender. Superficially, in this particular instance she rode sidesaddle and was unveiled, while Muslim women rode astride but veiled. More important, there was something masculine about her appearance and certainly about her bearing and behavior. There were many on the crowded streets of

Stamboul who argued that she was not a woman. Others, believing that she was a woman, were captivated by the pride and dignity of her queenly bearing.

Hester was proud of her acceptance by the Turks and noted that the best way to "gain the good will of any Turk" was "unaffected, easy manners, accompanied with great civility, totally devoid of obsequiousness."[9] This described Hester's natural behavior. The Turks admired her, and she admired them. "I must confess I think them a very superior people, they have no advantages, no education, yet they never say a silly thing. They have all high spirits, great composure of manner and a degree of good breeding which would make our courtiers blush."[10]

Hester decided not to spend another winter in Constantinople and in October 1811 she and her party embarked on a large caique. The boat was a wooden, lateen-rigged vessel, broad in the beam and shallow in draft. Consequently, it had a tendency to wallow in heavy seas.

With varying winds and weather, they made their way south from the Sea of Marmara, through the Dardanelles, into the Aegean Sea. They were halted at Price Island for five days by adverse winds and for ten days at Chios by a gale. Finally they left Chios and made their way to Rhodes, where they stopped briefly to take on food and water, and left on Saturday night, the 23rd of November.

Rhodes is the last landfall north of Alexandria, Egypt, so they set their course into three hundred miles of open Mediterranean. The wind was with them and they ran before it, making what Dr. Meryon estimated as half the distance in two days. Then the weather began to change; the wind shifted until it was from the south, forcing them to sail into the wind. The caique is not well suited for sailing into the wind, as its shallow draft causes it to slip sideways as much or more than any forward progress that is gained. But since they were so close to Alexandria, the captain decided to push on and fought the waves for the next twenty-four hours even as the gale was increasing.

Finally he gave up, came about, and ran before the wind, heading for Rhodes. The buffeting and pounding of the boat ceased but the

damage had been done and it was leaking. The pumps did not work
and all hands began to bail.

Hester was at her best in crises and this one was no exception.
She claimed that she never felt fear, and on this and many other occasions it appeared to be true. She rose, dressed herself, and directed
her maid to prepare a box with a few necessary items, and then set
out to comfort and encourage the crew. There was a cask of wine on
board and Hester drew and distributed the wine among the sailors.

They continued to struggle, but it was hopeless, and panic set in
among some of the crew and the servants. There was a little comfort
when they glimpsed the island of Rhodes, but it was too late: the
ship had heeled gunwale down and was so waterlogged that it would
not answer the helm. Clearly sinking, they launched the longboat
with great difficulty and everyone scrambled aboard. The longboat
was overloaded, so no luggage was permitted. Hester had her small
box, while Dr. Meryon carried a bag of coin, his saber, and a pistol.
Everything else was left behind, including a small dog that could not
be induced to jump. It was a frightening gamble as waves continued
to break over the longboat. At last they reached a rock off the coast
of Rhodes where they were able to beach the boat on the leeward
side and scramble ashore. There was a cave on the rock where Hester and her maid were able to squeeze in and gain some shelter. The
exhausted men slept on the spray-drenched rocks.

At midnight the weather eased and the captain decided to try
to reach the island, but only without the additional load of his passengers. Promising to light a fire on the shore to signal his safe
arrival, captain and crew shoved off, and after two hours the fire was
sighted. The castaways settled down to await their deliverance. They
waited all day, becoming convinced that they had been abandoned
when, just before sunset, a black speck appeared on the water. As it
approached, they made out the longboat and the crew without the
captain, who had declined to chance another risky passage.

The crew had been celebrating their first landfall and fortifying
themselves for the second trip by consuming a considerable quantity of *arak* (a strong licorice-flavored liquor). They brought bread,

water, and cheese as well as more arak. Continuing to drink and, in Meryon's words, becoming "riotous and insolent," in the middle of the night the drunken sailors decided it was time to return to the island. The passengers begged them to wait for morning, but they were obstinate and there was no choice but to go with them. At the mercy of the impaired skills of the pilot and crew, they somehow made it to the surf and were swamped by a great wave just as they touched land.

They had lost almost everything, including their clothes. When they started reprovisioning, Hester concluded that to find clothes that would allow her to dress as an Englishwoman would be next to impossible, to dress as a Turkish woman would prevent her from talking with Turkish men, and thus she must, of necessity, dress as a Turkish man. She described her dress:

> as an Asiatic Turk in traveling dress—just a sort of silk and cotton shirt; next a striped silk and cotton waistcoat; over that another with sleeves, and over that a cloth short jacket without sleeves or half-sleeves, beautifully worked in coloured twist, a large pair of breeches, and Turkish boots, a sash into which goes a brace of pistols, a knife, and a sort of short sword, a belt for powder and shot made of variegated leather, which goes over the shoulder, the pouches the same, and a turban of several colours, put on in a particular way with a large bunch of natural flowers on one side.[11]

She dressed similarly for the rest of her life.

Hester's party was spared further experience with local shipping by Captain Henry Hope, who had heard of their shipwreck and came from Smyrna to offer them passage on the frigate *Salsette*. The voyage was stormy, but they arrived in Alexandria on February 11, 1812, two years and a day after Hester left England. She disembarked to a thirteen-gun salute from the *Salsette*.

Travel from Alexandria to Cairo today involves a three-hour train trip, during which a meal is served, or a five-hour bus ride with no meal. Hester and her party departed on donkeys and shifted to flat-bottomed boats to cross Lake Madiah. They proceeded up a branch of the Nile to Aboukir Bay, then along the coast for a mile or two to Lake Edko, and again mounted donkeys. They rode to Rosetta, where they hired two *dahabeahs* (houseboats) with two eight-foot-square cabins each to take them up the Nile, and after sailing day and night they reached Cairo on the fifth night.

The ruler of Egypt was Mehemet Ali, an Albanian who, by way of the Turkish army, had maneuvered himself to a position where he was able to seize power from the Mamelukes by means of a merciless massacre.

Mamelukes were themselves descended from slaves of the Arab rulers of Egypt who had revolted in the thirteenth century and had remained in power ever since. By the time Mehemet Ali assumed power in 1805, the country was nearly ruined. His tactic for dealing with the Mamelukes was to hold a banquet and invite the leaders. When they entered the city gates, his troops, who had been positioned on the walls, opened fire and slaughtered them. This was one year before Hester's visit.

Hester was not intimidated, and when she was invited to the palace her main concern was what she would wear. Again she dressed as an Arab man, this time in a Tunisian costume of purple velvet embroidered with gold, wearing two Kashmir shawls, one as a turban and the other as a girdle. The pasha received her respectfully, sending "[f]ive of his finest horses, splendidly caparisoned" to bear her and her party to the Ezbekiah Palace, preceded by a party of officials bearing silver sticks to mark her social status.

The pasha, who had never seen an English lady before, received her in the garden of his harem and seated her on a beautifully embroidered divan of scarlet velvet. In an exceptional recognition of his guest's rank, he had risen to greet her when she entered. He plied her with sherbet and coffee, and offered her a *nargileh*, which she refused because she had not learned to smoke at this point. He further honored her by having her review his troops, which she did, mounted, and used the occasion to demonstrate her equestrian skills.

Hester and the pasha apparently got along quite well as Hester felt free to visit him frequently whenever she chose, and they also rode together. As Hester wrote to Stratford Canning, "I talked to him for hours together and everything I asked was done." And Hester, never one to avoid the delicate topic, wrote, "I visited the widow of Mourad Bey; I was on terms of great intimacy with all the wives and widows of the Mamelukes, who were murdered or who fled, and I gave him myself an account of my visits."[12]

On May 3, 1812, the party left Cairo for the Holy Land, and after an uneventful voyage they arrived in Jaffa. Having reached the Middle East, Hester was now immersing herself in a radically different culture. The way people thought, behaved, and lived in Egypt, Palestine, and Syria was totally different from anything she had experienced to this point in her life. In fact, she had passed her first test with her deft handling of Mehemet Ali, but there were many and more dangerous tests to come.

In Palestine and Syria she would find that outside of the cities and villages and even within them, tribes were the basic form of social organization. Bedouin form groups with common patrilineal descent, and it is the group that bears responsibility for avenging wrongs done to its members and compensating those whom its members have wronged. Multiple related groups may join together as a clan, and multiple clans form a tribe, which is led by a sheikh and is the dominant political unit. It is also the primary military unit, although tribes may join together in tribal confederations led by a dominant sheikh.

Deserts are dangerous, unforgiving places, and this has led to bedouin mores that are admired by and have become common to the entire Arab culture. A traveler in the desert may seek sanctuary at any tent he encounters, and whether he is a friend, an enemy, or a stranger he is welcomed, fed, and sheltered for up to three days. The traveler is ushered into the tent and seated near the fire, and tea and coffee are prepared. The hospitality is complete: whatever the host has, he presses on his guest, though it may be all that he has. It seems likely that this tradition arose as a desert survival mechanism—without it, no one would dare to venture from the safety of their own tribe. This hospitality and the generosity that accompanies it became embedded in the general Arab culture and is found away from the desert in villages, towns, and cities. Should one express admiration for an object in an Arab home, she is likely to find her host insisting that of course she must have it.

Hospitality and sanctuary did not make the desert safe for the traveler, however; there was still the constant threat of attack, and many were the instances when a traveler lost everything, including his clothing and sometimes his life. Protection included weapons, alertness, stealth, and, best of all, a guide who was related or allied to the tribe through whose territory one was passing.

To a large extent, Palestine, though a part of the Ottoman Empire, was still unfamiliar territory to Europeans. A few traveled there but at substantial risk, for bandits preyed on vulnerable travelers. The risk made little impression on Hester.

She stayed in Jaffa only long enough to assemble servants and transport for the trip to Jerusalem. When she set off, she rode at the head of the column with two grooms walking at her horse's head. The rest of the column included ten camels and four horses. She was obviously a dignitary and a rich target as well.

Their path passed through the territory of a mercenary sheikh named Abu Ghosh who exacted a tax from all travelers. While the sheikh's usual technique involved force, for some reason he decided to receive Hester and her party as guests. He killed a sheep and his four wives prepared a meal that included four different combinations of lamb and rice: lamb stuffed with rice, lamb coated with rice, lamb chopped up in rice, and lamb and rice wrapped up in vine leaves.

The sheikh was fascinated with Hester, not least because she was not at all frightened of him. When it was time to retire, one of her Mamelukes suggested that they post guards around their camp for the night. It was a reasonable suggestion considering their host's reputation, but Hester was struck by an inspiration. She asked the sheikh if he would provide guards for them, thus placing her safety in his hands. In this, one of her earliest encounters with Arabs, she had intuitively appealed to a fundamental value—the obligation of a host to protect his guest. Abu Ghosh sat up all night by the fire. After presenting the sheikh with a fine gift, Hester continued her journey, leaving a new friend in her wake.

Reaching Jerusalem, thus fulfilling part of the Brothers prophecy, they visited the Holy Sepulcher and were mobbed by crowds of people anxious to see the English lady. With relief, they left and returned to Jaffa, then continued on to Nazareth.

There Michael Bruce encountered a man dressed as an Arab who addressed him in perfect English. The man, who called himself Sheikh Ibrahim, was Johann Ludwig Burckhardt, the renowned Swiss orientalist. Hester was not impressed and seemed to be annoyed primarily by the way Burckhardt traveled: his ability to disappear into the local environment, an obvious contrast to her own style. "To go to Palmyra or anywhere else like a thief I do not like, to scalk about fearing to meet this or that tribe of Bedouins, I go as a friend of them all."[13]

From Nazareth they passed through Acre, visiting Tyre in what is now southern Lebanon, where only Michael made the excursion over the mole built by Alexander the Great's troops in order to view the ruins of the Phoenician capital. They proceeded on to Sidon where Hester received an invitation from Emir Beshir of the Druse to visit his palace at Deir Al Kamar, the capital.

The Druse, living today in Syria, Lebanon, Jordan, and Israel, are a small religious group within the Arab culture. Their religious beliefs developed out of teachings of the Ismaili sect of Shiism but other elements were drawn from Jewish, Christian, Gnostic, Neoplatonic, and Iranian sources. Their doctrine is characterized by strict monotheism and a belief in the divinity of al-Hakim bi-Amr Allah, the sixth caliph (996–1021) of the Fatimid dynasty of Egypt. The level of secrecy is such that the Druse themselves are divided into two groups, one of which consists of initiates into the secret teachings of Druse religious doctrine—the hikmah—and the other of those who are ignorant of those doctrines. Even today it is considered improper to question a Druse about his religious beliefs. While the society is very conservative, women hold a respected position in the community and are accepted into the initiated group.

Hester was fascinated by the Druse and said in one of her letters that she would have gone to Deir Al Kamar even if she had not received an invitation. As it was, the emir dispatched an entourage of twelve camels, twenty-five mules, four horses, and seven foot soldiers to escort her to his capital.

She stayed with the emir a month, seemingly undaunted by the man's vicious reputation: he had blinded three of his nephews and had his prime minister strangled. "Nothing ever equalled the honors paid to me by these men. The Prince is a mild, amiable man; but the Governor has proved a Lucifer, and I am the first traveller he ever allowed to walk over his palace which has been the scene of several massacres."[14]

Emir Beshir apparently convinced Hester that Sheikh Beshir (the governor) was the true villain. Even so, Hester spent two days with the sheikh and had the sobering experience of having an officer at her side tasting her food for poison. She said that she was used to that but "this man on his knees before me looked more solemn than usual" (126).

Caution not being Hester's particular bent, she wrote, "I understand feeling my ground so well with savage people, that I can ask questions no other person dares to put to them; but it would not be proper to repeat here those I asked even the sages, and still less their answers. Any one who asks a religious question may be murdered" (126).

The party moved on to Damascus and Hester wrote Suleiman Pasha to inform him of her arrival. The pasha graciously responded by sending a page with an invitation. He told her, however, that she must wear a veil as Damascus was one of the most fanatical cities in Turkey (as the Ottoman Empire was also known along with "the Turkish Empire") and the scandal of a woman in men's clothes and unveiled would be so great that she would be insulted at the least. This was almost exactly the wrong approach to take with Hester, although it is hard to think of a strategy that would have resulted in her wearing a veil.

So in mid-afternoon with the streets packed with people, she rode straight through the gates in her usual costume, unveiled, a "triumphal entry" as she described it in a letter to Lord Sligo (127). She was first lodged in a house in the Christian quarter, but even though the house "was reckoned a very fine house" (127), she did not approve of it and insisted that she be lodged in the Turkish quarter, "under the minaret of the Great Mosque" (127), the best quarter of Damascus. The house

> opened through a narrow passage into an oblong marble paved court. In the middle of the court was a large basin, shaded by two very lofty lemon trees, into which two brazen serpents poured a constant supply of fresh water. At one end of the court was a saloon with a tessellated marble pavement; at the other an alcove or recess for a divan or sofa, with a small apartment on each side. A double staircase led up to a considerable height on the outside of the left wall of the court; at one end, to two rooms, which Lady Hester occupied for sleeping and dressing-rooms, and at the other to a large saloon, which was destined to receive visitors. There were consequently but six rooms in all, yet this was considered a spacious house; for the Orientals sleep in the same room where they sit, their beds being removed in the day-time to large recesses formed in the walls for that purpose, and hidden by a curtain.[15]

Hester had a sure touch when dealing with the culture around her. Early in her stay in Damascus, the superiors of the two monasteries in Damascus presumed to visit Hester in her new home, assuming that they would be received as the distinguished persons they were. Hester refused to see them, and they were told that because their visit to the Turkish quarter violated the rules they normally observed, they were requested not to visit again. This episode was known among the servants and repeated to others in the city. It was considered evidence of her esteem for the Turks and contributed substantially to her popularity.

Far from being attacked or insulted, she was admired in Damascus. Crowds waited to watch her mount her horse, and when she rode, coffee was poured out on the road before her as a sign of esteem. When she entered the *suq* (bazaar), all rose to their feet, an honor that they would normally accord only the pasha or the mufti. She was saluted as the *meleki* (queen) and was received by the pasha with a display that included two thousand guards and attendants lining her route through the palace, a display that may have been intended to intimidate her as it did her dragoman, who was unable to speak at the critical moment. Hester, however, considered it a tribute and handled the affair with great aplomb, if not relish. The pasha did not rise to greet her as had other rulers, but Hester did not seem to mind.

Her visit to Damascus was unquestionably a personal victory, so Hester now turned her attention to the purpose for which she had come to Damascus: Palmyra. She had been warned that the trip was impracticable. Only three Englishmen had been known to have reached Palmyra and they had done so in disguise; at that, one of them, the explorer Burckhardt whom she had met in Nazareth, had been found out, stripped, and turned into the desert to survive as best he could. An irresistible challenge.

The high desert around Damascus was seething with instability. A force of fundamentalist Wahabi warriors was rumored to be approaching, local tribes were at war, and the strongest of these opposed the pasha. Twenty leagues (sixty miles) of waterless desert lay between Damascus and Palmyra.

Michael Bruce had gone to Aleppo from Deir Al Kamar to see the ruins and had become friends with John Barker, the English consul. Both of them were deeply concerned about the risks associated with Hester's visit to Palmyra and wrote to her suggesting various ideas. They told her that she must join a caravan to Palmyra, to which she replied that no caravan goes by the route that she intended to go and that if it did, nothing could persuade her to join it. Alarmed, the two men set off for Damascus bringing a tartaravan, described by Hester as a "wire thing" drawn by mules. Whatever it was, she vowed that "all the Consuls in the universe shall never persuade me to get into

[it]" and argued, "What an absurd idea, in case of danger to be stuck upon a machine, the tartaravangers running away and leaving you to the mercy of two obstinate mules! The swiftest horse one can find is the best thing, and what the Arabs owe their lives to."[16]

A few days after she had sent a messenger telling them that whether they came or not, she would have nothing to do with either caravan or tartaravan, there was news that a caravan from Homs to Damascus of several hundred people and fifty armed men had been attacked and sixteen were killed.

Less easily dissuaded was the pasha, who insisted on sending eight hundred or one thousand men with her—at her expense.

Hester was not being foolhardy, but rather was determined to rely on her preparations as superior to those being suggested by her would-be protectors. She had, for instance, become friends with the sons of Muhannah el-Fadel, the chief of some forty thousand members of the dominant Anazi tribe. Muhannah himself arrived in Damascus to negotiate with the pasha over six or seven thousand head of livestock that the pasha had seized. She invited Muhannah, his eldest son, and twenty-five others to dinner, and by her report they "were all enchanted" (135). With regard to the Wahabis, Muhannah assured her that "as one of his family, he shall guarantee me with his life" (135). She also had become acquainted with Sir David Dundas, "the head of everything military in Syria" (134), and he had offered her an escort of troops, but perhaps more important, he let it be known that he would remove the heads of anyone who harmed her (153). Nevertheless, she dropped her current plan for the trip from Damascus to Palmyra.

She did conduct what she described as "an experiment on the good faith of the Arabs" (141). With Michael Bruce looking after an ailing John Barker, and Dr. Meryon awaiting the arrival of a messenger from Acre, Hester told everyone that she was going to Hamah and set out on the road to that city on November 15, 1812. Along the way, she turned off briefly at Nebk to get a Frenchman and his wife to accompany her. The Frenchman, named Lascaris, was an agent for Napoleon and, having spread a great deal of money among the tribes, was on good terms with them. At a place named Tel Bysy, they left the main road and struck into the desert with only a single bedouin for a guide. This was particularly dangerous as rumors had been circulating concerning the rich English princess who was planning to visit Tadmor (Palmyra) and who "rode on a mare worth forty purses, with housings and stirrups of gold, and for whom the treasurer of the English Sultan told out every day 1000 sequins . . . that she had in her possession a book which instructed her where treasures were to be found . . . and that she had a small bag of leaves of a certain herb which would transmute antique stones into gold."[17] Because ransom was a major source of income for the bedouin, this must have been a powerful temptation.

Eventually, they approached the encampment of Emir Muhannah and placed themselves in his protection. In a letter to General Oakes she says,

> I went with the great chief, Mohanna El-Fadel into the desert for a week, and marched three days with their encampment. I was treated with the greatest respect and hospitality, and it was, perhaps, altogether, the most curious sight I ever saw—horses and mares fed upon camel's milk, Arabs living upon little else, except a little rice, and sometimes a sort of bread, the space around me covered with living creatures, twelve thousand camels coming to water from one tribe only; the old poets from the banks of the Euphrates, singing the praises and the feats of ancient heroes; children quite naked; women with lips died light-blue, and their nails red, and hands all over flowers and designs of different kinds; a chief who is obeyed like a great king—starvation and pride so mixed, that I really could not have had an idea of it.[18]

An incident occurred that revealed something about both Hester and the emir. It seems that at some point in their travel, Hester observed the tribe preparing for battle and questioned Emir Muhannah about it. Reluctantly, he told her that the problem was her presence with his tribe, that other tribes objected to his alliance with an infidel and consequently they were expecting an attack. He would, however, under no circumstances abandon or fail to protect his guest, she should not worry.

Hester replied that she would never be a source of danger to her friends and would leave so that the tribes could resolve their differences. With that she rode off alone into the desert.

She rode for hours as the sun climbed overhead until she spotted a cloud of dust in the distance that resolved slowly into several hundred bedouin charging toward her with spears raised. As the horsemen were almost upon her, she stood in her stirrups, and with a haughty wave of her arms cried, *"Avaunt!"* The riders reined their mounts to a skidding halt, possibly owing to uncertainty about the meaning of avaunt, but the threatening yells were replaced by cheers and celebratory gunshots. Hester, with proper disdain, accepted the acclaim calmly. It turned out that the entire affair had been a contrived test of Hester's bravery and she had passed with flying colors—the legend of the English princess continued to grow.

It is hard to guess to what extent Hester may have seen through this ruse and simply played along. With a seemingly intuitive grasp of Arab character and behavior, she may have suspected the plot, but without certainty, there was plenty of room for fear. Also, Hester loved drama, and the situation supplied that whether real or test. Either way, she played her role admirably.

The emir escorted her to a point near Hamah where she was joined by the rest of her party and spent the winter. The following March (1813) Hester and her party set off from Hamah on their way to Palmyra. Again she made prudent preparations for what seemed to others an imprudent undertaking. She had deposited 3,000 piastres (about £150) as the cost of her Arab escort but arranged to pay only a third of that sum in advance; the rest would be paid upon her safe return. Sir David Dundas again warned the Arab chiefs that he would cut off their heads if they failed to bring Hester back safely. Still, the major safety factor was the word of Muhannah el-Fadel that they were under his protection.

The caravan proceeded toward Palmyra, a village of 1,500 inhabitants. As they neared the oasis, a plume of dust announced a large group of riders.

> The chief and about three hundred people came out about two hours distance to meet us. He and a few of the grandees were upon Arab Mares, and dressed rather more to imitate Turks than Arabs, with silk shawls and large silk turbans. The men, at least many of them, had their whole bodies naked, except a pestimal, or petticoat, studded or ornamented with leather, blackamoors' teeth, beads, and strange sorts of things that you see on the stage. They were armed with matchlocks and guns, all surrounding me and firing in my face, with most dreadful shouts and savage music and dancing. They played all sorts of antics till we arrived at the triumphal arch at Palmyra. The inhabitants were arranged in the most picturesque manner on the different columns leading to the Temple of the Sun. The space before the arch was occupied with dancing girls, most fancifully and elegantly dressed, and beautiful children placed upon the projecting parts of the pillars with garlands of flowers. One, suspended over the arch, held a wreath over my head. After having stopped a few minutes, the procession continued. The dancing-girls immediately surrounded me. The lancemen took the lead, followed by the poets from the banks of the Euphrates, singing complimentary odes and playing on various Arabian instruments. A tribe of hale Palmyrenes brought up the rear, when we took up our habitation in the Temple of the Sun, and remained there a week.[19]

In another letter after she had left Palmyra, Hester told Mr. H. W. Wynn that she had been crowned Queen of the Desert under the Triumphal Arch at Palmyra. She was now a successor to the great Zenobia; the prophecy "You will be crowned Queen of the East" had been fulfilled. For Hester this had become a self-fulfilling prophecy; she now believed it and it influenced her actions as well as her decisions. At least in a limited sense, it was true.

While she had little interest in historical ruins, Hester did take the time to view those at Palmyra. She was aware of the rumors that she was searching for treasure, so to forestall that accusation she took the local sheikh with her and surveyed the domain she fantasized that she had inherited from Zenobia. In her letters Hester does not mention Zenobia, but her companions do. Dr. Meryon notes that she "sought the remains of Zenobia's greatness, as well as the remains of Palmyra."[20] And Michael Bruce observes, "Who knows but what she may prove another Zenobia, and be destined to restore [Palmyra] to its ancient splendour?"[21]

Their stay in Palmyra was cut short when four bedouin of the Faydan tribe were caught outside Palmyra, brought into the village, and imprisoned. Two of the men subsequently escaped and, fearing an attack by that tribe, Hester's party left and returned to Hamah where the residents, amazed at her survival, rejoiced at her return.

6

A Nun in Lebanon

Plague was sweeping over Syria, and if Hester and her party were to escape, it would have to be from a port. The only plague-free port was Latakia, so they left Hamah on the 10th of May 1813 and arrived at Latakia on the 22nd.

Craufurd Bruce was pressing for Michael's return to England, and the relationship between Michael and Hester was wearing thin. Michael was sent on his way. Apparently as a way of wrapping up her responsibility for Michael's development, Hester wrote a letter to Craufurd Bruce offering advice as to how Michael might continue to progress. He, for example, rode poorly as "his seat is loose and ungraceful,"[1] so she recommended that he go to a riding house. Then "[p]ray sit him down regularly to business for an hour or two every [day], if he does not get the habit of it now he never will."[2] And she was concerned about his table manners because he would be arriving fresh from dining on the ground and eating with his fingers.

Michael and Hester parted as friends and Hester still loved him, but her pride would not allow her to break her word to Craufurd Bruce. Michael promised her a part of his allowance but it would be far from enough to support the style of travel they had enjoyed. Financial uncertainty was heightened by evidence that Craufurd was himself having financial problems. In fact, he died in 1820, leaving his family in financial difficulties.

In spite of her best efforts, Michael never reached the potential that she saw for him. He took up law, married in 1818, and did become a Member of Parliament but only for a short period. His lasting claim to fame rested on those early years in the Middle East with Hester. She never saw him again.

Financial considerations influenced Hester in planning her travels. England and Europe were out of the question, for if she traveled to either it would appear that she was chasing Michael. The plague had reached Malta so that destination was closed as well. She settled on Mar Elias, a monastery in the mountains about two miles inland from Sidon, south of Beirut. The building, which Hester had seen while riding, was the occasional residence of the patriarch of the Greek Catholics, who graciously offered it to her for £30 a year.

Sidon is about twenty miles south of the Beirut airport on the coast of Lebanon. The ruins of a crusader fort lie at the end of a stone causeway that juts into the harbor, so when you look out to sea from the town you are seeing the same view that Hester saw in 1814. The roads leading inland from today's sprawling city pass through silver- and green-leafed olive groves and launch quickly onto the lower slopes leading into the mountains.

Deir Mar Elias, as the monastery was called, was on the top of a mountain, and the mountain lanes came finally to a difficult trail that led into a deep and barren valley and then up a steep slope to the monastery. Meryon described the site as "picturesque, but lonely and barren, on the top of a mountain without verdure, surrounded on every side with mountains equally sterile; excepting a few olive and mulberry trees on a shelving bank at the back of the building . . . From its elevated situation, the monastery commands a most extensive view of the sea."[3] The building was plain but adequate, and Hester shut herself up in Deir Mar Elias and lived in total seclusion. She had had a personal encounter with the plague and illness had taken its toll. It would be months before she recovered her characteristic drive.

In retrospect, when she settled into Mar Elias, Hester crossed the line and became a resident of the Orient rather than a traveler, a feature of the landscape rather than a transient sampler of its curiosities. However, there is no reason to believe that permanent residency was her intent. This move, like many of the previous phases of her journey, was largely dictated by circumstance.

During this period, as her correspondence began to return to its normally massive levels, Hester began to date her letters from "The Convent at Mar Elias,"[4] and signed at least one letter to Michael "the Nun of Lebanon."[5]

In July, the heat became unbearable at Deir Mar Elias and they moved to a Druse village named Mishmushy higher in the mountains. Hester said that she had not been more comfortable anywhere since leaving Malta, and after ten weeks she had recovered her energy. In October 1814, she started on a journey to Baalbek in the Bekaa Valley.

Baalbek is home to magnificent ruins beautifully sited in the Bekaa Valley between the Lebanon and Anti-Lebanon mountain ranges. It lies near the middle of that valley between the headwaters of the Orontes River that flows north and the Litani River that flows south and eventually turns west to the coast. From the walls of the ruins, the view is over green fields and trees to the peaks of the Lebanon Mountain Range, frequently covered with snow; in the opposite direction are tree-shaded streets and the ridgelines of the Anti-Lebanon Range. The ruins are layered with history: remnants of Stone Age dwellings are nestled in the Temple of Jupiter, as are the remains of a Phoenician temple and a Greek temple. The Temple of Jupiter was built by the Romans. The Phoenician temple was dedicated to Baal Bukas, the sun god of the city—hence the name Baalbek. Alexander the Great named Baalbek "Heliopolis," the City of the Sun, and a writer named Erich von Däniken, in a book entitled *Chariots of the Gods*, reports that the buildings of Baalbek, now in varying degrees of ruin, were built on a single slab of rock, and that how this rock was acquired and positioned is a mystery that is best explained in terms of extraterrestrial beings. In fact, the foundations consist of a number of huge blocks of stone, and it is something of a mystery as to how they were brought to the site. The ruins have been reconstructed some since Hester's time, but they must have been awe-inspiring even then. Hester was not fond of or impressed with ruins, but Baalbek must have been an exception.

They remained in Baalbek a fortnight and left on November 8 when warned that snow would soon close the pass over Mount Lebanon to Tripoli. They made it through the pass and down, past the famous grove of cedars and through the village of Bsharre where the poet Gibran Khalil Gibran was born some sixty years after their visit and now rests in a cave above the village.

They descended to a village named Ihdin, near the Monastery of St. Anthony at Mar Antonius. This monastery was famous for the hostility of the saint toward anything female that might penetrate the holy grounds. Hens, for example, were cooped lest they wander carelessly into the precincts, while cocks were permitted to wander at will. Thus Hester guided her party to Mar Antonius where she was lodged in a house outside the monastery, while the male members of her party were accepted inside the monastery. Shortly after her arrival, Hester sent a message to the superior announcing that on the next day she would host a dinner for him and for the sheikhs who had escorted her from Ihdin. She hinted that she would do this under authority that had been granted her by the sultan.

With the monks and servants expecting retribution from above, Hester mounted a she-ass and rode into the monastery. She made it a point to visit every room in the place, sat down to dinner, and after four hours departed.

Once again Hester was the subject of discussion, with some criticizing her sacrilege and others admiring her audacity. When she arrived at Tripoli, the entire population came out to see her. On the 16th of January 1815, the party set off down the coast of what is now Lebanon.

Hester's power in the area that is now Lebanon and coastal Syria was substantial, although entirely unofficial and undefined in terms of title or specific authority. It was observable in practice, though, and recorded in episodes and anecdotes. One episode particularly illustrates her status in the region, her reach, and aspects of her character.

A French colonel of engineers named Boutin was sent by Napoleon to become familiar with Syria and to learn Arabic. He visited

Hester at Mar Elias and Hester warned him against crossing the Ansary mountains. He took her warning lightly and crossed the mountains with two servants. Suspicions were aroused when his watch was sold in Damascus.

Hester ordered three men to trace the path Colonel Boutin was believed to have followed and they determined that he had been robbed and murdered. Hester wrote to the French consuls in the coastal towns and urged them to write to Constantinople to have the murderers found and punished. Nothing was done, as the Ansary were a powerful tribe and there was a reluctance to challenge them. Hester wrote to the European ambassadors to the Porte with the same result. Finally she wrote to the pashas of Aleppo, Damascus, Tripoli, and Acre asking each to contribute troops to a punitive expedition.

Mustafa Aga Berber, a district governor, was given command of the force. He wrote to Hester saying that because he was marching "at the Syt's [the lady] bidding to do the Syt's business," it was only fitting that she should arm her champion. This she did, sending him a brace of pistols. She also directed his movements, using her knowledge of the area and communicating through messengers. Mustafa swept into the mountains, executed the murderers, sent their heads to Damascus, burned their villages, and recovered the stolen property.

The audacity of this exploit rippled throughout the area, and Hester received the title "Protectress of the Unfortunate." The French Chamber of Deputies gave her a vote of thanks after an eloquent speech by Count Delaborde.

In a strange postscript to this affair, Hester, in the fall of the same year, chose to spend two months in Antioch in the midst of the Ansary tribe. She said that she undertook this journey to meet with Consul-General Barker and settle accounts with him, but the Duchess of Cleveland suggests that while that may have been part of the reason, the real reason was to avoid the Princess of Wales, who was scheduled to visit the Holy Land and likely would visit Mar Elias as well. The Princess of Wales was Caroline of Brunswick, now somewhat disreputable and estranged from the prince who would soon become George IV. It was still a strange place to go, even to avoid the

Princess of Wales. Hester had known the Ansaris before the episode with Colonel Boutin; in fact, she had been adopted by the tribe and spoke of them as her "family." Family notwithstanding, revenge was an accepted element of the Arab culture and there was every reason to expect that she would be abducted and killed by relatives of those killed or even those whose homes had been burned. Nonetheless she took up residence in a secluded and unprotected cottage outside the town. She was even warned, while there, that her life was in danger, but instead of moving to safety, she instead chose to lecture the peasants who gathered at her cottage, explaining that she did, in fact, take revenge on the murderers of Colonel Boutin "because she knew that all just persons abhorred the deeds committed against the defenseless in the dark—deeds such as must be disowned by the brave and the good everywhere."[6] We can only speculate as to why she wasn't killed. Dr. Meryon writes that it was because of the fear engendered by the vengeance exacted for Colonel Boutin. Whatever the reason, her legend grew.

THERE WAS A MAJOR CHANGE in Hester's life sometime after the expedition to Baalbek: her challenges came to involve more statecraft than travel. She had sequestered herself before, but now it was more a change of lifestyle than a temporary retreat. She was experiencing financial problems partly owing to an unsuccessful treasure hunting expedition that she had financed. It is tempting to suggest that her financial problems dictated severe limits to her travel. On the other hand, she had never retreated from such obstacles before and she continued to spend money freely on other projects and expenses. It may have been a question of what challenged her, what stimulated her quest for adventure. She had exhausted most of the possibilities of the Ottoman Empire and Syria in particular. Perhaps there were simply no more challenges worthy of her attention. Whatever the reason, Hester retired to Mar Elias and looked after her domain.

That she settled finally in the mountains of Lebanon was a fulfillment of a series of curious prophecies. The first, which I mentioned earlier, came from the fortune-teller named Brothers, who predicted that she would travel to Jerusalem and spend seven years in the desert. It was an unlikely prediction for a time when few Europeans visited the Holy Land and when Hester had done no more travel than her Grand Tour, showing no interest in the East. Then she encountered a mentally unbalanced Frenchman who called himself General Loustaneau, claimed he had served in the native Indian armies, and now lived by begging and prophesying. He intrigued Hester by telling her that Napoleon had escaped from Elba, a very unlikely event given that he was well guarded. Later, it turned out to be correct: Napoleon had escaped in February 1815 and Loustaneau had announced his vision on March 18th when the escape was not known in the Holy Land. She offered him a home at Mar Elias whenever he needed one. With Bible in hand, he claimed to be able to cite texts that would prove that her coming had been foretold in the Scriptures and that she was the only real queen. Finally one of her servants, an old Syrian named Metta, told her of a secret prophetic book that he could produce if she would lend him a horse. She did and he returned with a book in Arabic that contained a passage that he translated, "A European female would come and live on Mount Lebanon at a certain epoch, would build a house there, and would obtain power and influence greater than a Sultan's; that a boy, without a father, would join her, whose destiny will be fulfilled under her wing; that the coming of the Mahdi would follow, but be preceded by war, pestilence, famine, and other calamities; that the Mahdi would ride a horse born saddled, and that a woman would come from a far country to partake in the mission."[7] The "woman from a far country" remained a mystery until the year 1835, when the Baroness de Feriat, an English lady residing in the United States, wrote of her own accord out of admiration of Lady Hester Stanhope's character, asking to come and live with her when the prophecy was fulfilled.[8]

Then Emir Beshir made a gift to Hester of a beautiful bay mare and sent with her a she-ass "said to be a lineal descendent of the ass on which our Saviour rode on His entry to Jerusalem."[9] Some months later the mare gave birth to a foal with a growth on its back that formed a natural saddle of the Turkish style.[10]

It is difficult to know to what extent these prophecies influenced Hester's behavior. At times she ridiculed Brothers's prophecy, but as the years passed and people referred to her as a queen or a princess and when she was welcomed with a pseudo-crowning in Palmyra, it must have had some effect. Known to be fascinated by the mysterious and wondrous, the accumulation of these events and prophecies could well have inspired her. Certainly, the way she behaved in the Boutin affair and during the last major phase of her life was unmistakably regal.

A steady stream of visitors made their way to Sidon and on to Mar Elias to visit Hester, and whenever possible she would provide them with accommodation and entertain them, an expense that added strain to her already limited budget. In addition to the mostly European visitors, she never turned away a bedouin or anyone in need or distress. Women, including visitor's wives, were generally not welcome. Hester professed a general dislike of women and said that there were only three among the hundreds she had known whom she could speak of with unreserved admiration.

Her own staff numbered over twenty and included a secretary, chef, groom, muleteers, and water carriers. Mar Elias was becoming too small.

Higher on Mount Lebanon, Hester had seen a small house on the top of a hill that would allow her to build the accommodations she required. The house was near the village of Djoun and was called Dar Djoun. Hester moved there in 1817 or 1818.

Rooms, entire dwellings, cottages, offices, and stables were built around the house and enclosed within a wall. One of the rooms was a prison. A large garden with covered alleys, serpentine walks, summer houses, pavilions, and arbors was constructed adjacent to the compound and also enclosed within a wall. Meryon observes that the compound was constructed in such a way that no one could enter or leave unobserved and that once inside the compound, the layout of the buildings and rooms was a labyrinth. In the garden, two of the pavilions had trap doors in the floor leading to steps that descended into an underground room that, in turn, had doors in the wall that led to the outside. The size and nature of the construction are consistent with the idea that Dar Djoun was intended as a sanctuary for a potentially large number of refugees. According to Meryon, she kept a score of workmen constantly working on the compound and, in addition, she rented four or five cottages in the village of Djoun and purchased a ruined house there that she planned to turn into an inn.

It was Hester's old friend Mehemet Ali in Cairo who, seeing opportunity in the weakness of the Ottoman Empire, sent his son Ibrahim Pasha and an army of 50,000 up the coast from Gaza, seizing towns and laying siege to the town of Acre while terrorizing the countryside. Refugees, including some who had been condemned by Ibrahim Pasha, fled to Dar Djoun. The pasha demanded their surrender but Hester defied him with the reply that he must take her life first, for as long as she had breath, she would protect those who had sought protection under her roof. She won her point and after subduing Acre, Ibrahim Pasha ignored Dar Djoun but went on to take Damascus, defeat the Ottoman army, and threaten Constantinople. The Great Powers stepped in and saved Sultan Mahmud and the empire, but arranged a peace that conceded to Mehemet Ali the governorships of Aleppo, Tripoli, Damascus, and Sidon.

Earlier, in 1817, Hester's father had died. She had had no contact with him for many years but that is no insurance against grief: there is always the pain in the thoughts of what might have been. Her half-brother Mahon had become the fourth Earl Stanhope, and though she had not spoken to him in years, she took the occasion to write him a letter that he described as "most cruel and insulting."

Her sister Lucy had died in 1814, but the real blow came on May 25, 1825, when her beloved half-brother James committed suicide. As recently as the treasure hunting fiasco, she had talked of asking James to come and take her to Europe; now the last working link to her family was gone. She was estranged from her last surviving sister, Grizelda, as well as from Mahon. Grizelda wrote to her following James's death in the only communication between them in thirty years. Hester did not reply. In fact, we know nothing of

Hester's grieving except that from this time her way of life changed once more. Never again was she seen outside her garden wall.

Her break with England became complete with an incident involving one of her creditors. The British consul-general of Egypt had written to Hester demanding payment on behalf of a merchant. When Hester responded negatively, he referred the matter to the British Foreign Office, where it was decided to suspend her pension in order to repay her debts in Egypt. This was done by order of the young Queen Victoria, and Hester was informed by means of another letter from the consul-general. She in turn wrote directly to Queen Victoria telling her that she should have investigated the situation before taking action and that she would resign her pension rather than having it stopped by force and with it she resigned her status as an English subject.

Hester had now severed all connections. Few people in England remembered her and fewer still cared. Mrs. Williams, her faithful friend and attendant, had died and there were now no Europeans with her at Dar Djoun. She was very ill with what was probably tuberculosis. The local servants stole from her whenever the occasion would permit and the level of care she received from them is unknown; nor is it known who, if anyone, was with her when she died on the 23rd of June 1839.

Mr. Moore, the English consul in Beirut, and a Rev. Mr. Thomson, an American missionary, proceeded to Djoun from Beirut, arrived about ten the same evening, and interred Hester according to her instructions in a vault in the garden, the same vault in which lay the bones of Captain Loustenau, the son of the "General."

In the words of Rev. Thomson,

The Consul subsequently remarked that there were some curious coincidences between this and the burial of Sir John Moore, her Ladyship's early love. In silence, on the lone mountain, at midnight, "our lanterns dimly burning," with the flag of her country over her, she "lay like a warrior taking his rest," and we "left her alone in her glory." There was but one of her own nation present, and his name was Moore.[11]

Lady Hester Lucy Stanhope was a legendary figure during her life and even more so afterward, a woman who has been dead more than 150 years, yet whose story seems fresh and unique, a personality that would be notable today. She was legendary not only in the West, where a number of books have been written about her, but also in the Middle East, where her story is more widely known.

The legend is, in part, her own creation, for she had a flair for the dramatic and an attraction to adventure. Her correspondence is voluminous and does not fail to carefully describe her successes and to ensure that the reader is fully aware of the drama involved.

The personality behind the legend is well documented by multiple observers as well as by her own words. An outspoken woman, unconcerned about the effect of her words on others and equally unconcerned about public opinion, she created a wide swath of enemies, unaware or at least unconcerned with the effect that these enemies might have on her later. On one occasion, she gratuitously insulted bankers as a group at a dinner party that included close friends who were bankers. Years later, when she asked them for help, they refused her coldly. Her standard seemed to be honesty at all costs, even where the subject was simply a matter of her own opinion with no pressing reason for expressing it. She was loyal to the point of obsession, both to memories as in the case of Pitt and John Moore, and to the living such as James, the Bruces father and son, and inexplicably, the Grand Porte whom she had never met. She expected that same caliber of loyalty from those who served her and did little to reciprocate. She would, for example, only occasionally and then grudgingly admit to any good qualities on the part of Dr. Charles Meryon who served her loyally and often courageously through much of his life. On many occasions he would set off alone to make arrangements in advance of Hester's journeys.

Her courage was remarkable, although it is hard to separate courage from fearlessness, which she also possessed in great measure.

These characteristics, combined with her instinctive response to challenges, created the adventure that constituted much of her life. Had she been a soldier, "ride to the sound of the guns" would surely have been her creed.

Hester commanded a bundle of personal traits that can best be described as regal. She would accept no slight, no treatment that failed to meet her standards, and she felt and acted upon a responsibility to the less fortunate among her fellows. Her treatment as royalty in the Middle East was owing, in part, to misunderstanding by the Arabs. They confused her relation to Pitt as a relationship to the king of England. The pashas were presumably better informed, yet they treated her with deference as well. Probably the simplest answer is that if you want to be treated as a queen, act like a queen.

But that does not explain why she was so readily accepted by the Turks and the Arabs. Virginia Childs in *Lady Hester Stanhope: Queen of the Desert* suggests that the acceptance stemmed from the fact that Hester possessed qualities admired by the Arabs, and further, because she behaved as they did. It is likely that she is right; Hester's great dignity, her courage and fearlessness, her generosity and equestrian skills were all characteristics that were and are greatly admired by Arabs. Her behavior and lifestyle gradually became more and more oriental over the years until at Dar Djoun her life was devoid of European characteristics. She had even taken up smoking the nargileh. All of this may have impressed her guests, but it does not account for the almost instant acceptance and rapport she established with all she met. If anything, the way she dressed must have seemed bizarre to the Arabs, and while an attention-getter, her acceptance was probably in spite of this rather than because of it. This conflicts with her own assessments of the effects of her dress. She said that had she not adopted men's clothing after the shipwreck, she would have been nothing. If we accept that as accurate for a moment, it means that the Arabs viewed clothing symbolically, for there is no question that they knew she was a woman. She was celebrated far and wide as the *meleki* (the queen) or the princess or the *sitt* (the lady), and she was given complete freedom to visit and investigate the harems; she considered this one of her major accomplishments. So the sheikhs, emirs, and sultans either accepted her in spite of her clothing because of her reputation, or the men's clothing was a cue that regardless of her gender, she was to be accorded the standing of a man. We should note that her gender permitted her to do things that she could not have done as a man. Women are protected as well as oppressed in some Arab societies, and this may have worked to her advantage, particularly in her journeys into the Syrian desert.

Perhaps the most notable feature of Hester's early life was the degree to which she was on her own, even as a child. Her mother died, and she was left to an uninterested stepmother, an eccentric if not mentally ill father, and frustrated governesses with whom she maintained a state of hostility, and yet she thrived. There was no adult with whom she was sufficiently close to be able to pattern herself. Hester simply was not provided a script either to follow or to rebel against; she had to invent a script of her own. Thus marriage, which would have been the fate of most young women of her class, was not forced upon her, and though she received multiple offers, there was no compulsion to accept. With that obstacle avoided, the balance of her life became a blank slate that she could fill more or less as she wished and this she did with a creativity she may have inherited from her father.

So Hester wrote her own script and played out a life that was not only extraordinary for a woman of her era but also unique among the explorers and travelers of her day. A more abstract assessment of her life would suggest that the energy that propelled her out of England onto her unusual journey and life was the pressure of a forceful woman unrestrained by social norms colliding with a society that limited women to a narrow band of social roles. With a different structure, Hester could herself have been prime minister of England.

PART THREE

LADY JANE ELIZABETH DIGBY EL MESRAB
1807–1881

This fine English lady, so willowy, so fragile; this milky woman, so broken, so breakable, so sweet; with her caressing brow crowned with such fine tawny coloured hair; this creature whose brilliance seems luminous and evanescent, is an edifice of steel. No horse, whatever his mettle, can fight against her nervous wrist, her soft hand that nothing in the world can tire. She has the feet of a doe, small, dry and muscular beneath an indescribably graceful sheath of skin. She has a physical strength which makes her fearless in any combat; no man can keep pace with her on horseback; she would carry off the prize in a steeplechase with centaurs; she can shoot deer and hart without reining her horse. Her body is innocent of sweat; it breathes in fire from the atmosphere and is at home in water. Her passion is all African; her desire rises like a whirlwind in the desert, that desert whose burning immensity is painted in her eyes, desert full of azure and love, with its unchanging sky and its cool, starry nights.

> —Description of Lady Arabelle Dudley modeled after Jane Digby. HONORÉ DE BALZAC, *Lily of the Valley*

Figure 3. *Jane Digby, Lady Ellenborough* (1807–1881), an oval miniature by Knight after the portrait by Josef Stieler, commissioned by King Ludwig I of Bavaria for the Gallery of Beauties, in an ivory frame at Berrington Hall, Herefordshire. BER/P/30. © National Trust Images/ John Hammond.

7

JANE'S WORLD

Geordie—The Regency—David Roberts

Napoleon's invasion of Egypt launched a fashion trend in England and Europe. The material and images his expedition brought back created a romantic aura that influenced architecture, decoration, painting, and literature. Into the arms of this trend was born a lad who, in the Highlands of Scotland, was called Geordie. Wee Geordie was six years old when his life changed forever.

His grandfather was an admiral nicknamed "Foulweather Jack" because it seemed that every time he put to sea he encountered a hurricane. Then there was his father, John, son of Foulweather, a dissolute spendthrift who had married Geordie's mother for her money and then proceeded to ruin her financially. His mother, Catherine Gordon of Gight, had a violent temper that her marriage helped to make chronic, but she did love to read good literature. Geordie's sister married a man whose father bore the forbidding nickname "The Wicked Lord" and who objected strongly to the marriage. On top of everything Geordie had been born with a deformed right foot that subjected him to childish torment in school.

While he was Geordie in the Highlands of Scotland, he was born George Gordon Byron, and the classroom event that changed his life happened when, for the first time, his name was called with the appellation *dominus* or lord. The startled stares of his fellow students rendered Geordie speechless and then he burst into tears. It seems the Wicked Lord had been the fifth Baron Byron of Rochdale and he died with no immediate heir, leaving the title and Newstead

Abbey, his estate, to his hated daughter-in-law's brother. So George Gordon the sixth Lord Byron had to learn to cope, and he did by playing cricket and by becoming a powerful swimmer, a famous poet, an infamous libertine, a lover, and arguably the second most famous man in Europe after Napoleon.

His fame was built in almost equal parts on his amorous behavior and on his poetry. A bisexual, his affairs with women ranged from giddy, overwhelming love and long-term relationships to temporary lusty encounters, usually with married women. The strikingly handsome man with luxurious black curls exerted a magnetic attraction both on women and on many men, and if the quality of his romantic skills was significantly above average, the quantity of his encounters was exceptional.

Lord Byron was living and loving during a period of British history known as the Regency. George Augustus Frederic, the Prince of Wales, became regent in 1811 when his father, George III, was declared to be mad and unable to exercise the powers of the Crown. The prince was regent until 1820 when his father died and he became George IV. A dissipated man who became obese, he was drunk at his wedding and spent his wedding night under the grate of the bedroom fireplace unconscious. This may have been because of the fact that he was repulsed by his new bride, Caroline, who was apparently hygienically challenged. During her days as "first lady," Hester Stanhope had been one of Princess Caroline's ladies-in-waiting, and this is probably why the princess planned to visit Hester in Lebanon. For his part, the prince was married, though unofficially, to a widow whom he kept in Brighton on the south coast sixty miles south of London. To add a little balance to this description, the prince and subsequent king was keenly interested in and supportive of the arts and architecture. Music, literature, theater, and painting experienced a period of rich growth during his reign. He himself was constantly building and not the least of his creations is an oriental-appearing palace known as the Royal Pavilion in Brighton with a possible tunnel connecting the palace to what is now the Queens Hotel on the seafront. In 1984 I was working for Cheffick

Ltd., a company that, among other things, owned the Queens, The Prince, and the Royal Albion hotels on the Brighton seafront. While the Queens Hotel was being remodeled, two tunnel entrances were found in the basement: one was pointed toward the seafront and the other in the general direction of the Royal Pavilion. The entrances to both tunnels were sealed and, to my knowledge, the destination of the latter tunnel was never determined. The Queens Hotel is just a short walk from the Norfolk Hotel that became an important location in Jane Digby's life.

It would be unfair to attribute the moral tenor of the Regency era entirely to the Prince Regent or even to him and Lord Byron. They both did their best, but to be successful the equation requires an inspired and willing public. This was supplied by the aristocracy and the gentry. In this stratum of society, one married for political, economic, or social reasons; produced heirs; and then found romance with a mistress or a lover. Almost everyone knew, but if practiced with a modicum of discretion, the key players were covered by a veil of deniability while still providing subjects for juicy discussion.

Anyway, that was only half of Lord Byron's appeal; the other half was his poetry. Byron was entranced by the East and he had traveled as far as Greece and Turkey. His first major success was *Childe Harold's Pilgrimage*, an autobiographically based epic of the travels of the hero that reach from Lisbon to the Greek Isles and Istanbul. Eventually Byron exiled himself from England, though it has been suggested that it was a forced exile brought on by a scandal over his homosexual behavior. In either case, he lived the rest of his short life in Europe and mostly in Greece, where he took up the cause of Greek independence from the Ottoman Empire. It was during this period that he met Hester Stanhope, and they were mutually unimpressed. Byron despised females in general and was unable to tolerate a forceful woman such as Hester. He died in Missolonghi in Greece at age thirty-four.

Regardless of how far east Byron actually traveled, he reinforced Europe's attention in that direction and his personal mystique only added to the allure of the East.

Many other writers took up the theme of the Romantic Orient, as did dozens of visual artists as well. Some of the artists worked from images described in literature or sketches made by travelers, but for David Roberts there was no alternative but to travel to the source and to experience and sketch the land at first hand.

For the son of a shoemaker and a laundress, formal education was out of reach, but the boy had talent that was apparent to all. When circuses visited Edinburgh, David would study the sights and the animals, run home, and sketch them on a whitewashed kitchen wall for his mother. One of his father's customers, seeing the lions, tigers, and leopards on the wall, insisted that the boy should not be apprenticed to his father as a shoemaker but should be apprenticed to a housepainter: house-painting at the time included interior decoration that could be quite elaborate with murals, the illusion of three dimensions, and innovative use of color. As an apprentice, David was assigned to the laborious tasks of grinding and mixing paints, but his talent quickly pushed him into the artistic aspects of the trade. In their little free time he and the other apprentices set up a studio in the basement of a house where one of the apprentices lived. They called it the Life Academy and their first model was a donkey. The boys took turns feeding and caring for the animal, and it is said that in David Roberts's paintings the donkeys are always more accurately represented than the camels. David went on to painting stage sets and was quickly a success at that as well. One of the sets for the Edinburgh Theatre was for the performance of *Aladdin and the Forty Thieves*, and David was enchanted, sketching them all. Long before he set foot in the East, he believed that he knew the landscape by heart and, more important, a longing had been implanted. By the time he began landscape painting he was already well known. He soon began to travel and sketch: first to the Highlands of Scotland, then to Spain, and on to Morocco. After each trip, with a folio full of sketches, he would translate the sketches into watercolor and oil paintings. The Morocco sketches proved to be the lure that would tempt David Roberts onto a path to the east.

Boarding a steamer in Marseilles in September 1838, he arrived in Malta six days later and then traveled on to Alexandria, Cairo, and Nubia, through the Sinai to Petra, Jericho, Bethlehem, Jerusalem, Nablus, and Nazareth, and then north along the coast to Tyre, Sidon, and Beirut. In Sidon he commented on Lady Hester Stanhope's good judgment in choosing so fair a place to settle, while at that moment she lay dying in Dar Djoun in the mountains just above. From Beirut he climbed up and over the mountains to the town of Zaleh, which he thought was one of the prettiest towns he had seen, and then up the Bekaa Valley to Baalbek. Roberts was awed by the ruins and made detailed sketches of a number of the temples. In a little less than a year he was back in London hard at work translating the sketches into lithographs that would be included in a series of published folios entitled *The Holy Land, Idumea, Arabia, Egypt and Nubia*, consisting of 320 subjects in six volumes. Roberts was paid £3,000 for the use of the works and the folios were sold by subscription for £52.10; among the subscribers were Charles Dickens and Queen Victoria. In 2011 a set of the original folios was listed on the American Book Exchange for $495,000. By the time the first volume was published, David Roberts had been named a full member of the Royal Academy and was now wealthy as well as famous. His art had altered the way the West saw the East.

It was this milieu that enveloped Jane Elizabeth Digby from her birth on April 3, 1807.

8

EVERYTHING FOR LOVE

Cast against a background of loss, grieving, and romantic failure, the loss of General John Moore was the event that thrust Hester Stanhope into the journey that would last the rest of her life. Similarly, cycles of romantic hope and disappointment drove the life and travels of Jane Digby. In Jane's case, disappointment did not lead to a change of strategy but rather to a new fascination and a fresh attack. Her scorecard shows four husbands and at least six lovers. She had a vision of what love should be and a conviction that her ideal could be found; that she did not find him immediately was not owing to a lack of effort. She was an example of a class of successful people personified by the entrepreneur who invests everything in a new business, fails, loses all, and then picks herself up and struggles again, and again, until she achieves success. And Jane Digby did.

In the early nineteenth century, the upper classes of England were the nobility and the gentry. The latter were well-born, generally wealthy, and frequently landowners, and were entitled to a coat of arms. They did not, however, bear a title. The nobility included the royal princes and the peerage: those bearing the title of duke, marquess, earl, viscount, and baron. Lesser nobility included baronets, who could transmit their title to the next generation, and knights, who could not. In 1801, all titled individuals in England totaled fewer than 1,500 and this was in a total population of 8.5 million. The nobility and gentry together would number no more than 10,000. Thus Hester Stanhope, whose father was an earl, was a member of a select level of society even without her family's connections to political power.

Jane Digby was born into the same level. Her grandfather was Thomas Coke, the first Earl of Leicestershire of Holkham; her mother, Lady Andover, was the widow of Viscount Andover; and her father was Henry Digby, a naval captain with many prize ships and thus considerable wealth to his credit. With Lord Nelson at Trafalgar, he became a national hero when, misunderstanding a signal from the flagship ordering him to stand away to safety, he laid on all sails and bore into the enemy fleet, a daring and successful maneuver. Captain Henry Digby was honored by both houses of Parliament and awarded a gold medal. His career prospered, and he was eventually promoted to rear admiral, vice admiral, and admiral.

Jane was born in Forston House, Dorset. Forston House, a country estate, overlooks the Cerne Abbas giant. The giant, likely of Celtic origin, is formed by trenches carved into the hillside and filled with chalk. Not least of its remarkable features is an erect phallus that was lengthened by some seven feet during the Victorian era. While Jane's father was away at sea, her mother took her to spend extended stays at her grandfather's 43,000-acre estate, Holkham Hall in Norfolk.

Set in the midst of a park with lakes, forest, and a distant view of the sea, Holkham Hall was famous in Jane's day and is still magnificent today. The massive building, built in Palladian style between 1734 and 1762 by Thomas Coke, the first Earl of Leicester, still sits on 3,000 acres with a one-mile-long lake.

While her parents cared about her and were involved in her upbringing, the era and their class called for the services of a governess. Miss Margaret Steele was the daughter of a poor but scholarly clergyman. Educated as a lady but never married, when her father died she was forced to seek employment and found both a position and a lifelong relationship with Jane and her family. She would play a treacherous role in Jane's life.

Jane was adventurous and fearless: a potent combination. She could ride anything found in the stables at Holkham, and she led her brothers and cousins on expeditions through the maze of corridors and rooms of the great house. At age eight she wandered away with a troop of gypsies, was recaptured, and returned to Holkham Hall.

When Margaret Steele took command of Jane at age ten, she found that she had an apt pupil. Jane was adept at languages, loved literature, and had artistic talent that was encouraged in special lessons in painting and drawing given by Margaret's sister Jane Steele. She had no patience for the traditional feminine tasks such as needlework.

When Jane was described, it was always with some variation or elaboration of beautiful. At age sixteen, the description was "an enchanting child with 'a most lovely and sweet-turned face,' delicate pale-gold hair, wide-apart dark blue eyes with long dark lashes. She had a good skin and wild rose coloring . . . a pretty figure and was tall for her age."[1] The next year, Jane was introduced to London society.

Because her beauty was well known, her appearance in the London social swirl was eagerly anticipated. The problem was not going to be finding suitors but selecting the best candidate from among the many.

ON KING STREET in London, near the fashionable gentlemen's clubs of St. James Street, were the rather plain assembly rooms of an organization called Almack's. In the American Old West it would have been called a dance hall, but in Regency London it was the extremely fashionable and exclusive playground of the upper class. Its attraction was not the undistinguished supper that was served or the music; the Scottish reels, the English country dances, or even the French quadrille were available elsewhere. The sheer exclusivity associated with admission was the draw. Vouchers permitting one to approach the portals of Almack's were authorized by a group of Lady Patronesses that consisted of Ladies Castlereagh, Jersey, Cowper, and Sefton; Princess Esterhazy; Countess Lieven; and Mrs. Drummond Burrell. These ladies decided the acceptability of each applicant, and their standards were rigorous. It was said that no more than six of the three hundred officers of the Foot Guards were admitted and many peers of the realm were excluded. Even after receiving a voucher that allowed the purchase of a ticket, one had to be correctly dressed to enter and those standards were also rigid. Men must wear knee britches, and even the Duke of Wellington, lionized for his victory at Waterloo, was turned away when he showed up in trousers—it is said that he left good-naturedly.

A key function of Almack's was that of a marriage market, and it was for this purpose that Jane's parents submitted her after presenting her at court and hosting a ball in their home at 78 Harley Street. She quickly became a favorite, and one of her admirers gave her the nickname "Aurora" after the sixteen-year-old heroine of the fifteenth canto of Byron's *Don Juan*. Coincidentally, perhaps, *Aurora* was also the name of the frigate Captain Digby commanded in 1796 and in which he made several captures of valuable enemy ships. Not so coincidentally, Jane later assumed the name "Ianthe," which is Greek for Jane but which was also used in Byron's dedication of *Childe Harold*.

Byron was at the height of his popularity, and his life was almost finished. His poetry had done much to create the romantic aura associated with travel and with the eastern Mediterranean. Jane was both fond of poetry and a romantic. While it is not possible to prove a direct influence, it is likely, to the edge of certainty, that Byron's poetry colored Jane's perception of travel and of the East.

On the night of her debut, Jane met a widower eighteen years her senior. She might have met Edward Law, Lord Ellenborough, four years earlier at Holkham Hall when he and her grandfather had found common cause in defending "hygienically challenged" Queen Charlotte against a charge of adultery brought by her gross and lecherous husband, George IV. If a meeting did occur, the thirteen-year-old and the thirty-year-old presumably were not attracted to one another. Now, however, Lord Ellenborough was entranced and in full pursuit.

In fact, he had been in full pursuit of one woman or another since emerging from mourning, and it was rumored that several had rejected his proposal of marriage. He was a handsome man, tall, well built, but vain, particularly about his thick brown hair. One observer suggested that he wore his wig askew in order to draw attention to his hair. He also had a sharp tongue and a full complement of enemies. Some of his unpopularity stemmed from his friendship and support for his previous brother-in-law Lord Castlereagh, an immensely unpopular foreign secretary and the target of Hester Stanhope's "His Monotonous Lordship" remark. Still, Ellenborough was a wealthy and successful man whose father had been Lord Chief Justice of England and who could claim descent from the royal families of England—he was one of London's most eligible men.

Jane was, of course, naïve, and the problem of the age differential was mitigated by the fact that her grandfather Thomas Coke one year before at age sixty-eight had married the eighteen-year-old Lady Anne Keppel, who had already produced the first of a series of new uncles and an aunt. Lady Anne's independence and her authority at Holkham must have been an instructive example to Jane, who was only two years younger. There is also some evidence that Lord Ellenborough was pursuing Jane at a time when she was rebounding from a romantic attachment.

Thus, when Lord Ellenborough proposed, Jane happily accepted. He acquired a special license to have the marriage occur immediately, and while this could be seen as romantic or at least lustful, it is more likely that haste was necessary to clear the decks for political battles that would occur with the new parliamentary session. They were married at 78 Harley Street on September 15, 1824.

The honeymoon at the seaside resort of Brighton was said to be a failure, with rumors that Edward was distracted by the attractive daughter of a pastry cook at the Norfolk Hotel where they were staying. While this may be true, less than two months later the newlyweds were reaffirming their love in an exchange of poems, and this poetical display of affection continued throughout the year, whenever Edward was away. Visitors found them to be happy and affectionate with one another.

But the marriage was under attack from within. Lord Ellenborough was an ambitious man and his work was his passion. Having captured Jane in a swift campaign, it was as if he felt that no further effort was necessary. Jane, young and immature, had merely taken the first step and now needed to fill in a life under the heading of Lady Ellenborough.

THE "season" in Regency London was de rigueur for the fashion-able. Newly freed from the restrictions imposed by her family, it was an opportunity too attractive to be missed. Far from discouraging her participation, Lord Ellenborough introduced his young wife to his friends from the foreign legations, the smartest and fastest track in London society. Foreign was fashionable in Regency London, and even though England was at war with France, or perhaps because they were, elegant conversation was sprinkled with French words and phrases. Lord Ellenborough's political aspirations were toward the Foreign Secretary's Office, and he did craft a highly success-ful career, eventually becoming the governor-general of India. This ambitious man filled his guest lists with minor royalty, politicians, and members of the diplomatic corps and drew his friends from the same set. Jane quickly met Princess Esterhazy, wife of the Austrian ambassador, and Princess de Lieven, wife of the Russian ambassa-dor. Both of these ladies were Lady Patronesses of Almack's.

After launching Jane in the social whirl, Lord Ellenborough's work and time constraints—he also had a mistress—were such that he was unable to accompany Jane on all occasions. Regardless, she plunged in with enthusiasm and became a center of attention at Almack's and elsewhere.

While she was afforded a certain degree of protection before her marriage, after it she became fair game for the men-about-town; the customs of the circle to which she had been introduced were such that it was unfashionable for a woman to be faithful to her husband. The marriage bed was the correct venue for procreation, but not a particularly appropriate place for passion.

In 1827, three years into her marriage, Jane had not produced the heir that her husband was awaiting. Her stepgrandmother, Lady Anne Coke, had rewarded her aging husband with a third son, and Jane proceeded to Holkham to examine this new addition—perhaps for inspiration.

Four days before she arrived at Holkham, Sir Frederick Madden, a young librarian and scholar, had arrived and was busy at work cat-aloging Lord Coke's library. His diary records the event: "Tuesday,

March 14th. Lady Ellenborough, daughter of Lady Andover, arrived to dinner, and will stay a fortnight. She is not yet twenty, and one of the most lovely women I ever saw, quite fair, blue eyes that would move a saint, and lips that would tempt one to foreswear Heaven to touch them" (46).

If his cataloging had not been tedious before, it was now, and his days began to revolve around Jane. An accomplished musician, she played and sang for him in the salon. They walked, rode, and played whist in the evenings until on Saturday after whist, "Lady E. lingered behind the rest of the party, and at midnight I escorted her to her room—Fool that I was!—I will not add what passed. Gracious God! Was there ever such good fortune?" (49). Five days later Jane left Holkham and they never met again. In 1920, forty years after Jane's death, Sir Frederick Madden's diaries were unsealed according to his instructions. Until then, the brief romance had been secret.

One of Jane's ancestors, Sir Kenelm Digby, was born more than two hundred years before her in 1603, yet seemed to exert a curious influence on her life. His memoir, *The Private Memoirs of Sir Kenelm Digby*, was published for the first time in the year following her affair with Frederick Madden. His life read like a fictional romantic adventure, including a love affair with a most beautiful, desirable creature, a narrow escape from seduction by Queen Marie de Medici, and a faked death to escape the queen, the rumor of which reached Venetia Stanley, his lover. Venetia eventually took another lover, but then news reached her of Kenelm, who was still adventuring his way along the Mediterranean coast. On his return to England, he was knighted and made Gentleman of the Privy Chamber to the Prince of Wales. In a clever plan to recapture Venetia's love, he crept into her room as she slept, took off all his clothes, and crawled into bed beside her. Having so recently believed that he was dead, she was not pleased and ordered him to leave. He did and they were married in 1625. Three years after the wedding, Sir Kenelm outfitted two ships and set off on what became a highly successful voyage filled with victories at sea and the taking of prizes. *The Private Memoirs of Sir Kenelm Digby* was widely celebrated in England, and Jane, an avid reader, surely immersed herself in this romantic tale of her ancestor.

Another event in her twentieth year directed her attention toward the East. Henry Anson, one of the cousins who had spent extended periods of time at Holkham Hall, was three years older than Jane and a friend since childhood. He and John Fox-Strangways, another cousin, had set off for Syria and the Holy Land. Part of their plan was a very hazardous scheme to visit the city of Mecca disguised as Arabs. Had they accomplished this, they would have preceded Sir Richard Francis Burton by twenty-five years. Instead, the pair managed to visit Scanderoon and made it as far as Aleppo, where, in what may have been a rehearsal of their plan, they attempted to enter a mosque in disguise. Failing to remove their shoes, they were exposed as Christians, attacked by angry Moslems, and thrown into prison. Henry Anson contracted the plague and though eventually released, he died and was buried in Aleppo. Jane would visit his grave.

While the family was grieving over the loss of Henry Anson, Jane was thrown into close company with his brother Colonel George Anson. In fact, this relationship predated the Madden affair. George Anson was some ten years older than Jane but they had known one another as long as they could remember, and after Jane's introduction to the social swirl of London they were both popular and sought-after participants on the fast track. Colonel Anson was known as a womanizer, but a very handsome one, stylish and very acceptable.

As Lord Ellenborough was too busy, it was entirely suitable for Colonel Anson to escort his beautiful young cousin to various social functions. They were seen together frequently, but maintained sufficient discretion to avoid gossip and scandal. Still, Jane had given George a key to the side door of her home at Roehampton so that he could visit unseen when Lord Ellenborough was away.

Jane was totally immersed in the relationship, and while we do not know how Colonel Anson viewed the affair, it seems likely that he was aware of the difficulties looming and the impossibility of a future marriage. As long as an extramarital affair was discreetly pursued, it was condoned, even expected in their social circle. Any step toward a more permanent relationship would, by its nature, remove the shield of discretion. Divorce was possible, but it required an act of Parliament and the process itself became a source of great titillation and public gossip. Only the exceptionally wealthy could afford the process and few families could tolerate the humiliation of the public spectacle. That the Digbys and the Ansons would subject themselves to such scandal for a marriage was out of the question.

Somehow, we assume it was at George's initiative, the affair was brought to an end, but on February 15, 1828, Jane presented Lord Ellenborough with a son, Arthur Dudley. It is clear that Lord Ellenborough was not the father, and while other candidates have been suggested, Jane believed the father to be Colonel George Anson. It may be that Lord Ellenborough tolerated the liaison in order to gain an heir, but whether that is true or not, from the birth of Arthur Dudley, Jane and Lord Ellenborough ceased to cohabit.

Lord Ellenborough's work began to pay off when in 1828 he was made Lord of the Privy Seal in the Duke of Wellington's ministry. Possibly his hard work was a thinly cloaked excuse to avoid an inadequate marriage, but the evidence does not point in that direction. For one thing, his obsession with work predated his marriage to Jane and even dictated the wedding date. He is described as a dynamic and energetic man who was thoroughly absorbed in his work. This leaves the unflattering assessment that Lord Ellenborough saw his marriage as a transaction in which he acquired a beautiful young wife suitable to his station and the possibility of acquiring an heir, neither of which required the investment of extensive interest or energy on his part. Jane, while not gaining much in the way of a marriage, had acquired substantial personal freedom and unfettered access to the lively social life of Regency London. This potentially dangerous mixture became explosive with the arrival of Prince Felix Ludwig Johann von Nepomuk Friederich zu Schwarzenberg.

With an aristocratic and wealthy family, Prince Felix was a captain of mounted lancers in the Austrian army, and at this point in his developing diplomatic career he had been appointed secretary to Prince Esterhazy in the Austrian Embassy in London. Tall and thin with long thick black sideburns and moustache, he was good-looking, but even his looks were subordinated to the extraordinary magnetism of his eyes. He was alleged to have hypnotic power over women, to the extent that he was said to keep his sickly sister alive by his personal magnetism. An attractive womanizer with an aura of the foreign and exotic, he was also a wanderer whose philosophy was "To live is to travel; to travel, to live" (59).

This was a package of powerful attraction to Jane, who, primed by the poetry of Byron, the stories of Sir Kenelm, and the fateful adventure of Henry Anson, was bound in an unhappy marriage with geographic boundaries that rarely exceeded the south of England. Little wonder that not long after their first meeting at an embassy ball, Jane had lost her heart and any pretense of discretion. They were lovers almost immediately and this became obvious to the denizens of Almack's shortly thereafter. Within a month, Felix was known behind his back by a nickname. A horse named Cadland had won the Derby by beating the king's horse The Colonel, and some wit had observed that since Prince Felix had apparently displaced Colonel Anson in Jane's affections, he should be known as "Cadland" (61). And so he was. Cadland later became Cad, and the prince's subsequent behavior helped to define the meaning of the word as one who behaves in a dishonorable or irresponsible way toward women.

9

AFFAIRS TO REMEMBER

At this early point in their affair, Felix was as engulfed by emotion as Jane. They were passionately in love and everything else, including discretion, was secondary. There must have been some semimystical feeling of invisibility as well, for a major venue for their affair was 73 Harley Street, a few doors from her father's residence at 78 Harley Street where she had been married. Coincidentally, Gertrude Bell would later attend a school just down the street from these houses.

Jane employed a young man named William Carpenter as groom to care for the horses and accompany her to London, where with some variations in routing, they would arrive at or near 73 Harley Street and Jane would be met at the door by Felix. William would then take the carriage to some less obvious point and wait. The minimal attempts at subterfuge were ineffectual and only enhanced the fascination with which the neighbors viewed the developing situation. From the opposite side of the street it was possible to see into a bedroom window and at least one did. Thinking without the goad of rampant passion, it is hard to imagine how the lovers saw their situation. Did they assume that because they were so engrossed with one another and cared little for the rest of the world, the rest of the world must care little about them? Or did they feel protected by that invisibility that seems to accompany love? Or did they simply not care?

Unfortunately, the invisibility accompanying love is like a one-way mirror that gives only the illusion that you are alone and cannot be seen, for the neighbors did see and one later testified that "he had watched Prince Schwarzenberg lacing Lady Ellenborough's stays in the window of his bedroom, and that often he had seen them in bed together for hours at a time."[1]

Beyond these almost daily meetings at Harley Street, the couple threw themselves into the social events of the London season. They made it a point to arrive and leave separately, but this deceived no one, and the affair became a titillating topic of conversation among the aristocracy and lower levels as well. The gossip had actually reached Europe, and Jane was famous as the beauty that had captured the heart of Prince Schwarzenberg.

Rumors of Jane's behavior reached the Digby family, and Margaret Steele, her old governess, took it upon herself to step in. On a visit to Roehampton, she faced Lord Ellenborough and told him that she was concerned that Jane's reputation was being damaged by the company she was keeping. He laughed at her and told her that she was being overscrupulous.

In fact, Lord Ellenborough's behavior raises significant questions that in turn generate speculation and no real answers. It is hard to believe that he was unaware of the affair. He was in constant contact with the Esterhazys, the de Lievens, and the St. Antonios, and these were the same circles in which Jane and Felix were being entertained. There is some evidence that his friendship with Countess St. Antonio was not entirely innocent, and the countess was, on occasion, hostess to Jane and Felix. Lord Ellenborough was not an obtuse man who might remain happily unaware though surrounded by hints and innuendo. The most likely scenario is that he was aware of his wife's affair but chose to ignore it as long as he was left with plausible deniability. It was a marriage in which he had little emotional investment from the beginning and now it was broken. If he was to be cuckolded, at least it was by an elevated level of aristocracy and it did leave him free to pursue his career as well as his own amours. Perhaps he found the affair stimulating. Events, however, were spiraling out of control.

Brighton is on the south coast of England about sixty miles from London—an hour on today's fast train. Edged by beaches composed mostly of rocks and pebbles, it was made fashionable by the Prince of Wales, soon to become George IV, who was drawn to sea bathing as a way of perfecting his health. He built what is now called the Royal Pavilion: an oriental, mostly Indian-appearing confection of a building that became symbolic of his excesses. His libertine behavior helped to mold Brighton's bohemian image.

It was to the Norfolk Hotel in Brighton that Jane and Edward had gone on their honeymoon and where they had often visited in the years since. On February 6, 1829, Jane, accompanied by her son Arthur and two nurses, traveled to Brighton in order to give Arthur a change of air. The small entourage was installed in the suite in the east wing that the Norfolk normally reserved for the Ellenboroughs.

Driven mostly in the early dark of English winter, a bright yellow carriage rattled down the road to Brighton and arrived at the Norfolk shortly before seven in the evening. Prince Felix Schwarzenberg was given an apartment in what the staff described as the west end of the hotel.

On being shown to his room, the prince asked the servant if the hotel was crowded and was informed that there was only one other guest—Lady Ellenborough. The prince said that he had met Lady Ellenborough and would like to call on her, and sent his card to her room. She replied that she would be happy to receive him after dinner for tea.

Both the prince and Lady Ellenborough took dinner in their rooms. After dinner William Walton, the waiter, conducted the prince to Lady Ellenborough's rooms and left them to bring the tea. At 10 p.m., Walton returned to collect the tray and as he entered the prince rose and bade the lady good night. He returned to his rooms.

At midnight with the staff asleep, the night porter was waiting to let in a newly arrived family that had gone to the theater when he saw the foreign gentleman come down the stairs from his bedroom and climb the stairs toward Lady Ellenborough's. Intrigued, the porter/voyeur followed him and saw him enter Lady Ellenborough's bedroom.[2] He tried to look through the keyhole but the door was locked and the key still in the keyhole. Later, when testifying in divorce proceedings before the House of Lords, he was asked what he had heard outside the door. "I could hear them kissing, and a noise that convinced me that the act of cohabitation was taking place."[3]

After this assignation, the lovers seem to have used even less caution. Jane, in particular, bubbling with happiness, made little effort to conceal the fact that she was the mistress of Prince Felix. This was scandalous: a violation of the code that accepted liaisons only if they were conducted with discretion. Then there were the political implications of a scandal that involved an Austrian diplomat and a cabinet minister's wife.

Prince Esterhazy became involved and issued a severe warning to Felix, who then moved his lodgings to 11 Holles Street where the trysts continued as before. But the end was drawing near.

A fundamental problem arose as it became obvious that Lady Ellenborough was pregnant. Because she had not slept with her husband since Arthur was born, there was no doubt as to the prospective father. Prince Esterhazy headed for cover by requesting a new secretary and Prince Felix was recalled to Vienna. Lord Ellenborough was still oblivious to his wife and her condition and so it was necessary for Jane to confront him directly. Though there is no way to know the details of their confrontation, the aftermath was a muddle of family interference and poor advice that saw Jane remanded into the custody of her mother, her aunt, and her ex-governess, who composed a letter that was subsequently used against her in the divorce proceedings.

Jane was twenty-one years old: an innocent deeply in love, willing and determined to follow her lover wherever he might go regardless of the consequences. Her lover did not measure up. He had ruined her reputation and was now running in order to avoid any consequences. Jane was on her own.

Lord Ellenborough eventually decided to pursue a divorce even though the proceeding was so involved and expensive that during the first half of the nineteenth century the average number granted was only about two a year. The process involved a suit in the ecclesiastical courts, a common law recovery of damages from the erring

102 • LADY JANE ELIZABETH DIGBY EL MESRAB

102 • LADY JANE ELIZABETH DIGBY EL MESRAB

partner's paramour, an application to the House of Lords for an absolute divorce with permission to remarry, the forwarding of a bill to the House of Commons for the thorough consideration of another committee, and finally royal assent.

By this time in 1830, Jane was in Paris, having left England in August 1829 for Basel, Switzerland, for confinement and the delivery of Mathilde on November 12, 1829. Felix had managed to visit Basel for the first time two days before the birth of his daughter. He left shortly after the birth and came back to visit at Christmas before Jane and Mathilde (nicknamed "DiDi") left for Paris in February 1830. On the 22nd of the month, the Earl of Shaftesbury presented An Act to Dissolve the Marriage of the Right Honourable Edward Baron Ellenborough with the Right Honourable Jane Elizabeth Baroness Ellenborough, his now wife, to the House of Lords. After the second reading on March 9, testimony began that would eventually include the lacing of stays, the midnight visit in the Norfolk Hotel, and the damaging testimony of Miss Margaret Steele that Jane had admitted her liaison with Prince Felix in the Norfolk Hotel, and her acknowledgement that she was pregnant and that the father must be Felix. On April 8, 1830, the bill returned from Commons, received royal assent, and the divorce was complete, although not without substantial criticism of Lord Ellenborough for his disinterest in and neglect of his young wife. Parliament also omitted the customary penalty clause that would forbid the guilty party from marrying the co-respondent.

As Jane was becoming aware of the weakness of the man for whom she had sacrificed everything and the real cost of her sacrifice, she was forced to bear the additional burden of the death in February of Arthur Dudley Law, the child she had deserted.

PARIS IN 1830 was unstable, with Charles X an unpopular monarch and fond popular memories of Napoleon, whose son, the Duke of Reichstadt, was a hostage in Vienna. It is a strong indication that Prince Felix's career survived the scandal that he was assigned to this post at a critical juncture.

Prince Felix and Jane lived in style in the Faubourg St. Germain in the heart of fashionable Paris, but Jane was ostracized from much of the society to which she was accustomed. Felix had no intention of marrying her because as a Roman Catholic he was forbidden to marry a divorced woman and also because of the effect that their scandalous past could have on his career. Because of their unorthodox status—a divorced woman living with a man who apparently did not intend to marry her—Felix was not able to take her to official functions and sometimes escorted other women. The critical nature of the political situation meant that he often neglected her because of his work, an irony that was probably not lost on Jane.

Jane delivered a son, whom she named Felix, in late December 1830, but the child lived only a few weeks. By June 1831, the prince was gone. After a violent quarrel in May, he ran from France as he had run from England, leaving Jane to deal with the shambles of her life alone.

After some hesitation and consultation with her mother, Jane decided to leave Paris for Munich and did so in August 1831. Why Munich? A likely reason is that the English ambassador to the Bavarian court, Lord Erskine, was a close friend of the Coke family and might provide at least some social support in the strange city. Also, Munich was a lively city with great ferment in the arts and was in the midst of an architectural revival. The stimulus of this renaissance was King Ludwig I, a somewhat eccentric ruler who was fascinated by beauty in all of its forms: art and architecture as well as female. He was particularly drawn to the classical beauty of Greece.

Jane made her way to Munich, and within days she was spotted by the king, who then insisted on meeting her. Shortly thereafter, he commissioned a portrait by Carl Stieler, the court painter, to be hung in the so-called Gallery of Beauty in the palace where Ludwig was known to visit each day for poetic inspiration.

Jane's ability to be discreet had apparently been strengthened with practice, for the extent of her relationship with Ludwig remains clouded and uncertain. Almost immediately, they were rumored to be lovers and such evidence as is available does suggest that she was the king's mistress. Had this relationship continued, she might have salvaged her reputation in England, where being a royal mistress conferred social status. But the affair lasted only a short time, though they remained good friends for many years. Ludwig was another wanderer at heart, and it is possible that his fascination with Greece influenced Jane and the course of her future travels. In the immediate future, however, was a marriage.

BARON KARL THEODORE VON VENNINGEN ÜLLNER was one of the most eligible young men in Munich. From a noble family whose title went back centuries, he was tall, powerfully built, and handsome, with red hair. He was an excellent horseman and that is how they met: on horseback in the Auf Garten in Munich. For Karl Venningen it appears to have been instant love as he immediately began a determined campaign to win Jane.

Felix Schwarzenberg was, in Jane's mind, still in the picture and Jane had visions of their reunion. Such an idea was not entirely unsupported as Felix had maintained a rather heavy correspondence with her after their separation. Whatever his motives, it was not to be.

Jane became pregnant and traveled to Italy to give birth to Filippo Antonio Herberto Venningen on January 27, 1833. It was suggested that the child had been fathered by King Ludwig but it seems certain that the father was Karl Venningen.

Felix finally withdrew himself from the field, and Karl Venningen and Jane were married on November 16, 1833. In spite of the marriage, popular opinion still held Jane to be King Ludwig's mistress with some suspicion that the king had arranged the marriage for his own convenience. Jane did continue her relationship with the king after her marriage, and her correspondence is carefully ambiguous.[4] On Karl Venningen's part there was no ambiguity or uncertainty; he was deeply in love with Jane. As Baroness von Venningen, Jane was now accepted at court and by the rest of Munich society that had previously snubbed her.

In September 1834, Jane bore her fifth child, Bertha. While Herberto or Heribert as he was actually called was the image of Karl

Venningen, Bertha did not resemble either Karl or Heribert and as a child was struck with mental illness that led to her confinement in an asylum by the age of twenty. Madness was a plague of the Wittelsbachs, and the child's illness added to the suspicion that her father might be King Ludwig.

In the spring of 1835, Jane began a curious acquaintance with Honoré de Balzac, who had already received acclaim, in particular, for the December 1829 publication of *La Physiologie du marriage* in which he dealt compassionately with unfaithful wives. They had friends in common, and it is likely that they met through them. While an intimate relationship has been suggested, it seems unlikely, although Balzac knew Jane well enough to make her the model for Lady Arabelle Dudley in his novel *La Lys dans la Vallée* (The Lily of the Valley). In addition to the details of family, personality, and life that are common to Lady Arabelle and Jane, there are multiple clues such as the surname Dudley, the name of her son, and Felix, the name of her lover.

Given that Lady Arabelle and Jane are one and the same, the astonishing aspect of the story is an almost clairvoyant portrayal of Jane's future. In a number of passages such as the epigraph to part 3 in this book, he relates her to the East and to the desert, and he links her to Lady Hester Stanhope, who at that time was still alive and living in grand isolation in the mountains of Lebanon. He has Lady Hester send her an Arabian horse, which she in turn gives to her young lover so that he might ride at night to meet her. The fictional gesture links Hester and Jane in oddly realistic ways. Both women were exceptionally skilled on horseback and very interested in horses. For Hester to give someone a horse as a present and for Arabelle (Jane), in turn, to make such a gift to a lover were lavish acts completely in character for both women. And not too far in Jane's future, a lover would be riding to her by night. As Balzac created Arabelle, Jane was twenty-four years old and years away from the East and the deserts that were to be her home. Even she could not possibly imagine the twists and turns that the path of her life would inscribe. Yet somehow Balzac was able to relate her to Hester

Stanhope, whose own life had inscribed a path that would have been considered too bizarre for fiction. Of course the book may have constituted a self-fulfilling prophecy in that it would certainly have been read by Jane and may have provided a guide for her romantic nature.

In the epigraph quotation, Balzac notes of Arabelle, "Her body is innocent of sweat,"[5] and thus creates a small connection between Arabelle (Jane) and Stelliana (Venetia), whom Kenelm Digby had described in the same terms almost three centuries earlier in *The Private Memoirs of Sir Kenelm Digby*. Balzac could, of course, have easily read the memoirs and noted a connection with Jane, but no one else had.

Finally, Balzac limns Jane precisely when he describes Arabelle:

> But to hold one's head high and love without regard for rules; to die for one's chosen idol and cut oneself a shroud out of his bed sheets; to subordinate heaven and earth to one man and filch from the Almighty the right to create a god; not to betray him to anything, not even virtue—for surely to refuse oneself to him in duties name is tantamount to giving oneself to something which is not *him*! (whether it be a concept, or another man, it is still betrayal!)— these are the heights to which lowborn women cannot aspire; they only know two common highways, the broad road of virtue and the muddy footpath of the courtesan![6]

The fascination with all things Greek that had been stimulated by King Ludwig became even more intense with the crowning of his son Otto as the king of Greece. As Otto took power, there was a migration in both directions between Bavaria and Greece. One member of a Greek delegation to the Bavarian Court was Count Spyridon Theotoky, a handsome young scion of a prominent family from Corfu.

The count offered a stark contrast to Baron Venningen: dashing, careless, and festive. He arrived at a time when Jane was being forced to confront the end of her youth and the sober responsibilities of maturity and motherhood. It was no contest, and when they met, presumably at a ball, Count Theotoky was entranced. The attraction was mutual, and Jane, with all senses delightfully reawakened, sank deeply into love.

Spyridon was four years younger than Jane and apparently no more interested in discretion. Not long into the Munich season, the Venningens suddenly left and returned to the family estate at Weinheim near Heidelberg. The count followed quickly and took up residence in Heidelberg. Thus began a course of assignations that became legendary. The baroness, who rode like an Amazon, would ride out during the day to meet her lover, and when that was not sufficient, she would ride at night and return with the first rays of dawn.

The crisis came when the lovers decided to escape, and during a ball slipped out and headed toward the frontier by coach. There are several versions of this story but in at least two of them, the baron learns of the flight, pursues and overtakes them, drags the count from the coach, and challenges him to a duel. Spyridon was a lover but not a warrior and at a distinct disadvantage. He fired first and missed, whereupon the baron fired and hit him in the left breast. The count fell to the ground bleeding profusely, and Jane fell upon him sobbing. The count showed some character when, while all thought he was dying, he sought to protect Jane by admitting his love for her but denying that he had behaved dishonorably. The baron demonstrated his own character by taking the count back to their home so that he could die in comfort.

The count did not die, however, and it was almost three years later, in March 1839, that he and Jane took up residence in Paris. In the intervening years, she and Baron Venningen had visited England, a trip that demonstrated that her reputation was almost repaired even if the sad memories were not. Now in Paris with Count Theotoky, she set about dealing her reputation another serious blow. The pair falsely represented themselves as married and a year later, in March, Jane gave birth to a son whom they called Leonidas.

Jane asked the baron for a divorce and at first he refused. Later, after learning of the birth of Leonidas, he conceded. In a farewell letter to Jane, he forgave her completely:

Chére amie,

When you receive these lines, I shall be far away from Paris. But my last word must be for you, to tell you once more that which I told you so many times in person—that my friendship and my attachment to you will end only with my life, and that each time I shall have to prove it to you will be a source of great satisfaction to me. May you find in those faraway lands where you will live the happiness I tried in vain to give you and which I regret so deeply is now forever lost to me. . . .

May I learn some day soon that you are completely happy. Think then, under that beautiful sky of the Orient, that in cold and sad Germany a warm and faithful heart is beating for you, a heart which will *never* forget the happiness and the heavenly bliss you gave him during several years. . . .

Everything always to you,

Karl[7]

Baron Karl Venningen never remarried and did remain a friend to Jane until he died in July 1874 while riding in the Hofgarten, where he had first seen the beautiful Lady Ellenborough in the fall of 1831. This was the noblest man Jane had yet loved and arguably the finest that she would ever love. His loyalty points once again to those now opaque qualities that drew men to Jane with such fervor and devotion. Beauty would not have been sufficient. There must have been qualities of mind, of presence, of sensuality that we can only imagine.

Jane gave a revealing glimpse of herself when she wrote to Ludwig,

The Baron and I go on what the world may call "well" together; the difference that exists in our characters cannot be changed. His *really* noble qualities are justly appreciated and esteemed by me. I am attached to him from affection and habit, but between ourselves, his want of *demonstration* and *warmth* of feeling stifles a passion I fain would feel, and which, once felt, and *returned*, would prevent my wandering even in thought to other objects.

The misfortune of my nature is to consider "Love" as *all in all*, without this feeling life is a dreary void. No earthly blessing can compensate its loss, and having at first setting out in life sacrificed *all* without regret to one great and absorbing passion, the necessity of loving and *being loved* is to me as the air I breathe and the sole cause of all I have to reproach myself with.[8]

The divorce was granted in 1842 along with an order that forbade Jane to enter Bavaria or any of the German states again.

In 1841, Jane and Spiro were unwilling to wait for the divorce that Baron Venningen was slowly pursuing. Jane converted to Greek Orthodoxy, her marriage was dissolved by the Greek Orthodox Church, and she and Spiro were married in a Greek Orthodox ceremony.

In March, the new family left for Greece and began an idyllic sojourn of almost two years. With Leonidas and a newly hired French maid named Eugénie, they traveled first to the island of Tinos in the Greek Cyclades where Spiro's father, Count Johannes Theotoky, was governor. The rugged island was not far from the island of Milos where Sir Kenelm Digby had written his memoirs some three hundred years earlier. Jane seemed to revel in the isolated surroundings and spent entire days exploring the island on foot. More significantly, for the first time in her life, after six children, she began to function as a mother. The custom of her time and class was for the children to be raised by nurses and governesses, and this was the case with her earlier children. Parents were remote from their children and in Jane's case there had been no bonding. She rarely mentioned the children in her letters. This time was different. It may have been because the house on Tinos was so small that there was no room for a governess, or because Leonidas looked just like her, or because he was so like her in temperament, but whatever the reason, Jane became attached and a mother to the boy.

There were dark clouds and they had to do with her family in England. Both her grandfather and her father died in the summer of 1842. Jane, who had never reconciled with either man, burdened by guilt under the best of circumstances, was devastated. She was well aware of the unhappiness she had caused both men, and now there was no way to recover.[9]

By the end of the year, Spiro was called to Athens to serve as aide-de-camp to King Otto. Jane immediately found a lot and began building a house in a fashionable neighborhood. Known again as Ianthe, she soon managed to charm King Otto and antagonize Queen Amalie. The queen prided herself on her horsemanship and her dancing, while in both categories, Jane was her equal or better, and when Jane rode through the streets, she was mistaken for the queen and cheered. As usual, there was speculation that Jane was King Otto's mistress, but it does not seem likely.

In 1846, Jane and Spiro's marriage was beginning to crumble. Spiro was an extremely handsome man and attracted more than his share of feminine attention. Jane learned that Spiro was unfaithful and also that he had taken advantage of her financially. Their love of Leonidas was holding the marriage together.

In the summer, they traveled to Italy and leased a three-story house in Bagni di Lucca, not far from Pisa. An open stairway guarded by a polished banister climbed to the top floor where the nursery presumably was located, and while Jane was talking with friends in the entry, Leonidas climbed on the banister to slide down to her from the third floor, but instead lost his balance and fell to his death at her feet.

Jane was devastated, and with her guilt about previous failures as a mother, she felt that this loss was retribution, and she carried the pain with her the rest of her life. With this last link gone, the marriage was over; Jane ordered Spiro out of the house and offered to maintain his financial allowance if he would leave Greece. Spiro and his mistress left for Italy.

For the next several years Jane was footloose and restless. She traveled extensively in Turkey, even becoming fluent in Turkish. She visited Egypt and traveled up the Nile. The next adventure, however, was waiting at home in Athens.

10

FROM BANDIT TO BEDOUIN

The Palikar were mountain men from an area close to the border of Albania, a volatile cross between patriots and brigands, instrumental in the war of independence from Turkey that was won in 1828. Some of them were highway robbers, and it had reached the point that travelers outside of Athens were liable to be relieved of all their possessions, stripped, and left to walk naked to the nearest town. To placate the Palikar and hopefully restore order to the countryside, King Otto appointed General Xristodoulous Hadji-Petros, "King of the Mountains," as his aide-de-camp, replacing Count Theotoky. General Hadji-Petros had fought in the war of independence and was now commander of the Palikar. Almost seventy, a widower, he looked much younger and was still an imposing figure. In his native costume, he was easily the most romantic figure at court, and he took a house in Athens in the Hodos Sokratans area close to Jane's.

The love affair began in 1852 and is not that hard to understand. From Xristos's side it was almost unbelievable good luck; a young, beautiful, and wealthy foreigner who could outride and outshoot many of his own men was in love with him. For a restless and bored Jane, Xristos may have symbolized freedom and adventure. Certainly the life that he lived was consistent with the life that she would live in the future. Xristos also had a daughter named Eirini (peace), a child in fragile health who happily absorbed the mothering and love that Jane could no longer lavish on Leonidas.

Life at court was not easy for Xristos, and King Otto solved the problem by appointing Xristos general in command of a garrison in

Lamia, a small town in the north, and governor of Albania. Jane sold her house in Hodos Sokratans and joined Xristos in Lamia.

Here she found her life of freedom and adventure. When Xristos led his troops out of Lamia, Jane rode by his side. She shared their primitive food and resinated wine, and slept under the open sky as they did.

Her behavior created a scandal in Athens and moved Queen Amalie to action. There were rumors that the queen was enamored of Xristos and that she and Jane were rivals. More to the point, King Otto openly admired Jane, and she had become his confidante; there were rumors of an affair. Again, it seems unlikely, but certainly there was jealousy on the queen's part and it was she rather than the king who was in control. She stripped Hadji-Petros of his command and the governorship.[1]

Xristos then wrote a letter to the queen in which he argued that he was a poor man and that he was living with Jane not because of love but because of her wealth. The queen rejected his appeal and made the letter public. Jane ignored the treachery as she had previously overlooked faults in her lovers, but the end came when she learned that Xristos was having an affair with Eugénie, her maid.

Jane left on what was intended to be a lengthy trip to Syria, ostensibly to acquire Arabian horses for her stable, but it would last for a lifetime, and the love that she had been so unsuccessfully seeking would rise from the desert, from Palmyra. Having apparently decided that a good maid was too important to waste because of a man, she took Eugénie with her.

A writer named Edward About met her when Jane was forty-five and left this description:

Ianthe is the incarnation of health and physical beauty. She is tall and svelte without being thin. If she were a shade taller it would be impossible to find a woman more beautifully made. Her feet and hands indicate her aristocratic birth. Her features are of an almost incredible purity. She has large blue eyes, deep blue like the depths of the sea, and beautiful chestnut hair lit with warmer golden tints. As for her teeth she belongs to that section of the *elite anglaise*, who have pearls in their mouths beside which other women's teeth look like piano keys. Her well preserved skin has the milky whiteness which belongs so essentially to England and which blooms best under thick English fogs. But at the lightest emotion she colours. You would say almost that this fine transparent skin was little more than a net behind which the passions one sees agitating in their prison are trapped.[2]

About's vision is at least tinted by his knowledge of Jane's past, but allowing for the tint, Jane is still beautiful, a woman who appears to be closer to thirty than forty-five. But Jane was an introspective person who was not only aware but guilt-ridden over the pain she had caused, and she wore the scars of age on her heart if not her face. Of the six children she had borne, she had been a mother to only one, and he was dead.[3] She had recently learned of the death of Prince Felix Schwarzenberg at age fifty-one. Schwarzenberg had reached the career pinnacle he sought by becoming prime minister of Austria, but the debris he left in his path included a grief that time had dulled but not erased. At a minimum Jane's voyage must have begun with sadness and feelings of failure. Yet to live is to travel, and so she went. Three days after her forty-sixth birthday, Jane embarked at Piraeus bound for Jerusalem, Damascus, and Palmyra.

BEIRUT, which is one of the world's loveliest settings for a port, with snowcapped Mount Lebanon rising beyond nearby hills, was not accessible because of a rigid quarantine, so Jane stayed on board and sketched the city, hoping to explore it later. The ship then sailed down the coast to Jaffa, where she was able to disembark. Her plan was to travel to Jerusalem, explore Palestine from there, and finally make her way to Damascus and on to Palmyra. To do this she had to hire animals and drivers as well as a dragoman (interpreter/guide).

The trip to Jerusalem took two days, and when Jane looked down on the walled jumble of the city she began what she later described as a new life. The dragoman would not be able to guide Jane to Damascus and it was necessary that she hire a new dragoman. The problem was solved by a chance meeting. While Jane was riding from Jerusalem down to the Jordan River she met a young bedouin sheikh named Saleh.

Among other things, Jane was unusual in her class and era for an apparent absence of racial prejudice. Perhaps this was why she was more open to an appreciation of the Arab culture. In a letter to her mother written during this period, she said, "My heart warms towards these wild Arabs. They have many qualities we want in civilized life, unbounded hospitality, respect for strangers or guests, good faith and simplicity of dealing amongst themselves, and a certain high-bred innate politeness, quite unlike the coarse vulgar Fellah."[4]

According to one widely circulated story, Jane met Saleh while shopping for a thoroughbred horse. Saleh had such a horse but assured her that the horse was unbreakable. Jane had the horse brought to her and saddled and mounted her with little difficulty. As she galloped by the sheikh, he was galvanized with excitement and lust. When she offered to buy the horse, he told her that she could buy the animal but not with money. The attraction must have been mutual for Jane began to share his tent and decided that they would marry.[5] While that did not happen, the affair did mark an important turning point. Jane began to think of Syria as a home rather than as a temporary sightseeing destination. Xristodolous became a fading memory. Saleh was unable to accompany Jane to Damascus because it was beyond his tribal boundaries, so the two parted in anguish with pledges of eternal love, and Jane traveled on.

More than one city in the Middle East claims to be the oldest continuously inhabited city in the world, and Damascus is one of these. Artifacts have been found dating to 3000 BCE. When Jane wound her way around Mount Qasiyun and beheld the oasis nestled beside the tree and garden-lined Barada River, with minarets pointed into the vault of blue sky, it was pure enchantment, and she soon decided that she would live there. The village where she would live lay a little more than one mile above the walled city at the foot of the

Qasiyun hills, now well within the sprawl of modern Damascus. The house, gardens, orchards, and animals came later; first, there was the long-planned trip to Palmyra, roughly 128 miles of desert and mountains northeast of Damascus, abutting the Arab town of Tadmor. In Jane's day, the trip still took eight to ten days on horseback and was almost as dangerous as it was when Hester made the trip. Water was a problem, solvable only by knowing the locations of the few wells scattered across the desert, and local tribes still considered travelers as targets of opportunity. One solution, not always reliable, was to hire an escort of bedouin to accompany the traveler.

The area to be traveled was controlled by the Mesrab tribe, a branch of the dominant Anazeh. The tribe was less wealthy than the other Anazeh tribes, but the previous sheikh, in what was an unusually enlightened gesture, had a learned man teach his sons. The major beneficiary was not Mohammed, the current sheikh, but his younger brother Medjuel who could not only read and write, but also speak several languages and was widely read. With the intellect came personality and charm, all packaged in a five-foot three-inch frame. It was Medjuel who was chosen to negotiate with Jane.

Jane was bombarded with objections to her proposed trip, with most, including the British consul, considering it lunacy. For Jane, who had lived and ridden with Greek brigands, the dangers were far from frightening and she quickly reached agreement with Medjuel on a fee of 8,000 francs. The cost to Medjuel involved his heart. Jane, always open about her love affairs, told Medjuel about her affair with Saleh and her plans to live in Syria. Medjuel was smitten and shortly after proposed marriage.

A description of Medjuel was provided by Emily Beaufort, Viscountess Strangford. Medjuel had guided the viscountess to Palmyra some six years after the trip with Jane.

> He is like all true Bedoueens, a small man about five feet, three inches in height, slightly made, but erect, very graceful in all his motions, and with a light, easy step. His face is really beautiful— of a perfect oval; a long aquiline nose, delicately-formed mouth,

and small regular teeth of dazzling whiteness, and large black eyes that could be soft and sweet as any woman's or flash with a fierce, wild eagle glance that really made one start. He wore a short black beard, and long crisp ringlets under his *kefiyeh*, which was of the very finest and brightest Damascus silk, bound round his head with the pretty *akgal*—a double wreath of camels' hair tied and tasselled with coloured silks. His dress was a *kumbaz* or long tight gown of striped and flowered silk, with wide, open sleeves hanging down to the knee; then his sheikh's cloak or pelisse of bright scarlet cloth bound with black braid across the chest, this, with the scarlet leather boots worn over stockingless feet and reaching to the knee, is the distinguishing dress of the sheikh. Over all came a *mash'lah*—a shapeless but very comfortable cloak—sometimes of thin white cloth edged with color, sometimes of coarse, thick brown and white camel's-hair cloth, sometimes of the same material in black, violet or brown, with a handsome pattern in gold thread woven in up to the shoulders. . . . A silk scarf wound many times around the waist, into which a couple of revolvers and a big knife were stuck, and a sword hung round the neck by a crimson cord, completed the costume. As to his manners, the "best-bred" English gentleman is not more polished than he, and the Bedoueen chief joins an easy chivalrous grace to his quiet dignified demeanour, which has a double charm.[6]

Jane, however, was still preoccupied with Saleh and the fact that Medjuel was married did not help his case. So the relationship of guide and client continued.

During the trek to Palmyra, Jane and her escort were set upon by a gang of bedouin. With raised lances and wild cries they engaged and defeated the escort with little trouble, forcing Jane to turn to Medjuel for protection. Medjuel took up his lance and gallantly defended her, creating surprise and then alarm on the part of the attackers, who subsequently disappeared into the desert. The entire episode was probably a sham, a staged affair in which the bedouin would relieve the travelers of any valuables that remained after they had paid for their escort. Medjuel may or may not have known about the planned attack in advance, but he certainly would not have been surprised. It may be that Jane's asking for protection appealed directly to Medjuel's sense of honor and caused him to ad lib his performance or it may have been planned from the beginning. In either event, Medjuel became a hero in Jane's eyes.

Medjuel's new status elevated him to good friend but no further. Jane later told friends that even by the end of the Palmyra trip, Medjuel had not kissed her. She had admitted to far more intimate details on other occasions so it seems unlikely that she would lie about this.

Together they explored the ruins of Palmyra with Medjuel telling stories that wove the tales of the Mesrabs into the tumbled stones. Later, on other visits, Jane would sketch the ruins, and gradually she became an authority on Palmyra.

After this trip, Jane made a brief trip to Athens and returned to Damascus to find that Saleh had been unfaithful. It is unlikely that Saleh had ever been serious about marriage to Jane and now he had acquired a very young woman named Sabla. One might have thought that Jane the sophisticate could shrug off the loss of an illiterate lover, but that was not the case. She had invested heavily in dreams and plans revolving around Saleh, and now was heartbroken. The whole idea of a new life in Syria seemed to rest on Saleh. Jane was tempted to swear off men but decided instead on a trip to Baghdad.

While she still regretted the loss of Saleh, her thoughts turned more to Medjuel and in her return from Baghdad at Hamah they were back in El Mesrab territory. She began scanning passing faces, looking for Medjuel; by Homs, she was talking about him with passing bedouin.

Medjuel had not forgotten his beautiful English client; in fact he had followed her progress by the desert grapevine, and as they approached Damascus, he rode out to meet them, bringing Jane a homecoming gift of an Arab mare. They rode into Damascus together.

Medjuel and Jane were married in Homs; a marriage that had not been without obstacles. His family was opposed, partly on the ground that she was not *asil* or noble. That she was from the English nobility meant nothing to the Mesrabs, who were one of the noblest families in the desert. For her part, Jane had to overcome a residual fear that Medjuel might be marrying her for her money: she had recorded a substantial list of lovers who were also fond of her purse. In fact, Medjuel was not at all materialistic and went out of his way to avoid Jane's money.[7]

Their marriage included an unusual pact. Medjuel had sent his previous wife and her dowry back to her family, the bedouin form of divorce. But in case he should be tempted to add a wife in the future, they agreed that he would not burden Jane with that knowledge. The uncertainty inherent in this agreement was to cause Jane anxiety and pain.

In the beginning, Jane faced some hostility from his tribe, but eventually she worked her way into their affections, and they began calling her their *umm al laban* or mother of milk, a reference to the whiteness of her skin.

Their first home was in Homs, and later Jane built a house in Damascus. The house in Damascus was designed with three sides around a courtyard and two levels. Medjuel and Jane both had apartments on the top floor along with separate apartments for guests. All apartments had access to the roof where the family gathered on hot nights. The north-facing room on the first floor was a large Arab *diwan* with carpets and cushions spread across the floor. In Jane's apartment was an English drawing-room.

> But the garden was her chief pride. In the courtyard was a large oblong pool fed by water from the river, with raised sides upon which one could sit to trail a hand and watch the fish hiding under the lily pads. Four fountains bubbled gently to provide the soft sounds of trickling rather than splashing water. Doves fluttered from a dovecote, and she had planted trees—citrus, flowering hibiscus, pomegranate, mulberry and, to remind her of England, a pear tree, unheard of in Damascus. There were also old-established trees which gave welcome shade and to these she added a horse chestnut. She laid paths which wound informally through English herbaceous borders, and rose-beds which vied with native

plants and palm trees. Climbing roses and jasmine scrambled in profusion up arches, along walls and over the little kiosque she had built, where she could sit and read.[8]

The garden was quite large, as members of the tribe were invited to camp there when in Damascus. There was room to graze the horses and camels as well as to contain a large variety of smaller animals, including gazelles, salukis, cats, various birds, and a pelican, that she collected and sheltered.

Jane loved the house, but she loved the desert as well. As a wedding gift to Medjuel, she had contracted for the fabrication of a bedouin tent worthy of a sheikh: almost 100 feet long and 36 feet wide, the black tent of tightly woven goat's hair was impervious to wind and rain and built in such a way that all sides could be raised and lowered at will. Space within the tent was organized around a large diwan capable of holding fifty guests and included rooms for servants and for storage.

In the early years of their marriage they spent half the year in the desert. When in the desert, Jane behaved as a bedouin wife: milking the camels, cooking, and washing Medjuel's hair, face, hands, and feet. She adopted the blue cotton gown of the bedouin and toughened her feet to the point that she could walk barefoot over the flint- and rock-scattered surface of the desert. She had dyed her hair black to avoid the Evil Eye, which was attracted by blonde hair, and she outlined her eyelids with kohl. On some occasions she wore a veil over the lower half of her face, leaving only her remarkable blue eyes in view. The major difference between Jane and the other bedouin wives was that Jane, an expert horsewoman, was allowed to ride a mare while the others rode camels. She was equally skilled on camels and had learned to mount as the bedouin did by standing on the camel's neck and springing into the saddle when the animal lurched to its feet.

Over the years, Jane became skilled in the ways of the desert and at one point guided a group of English tourists to Palmyra, the same trip on which Medjuel had guided her years before. On other occasions she rode into battle with Medjuel, though the Arab version of "war" was not the same as that prevalent in the rest of the world. The object of war in the desert was to capture the camels, horses, tents, and other property of the enemy and not to take lives. Any lives lost had to be compensated by the winning tribe and thus a serious effort was made to avoid killing. The *ghazus*, or raids, were virtually a form of sport among the bedouin. Nonetheless, there was Jane, expert horsewoman and shot, black hair flying, galloping into battle at the side of her husband.

When she first came to the desert, tribes were armed with spears, swords, and knives. Gradually this weaponry was replaced with firearms, and Jane with her money assumed a large role in rearming the Mesrabs. In fact, largely because of Jane, the Mesrabs went from the status of a rather minor tribe to one of the important tribes of the desert.

THE BEKAA VALLEY in what is now Lebanon was once known as the granary of the Roman Empire, and its abundance still fed the people of the nineteenth century. In 1859 it failed to produce a wheat crop, and then an appalling winter struck and ruined the olive crop. When in the spring of 1860 an almost biblical plague of worms destroyed the corn crop, the stage was set for a disaster. The spark was provided in May, on the coast near Sidon, when three Druse were murdered. An immediate reprisal took four Maronite Christians, and the religious direction of the cataclysm was set.

The slaughter was frightful. Across the countryside, children, women, and men were put to death and their homes burned. As the disaster spread toward Damascus, Medjuel, who had left on a trip to Homs where his first wife, Mascha, had died, returned hurriedly to the city and prepared to defend his Christian wife. Jane, for her part, was afflicted with guilt for the injustice she had done to Mascha by taking the love of a man as wonderful as Medjuel. This was typical behavior for Jane who, while lenient and nonjudgmental with others, was very hard on herself.[9] She grieved over a long list of sins and injustices she had inflicted on others, including the children she had deserted and her family.

The fame of the Sitt El Mesrab had spread widely across Syria and this, of course, was a cause for anxiety. However, it seemed to be having an opposite effect as tribesmen and others moving toward the city stopped to offer Medjuel their assistance in protecting his home and his Christian wife. Medjuel politely refused their offers and prepared his own defenses.

One of Jane and Medjuel's friends was a man famous throughout the East. Emir Abd el Khader was a hero of the Algerian resistance to France. For fifteen years he had fought the French and had won several victories. In the end he had been captured, imprisoned, and ultimately exiled to Syria. In a palace in Damascus, he lived with an armed and disciplined band of loyal followers. When the massacre began in Damascus, Abd el Khader went into the streets and harangued the angry mob, and when that failed gathered Christians and shepherded them inside the walls of his palace.

Christians were slaughtered in the streets, and women and girls were raped in front of jeering crowds. The next morning Jane dressed in her bedouin clothes and, wearing a veil, rode into the streets. The streets around the smoking ruins were glimpses of hell. Corpses were swelling in the great heat accompanied by swarms of flies and scavenging dogs. Jane did what she could for the survivors, sheltering some in her own home and helping Abd el Khader with the refugees in his palace. She never mentioned her role in her own letters and memoirs, but European survivors reported on her actions and her heroism was widely known in Europe.[10]

ON AUGUST 11, 1881, at age seventy-four, Jane died of dysentery. She was buried the next day in the Protestant cemetery in Damascus. There are two stories of her funeral. In *A Scandalous Life*, Mary S. Lovell cites Roland Mitchell, who was an eyewitness, as saying that the cortege was led by a carriage bearing her coffin followed by Medjuel in scarlet and gold robes leading Jane's white mare and followed by a band of bedouin as an honor guard. In the first biography of Jane, titled *A Portrait of Ianthe* by E. M. Oddie, the author says that Medjuel was riding alone in the first carriage following the coffin when he leapt out, startling the other mourners, and ran away from the procession. Later at the graveside, he raced up riding Jane's white mare and sat watching as they lowered her into the ground. Take your choice.

PART FOUR

ISABEL ARUNDELL BURTON
1831–1896

Lovers don't finally meet somewhere.
They're in each other all along.
                    —BARKS, *The Essential Rumi*

Figure 4. Louis Desanges, *Isabel Burton as a Bride.*
Print Collection, Miriam and Ira D. Wallach Division of Art, Prints and Photographs, New York Public Library, Astor, Lenox and Tilden Foundations.

11

ISABEL'S WORLD

The Industrial Revolution—Khartoum—
The Battle of Omdurman

The latter half of the nineteenth century was marked by the fruitful intersection of peace between Britain and Europe, the accelerating pace of the Industrial Revolution, and the peaking of the British Empire. The British economy rested more and more on manufacturing and trade, with the colonies providing a ready market for manufactured goods and Britain becoming more dependent on the colonies for agricultural goods. As the British agricultural sector dwindled, displaced farm workers migrated to towns and cities where there were jobs, but wages were low, working conditions were poor, even dangerous, and living conditions were appalling.

IN RECOGNITION OF HER EMPIRE, Queen Victoria had been given the additional title of Empress of India. The Suez Canal was a critical link between Britain and India, so in 1874 with Egypt bankrupt, when the khedive offered to sell his shares in the Suez Company, Britain jumped at the opportunity and ended up holding 44 percent of the outstanding shares. By 1882 the khedive's mismanagement of Egypt was such that Britain occupied Cairo and, though it was still under the nominal suzerainty of the Ottoman Empire, took control.

Among the Sufi orders of the Sudan, bordering Egypt to the south, there was a widespread belief that in the Muslim year 1300 after Hegira (1882 CE), the Mahdi or Expected One would appear and his appearance would presage the end of the world. And so it happened that in 1881 Mohammad Ahmed ibn Abdullah, himself the son of a sharif or descendent of the Prophet Mohammad, had been living as a hermit, praying, fasting, and studying the Quran on a small island two hundred miles up the White Nile from Khartoum, when he decided that he was the Mahdi and proclaimed that it was his role to reestablish the purity of Islam. He would accomplish this task with the sword. The British tried to suppress the Mahdi's revolt by sending an army of 10,000 Egyptians under the command of a retired British officer named Hicks into the Sudan. The force was annihilated by an army of 50,000 Sudanese.

In 1884, the British sent a highly regarded officer, General Charles George Gordon, to Khartoum to assess the difficulty of evacuating the Egyptian garrisons from Sudan. He was then reappointed as governor-general of the Sudan—he had held that position before—and ordered to organize the withdrawal of the Egyptian garrisons and abandon the country to the Mahdi. His response to his orders was ambiguous at best, and it appears that he had no intention of abandoning Khartoum, much less the Sudan. By summer 1884 the Mahdi had laid siege to Khartoum.

Gordon was a famous man in England, largely because of his exploits in China in the suppression of the Taiping rebellion. His nickname was "Chinese" and Charles "Chinese" Gordon is the way he is known by many to this day. He was handsome, with curly hair, "bright blue and fearless eyes"; a man of deep complexity, eccentric in the grand English tradition, possessed of great religious faith, courageous, ruthless at times, compassionate, and tender. During one battle in China he came upon a naked Chinese child, picked the child up, and carried him in his arms as he directed the operation. Later the child was educated at Gordon's expense. Gordon's reputation and fame were such as to generate great public demand for his relief in Khartoum. The Mahdi had offered Gordon the opportunity to surrender with guarantees of safety for both him and the garrison. As the relief force neared Khartoum, the Mahdi realized that he had to move, so giving orders that Gordon was to be taken alive, he attacked the city. In full dress uniform, as the dervishes approached,

Gordon left his palace and stood on the landing at the head of the stairs. He made no effort to defend himself but the frenzy of battle overcame his attackers and he was thrust through by a spear. The relief force was less than two days away from Khartoum. When they neared Khartoum, the sight of the smoking ruins told them they were too late. General Charles "Chinese" George Gordon had achieved what he believed to be a "triumphant release" from life.

Imperial Britain was a land of long memories, and twelve years after Gordon's death an army set out to avenge him. Unfortunately, the Mahdi had died, of natural causes, not long after Gordon. He was succeeded by the khalifa Abdullahi, who still maintained a grip on the Sudan and had inherited the Mahdi's mantle as an object of revenge.

In 1892, Horatio Herbert Kitchener was made *sirdar*, or commander in chief, of the Egyptian army with the rank of major general. This man was by no means a desk-bound general, nor was he new to Egypt or the Sudan. In fact, he had been involved in the effort to relieve Khartoum and was a great admirer of Gordon. In 1896 he gathered an Anglo-Egyptian expeditionary force to invade the Sudan and track the khalifa to his lair in Omdurman immediately across the river from Khartoum. Omdurman had been a small village when Gordon fell, but after the Mahdi moved his capital there it grew into a major city. Much of Kitchener's service had been with the Royal Engineers, and his thinking seemed to revolve naturally around lines of supply, so it was not too surprising that his campaign involved laying a rail line into the Sudan and building, launching, and manning gunboats that would provide both firepower and supplies to support the infantry and cavalry on their route parallel to the Nile. The success of this expedition was something of a foregone conclusion because the dervishes, though vastly outnumbering the expeditionary force, were armed with spears and antique weapons. Still, there was a massive battle in the hills and on the plain north of Omdurman. In terms of the world that Isabel, Gertrude, and Freya would inherit, the Omdurman campaign was another episode in what seemed then and still seems to be an interminable conflict between East and West, and among the people involved were some who would have a direct impact on their lives.

A supporting player in the Sudan campaign was Lieutenant Colonel C. V. F. Townshend, who less than twenty years later would lead another expeditionary force from Basra up the Tigris River in a campaign against Baghdad. General Townshend would get as far as Kut el Amara, where he would be stymied, then besieged, and where he would eventually surrender. All this while Gertrude Bell, the only female member of Indian Expeditionary Force D, would be dealing with intelligence in Basra.

A direct impact on Gertrude Bell's life would be caused by Kitchener himself, who would become Field Marshal Kitchener and Earl Kitchener of Khartoum and of Broom. In this capacity and with the collaboration of another Omdurman campaign graduate, he would lead Britain into one of its wartime disasters. The collaborator at the time of Omdurman was a young subaltern attached to the 21st Lancers who was also a correspondent to the *Morning Post*. The young lieutenant was disliked by the other lancer officers and also by Kitchener because, among other reasons, they disliked the press and its representatives. The lieutenant for his part did not care much for his fellow officers and thought Kitchener was guilty of "A gross piece of mismanagement." He also observed to his mother that Kitchener might be a general but he was certainly not a gentleman.

In spite of Kitchener's dislike of the young lieutenant, his lancers were spoiling for a fight, and in the Charge of the 21st Lancers at Omdurman they rode into history with a legend comparable to the Charge of the 17th Lancers as part of the Light Brigade at Balaclava. The irony is that Lieutenant Winston Spencer Churchill, the disliked collaborator-to-be, used the magnificent magic of his prose to help push the charge into legend.

And, much later, Earl Kitchener of Khartoum, Secretary of State for War, would collaborate with Winston Spencer Churchill, First Lord of the Admiralty, in leading his country into a major disaster at Gallipoli.

12

CREATING A DREAM

Six feet tall; broad chest and erect posture of a soldier; the swarthy face of a gypsy with a deep scar on the left cheekbone, souvenir of an unfriendly African spear; thick, drooping black moustache; and a fierce, hawklike gaze that was intended to intimidate and held more than a hint of the violence of which its owner was capable—this picture partly describes Richard Francis Burton at age thirty-three, when he was already a widely known and celebrated explorer. A more complete description would note that he was a scholar with six books to his credit; a linguist fluent in Arabic, Hindustani, Gujarati, Marathi, Sindhi, Punjabi, and Persian as the first of the twenty-nine languages he would eventually master; a dervish and Sufi master; and an expert swordsman. If even more complete, it would describe Burton as an amateur anthropologist with a lifelong interest in the sexual behavior and misbehavior of mankind along with a corre-sponding compulsion to record what he learned with clear and convincing detail, and it would describe him as a man unafraid to express his opinion, even when it concerned English women's need for sexual emancipation.

When Burton arrived in Bombay, Jane Digby's ex-husband Lord Ellenborough had become governor-general of India, though that would have meant little to a fresh subaltern whose father had been a colonel but whose family was not among the nobility. Burton was assigned to the 18th Bombay Native Infantry stationed at Baroda in Gugarat.

While most of the British officers spent their time in the regimen-tal compound with tablecloths and silver in the regimental mess, and cheroots and whist after dinner, Burton found his way into the maze of streets, shops, bazaars, and tenements of the local community. As did his fellow officers, Burton took a native "wife," or *bubu*, in an arrangement prearranged to terminate when he left India. The relationship was not intended to produce children, but a family in India today carries the surname Burton and claims to be descended from a "sir," an officer in Baroda. Burton was an enthusiastic participant in the practice and had relationships with a number of women during his stay on the subcontinent. Apart from the sexual services inherent in the arrangement, the bubu became a tutor in both the native culture and language, or a "walking dictionary," as Burton described his bubu.

Within two years of his arrival, having mastered several languages, Burton began undertaking undercover assignments. With the combination of his natural appearance, his language skills, and his knowledge, he was able to pass for a laborer, a trader, or, what was apparently his favorite, a dervish. These assignments freed him from the boredom of garrison life for long stretches of time. The downside was that it was extremely risky. While there is some disagreement among writers, it appears that Burton had genuinely accepted Islam, including a painful adult circumcision; his life depended on isolated and suspicious Muslims believing that his behavior was not a pretense.[1] These assignments continued throughout Burton's service in India, and during that time he conceived what was to be his most daring exploit.

MECCA AND MEDINA are the first and second most holy cities in Islam (the third is Jerusalem). The sacred cities are closed to non-Muslims, but to Muslims they are the goal of a pilgrimage, the *haj*, which should be taken at least once in a lifetime, if health and finances permit. Other Europeans had been to Mecca before Burton and one, in particular, he admired greatly. Johann Ludwig Burckhardt, the Swiss whom Hester Stanhope had disdained because of his disguise, was an explorer, adventurer, and scholar of the same stature as Burton. Burckhardt made the haj in 1815 and returned later to spend three months in Mecca observing and recording his observations.

Because he would not be the first to accomplish the feat, one might wonder why Burton wanted to make the journey at all. The answer is simple; Richard Burton was a Muslim and he wanted to accomplish one of the "Five Pillars of Islam." The next question as to why he chose to make the trip in disguise and thus at great risk is, like the man himself, somewhat more complicated. Burton could have made the haj as an Englishman who had converted to Islam just as thousands of Europeans and Americans do today. Instead he disguised himself as Abdullah, a doctor from Pakistan, and traveled in intensely uncomfortable and often dangerous conditions. Burton himself addressed the question and said, in effect, that it was a matter of both pride and the challenge of making the trip as a born believer rather than as a preferentially treated Englishman. He said that his pride would not allow him to be seen as a convert, "a renegade," and an object of contempt.[2] With all of his faults and strengths, Richard Francis Burton was the muscle and blood embodiment of what would become a young woman's dream.

ISABEL ARUNDELL was born on March 20, 1831, when Richard Burton was ten years and one day old. Her father was a wine merchant, not particularly wealthy, but the family was aristocratic, with powerful connections. At one point Isabel lived in a wing of Wardour Castle in Somerset, and her family had long before been granted a title by the Emperor Rudolph of Habsburg, confirmed by James II, that eventually allowed Isabel to be known as Countess Isabel Arundell of Wardour. Early on, she acquired the nickname of "Puss" because of a way she had of pointing her nose and cocking her ears, a name that would follow her through her life.

As was typical for the time, Isabel and her brothers and sisters stayed upstairs with their head nurse and three nursery-maids. They saw their parents only briefly after dinner when they were dressed up and paraded, to be seen and not heard. At age ten she was sent to the Convent of the Canonesses of the Holy Sepulchre at New Hall in Chelmsford, Essex, where she seems to have had a happy experience. She was removed at age sixteen, and that was the end of her formal education. By this time, her parents had moved to Furze Hall, a modest estate near Ingatestone, perhaps six miles south of Chelmsford, that includes a comfortable farmhouse in a setting of gardens and pastures that looks like a small park, an ideal environment for an adventurous young woman, for that is what Isabel had become during her years in the convent. With her brothers she explored the surrounding country, and in the winter there was sledging, skating, and sliding. At other times, she had solitude and passed time reading and contemplating in the woods.

Significantly, her favorite book was Benjamin Disraeli's *Tancred; or, The New Crusade.*[3] The story line follows a young man, Tancred, Lord Montacute, the scion of a wealthy aristocratic family, as he pursues the satisfaction of his spiritual needs. Sorely disappointed by the Church of England, he conceives the idea of a pilgrimage to the Holy Land, buys a yacht, and off he goes. The book is heavily laced with romance, longing, adventure, and mystical overtones. He falls in love with a Jewish princess who later, after he had been captured and held for ransom by her grandfather, saves his life. He goes on to meet a queen who falls in love with him and also manages to capture the Jewish princess. Coincidentally, this was supposed to be the queen of the Ansary tribe, the same warlike tribe that felt Hester Stanhope's vengeance after they had killed Colonel Boutin. The princess escapes with the help of her brother; Tancred realizes he is in love with her, and so on. The story wanders over a set that includes Jerusalem, the ruins of Petra in what is now Jordan, Damascus, and northern Syria.

We do not know what it was about the book that captivated Isabel but, in view of her later life, we can guess. The book is actually a vehicle for a not-so-subtle message to the effect that Christianity owes a substantial debt to the "Jewish race" and the definite superiority of that race. It is unlikely that Isabel missed the message, but it is hard to know what effect if any that might have had on a lifelong devout Catholic. It portrays the book's mostly Jewish bedouin tribes in a positive light, and this may have conditioned her expectations and perceptions of native peoples in general and bedouin in particular. But the most likely influence was simply the romantic coloration of the Near East as a setting. When a young man falls asleep in a kiosk by a fountain in a shaded garden hidden in a gorge in Bethany and wakes to find that he is being contemplated by a beautiful princess, the overall effect is teenage or even middle-age fantasy. Jerusalem, because of its religious significance, is naturally attractive; Petra with its multihued cliffs and carved tombs carries a romantic, even mystical aura; and just the name Damascus is romantic. It is not hard to believe that an intelligent and adventurous young woman might make the objective of Tancred's pilgrimage a goal of her own. She wrote, "I did not know it then, I do now: I was working out the problem of my future life, my after mission. It [*Tancred*] lived in my saddle-pocket throughout my Eastern life. I almost know it by heart, so that when I came to Bethany, or the Lebanon, and to Mukhtara—when I found myself in a Bedawi camp, or amongst the Maronite and Druse strongholds, or in the society of Fakredeens—nothing surprised me . . ."[4]

Tancred was certainly not the only reason, but Isabel noted that "I was enthusiastic about gypsies, Bedawin Arabs, and everything Eastern and mystic and especially about a wild and lawless life."[5] Because there were few bedouin in Essex, gypsies captured Isabel's attention. She was strictly forbidden to associate with them, but when "oriental gypsies" were present in the lanes, she would visit them in their camps. She became a friend of Hagar Burton, "a tall, slender, handsome, distinguished, refined woman, who had much influence in her tribe."[6] Hagar called her Daisy and on their last day together cast Isabel's horoscope and wrote it in Romany. Hagar translated it for Isabel:

> You will cross the sea, and be in the same town with your Destiny and know it not. Every obstacle will rise up against you, and such a combination of circumstances, that it will require all your courage, energy, and intelligence to meet them. Your life will be like one swimming against big waves; but God will be with you, so you will always win. You will fix your eye on your polar star, and you will

go for that without looking right or left. You will bear the name of our tribe, and be right proud of it. You will be as we are, but far greater than we. Your life is all wandering, change, and adventure. One soul in two bodies in life or death, never long apart. Show this to the man you take for your husband.—HAGAR BURTON[7]

Some writers suggest that Isabel made up this prophecy after the fact, and one must admit that she was capable of such myth creation. On the other hand, there is no evidence to support such a contention. If it was what she claimed, could it have influenced her and become a self-fulfilling prophecy? Of course, or it could be the mystical event that she thought it was. I find it interesting no matter which of these explanations may be correct. Richard Burton also found it interesting and credible. This linguist, who was himself fascinated by gypsies, saw the prophecy written in Romany and was impressed enough to write that "[a] certain Hagar Burton, an old fortune teller (divinatrice) took part in a period of my life which in no small degree contributed to determine its course,"[8] and then went on to inquire after Hagar Burton whenever he encountered gypsies anywhere in the world. He never found her.

It was just as well that Isabel was wandering the fields and woods at this time, for in her own words,

This was the ugliest time of my life. Every girl has an ugly age. I was tall, plump, and meant to be fair, but was always tanned and sunburnt. I knew my good points. What girl does not? I had large, dark blue, earnest eyes, and long, black eyelashes and eyebrows, which seemed to grow shorter the older I got. I had very white regular teeth, and very small hands and feet and waist; but I fretted because I was too fat to slip into what is usually called "our stock size," and my complexion was by no means pale and interesting enough to please me.[9]

For Isabel's parents, her behavior, though innocent, bordered on the eccentric, and they were approaching that critical period when they must find a "suitable match." By 1849 they had moved to London and Isabel had "fined down," to use her mother's phrase, but her eccentricity was not far below the surface.

The entire "season" of twelve weeks had a fairy-tale quality for a young woman who had spent most of her recent years immersed in the placid English countryside. She threw herself into the experience and savored the various diversions. Her first opera entranced her, and the first ballet was pure pleasure; days were spent sightseeing in London, then a city of about two million, and her early evenings were often spent riding in a carriage on Rotten Row in Hyde Park, where fashionable London went to see and be seen.

Her debut was arranged by the Duchess of Norfolk and was at a fancy ball at Almack's, the same room where Jane Digby had met Lord Ellenborough twenty-five years before. The experience was just short of overwhelming—the sparkle and color of an elegant room, beautiful dresses, attractive people, music, the scents of perfume and flowers—and Isabel absorbed the experience. She had been told that she would be lucky if she got four dances but, in fact, she had been engaged for seven or eight soon after she entered the room. Altogether a very satisfactory debut and a state of affairs that continued throughout the season.

All was not well, however, as Isabel was unimpressed with and uninterested in the eligible young men. The problem seemed to be that Isabel had drawn up a set of specifications for her "ideal" and was not willing to compromise. None of the lads had managed to measure up.

From her diary:

As God took a rib out of Adam and made a woman of it, so do I, out of a wild chaos of thought, form a man unto myself. In outward form and inmost soul his life and deeds an ideal. This species of fastidiousness has protected me and kept me from fulfilling the vocation of my sex—breeding fools and chronicling small beer. My ideal is about six feet in height; he has not an ounce of fat on him; he has broad and muscular shoulders, a powerful, deep chest; he is a Hercules of manly strength. He has black hair, a brown complexion, a clever forehead, sagacious eyebrows, large, black, wondrous eyes—those strange eyes you dare not take yours from off them—with long lashes. He is a soldier and a man; he is accustomed to command and to be obeyed. . . . This is the creation of my fancy, and my ideal of happiness is to be to such a man wife, comrade, friend—everything to him, to sacrifice all for him, to follow his fortunes through his campaigns, through his travels, to any part of the world, and endure any amount of roughing. . . . Such a man only will I wed. . . . But if I find such a man, and afterwards discover he is not for me, then I will never marry. . . . and if he marries someone else, I will become a sister of charity of St. Vincent de Paul. (37)

This specification of Isabel's "ideal" so accurately describes Richard Francis Burton that it is difficult not to suspect "diary-tampering." On the other hand, if a woman still believes that a man matches this ideal after forty years of acquaintance and marriage, it is even more remarkable. Understandably, it tended to limit the field at Almack's in 1850.

At the end of the season, Isabel's parents swallowed their defeat and took their romantically challenged daughter and the rest of the family to Boulogne.

Boulogne was second only to Paris according to Isabel's mother, and it was economical, thus attracting an English expatriate community. However, because the Arundells would only socialize with the topmost level of that group, the social life was rather thin and soon boring. Isabel, though, managed to become fascinated with the fisherwomen of Boulogne. This earthy subculture, led by a queen, was the most exotic group that Isabel was able to find. She became friends with Queen Caroline of the fisherwomen and seemingly had found a temporary substitute for the gypsies she had left behind in Essex. In a further assault on boredom, she and her sisters stole cigars from their father and taught themselves to smoke, thus beginning a lifelong habit for Isabel. She eventually gave up cigars, but found cigarettes to be graceful and enjoyable and the oriental *nargileh*, or water pipe, even more so.

Their parents kept a tight rein on the girls and they were not permitted to walk alone except on the ramparts of the city, where they were presumed to do quiet reading. On one memorable day "the vision of my awakening brain came towards us."

> He was five feet eleven inches in height, very broad, thin, and muscular: he had very dark hair; black, clearly defined, sagacious eyebrows; a brown, weather-beaten complexion; straight Arab features; a determined-looking mouth and chin, nearly covered by an enormous black moustache. . . . But the most remarkable part of his appearance was two large, black, flashing eyes with long lashes that pierced one through and through. He had a fierce, proud, melancholy expression . . . He looked at me as though he read me through and through in a moment, and started a little. I was completely magnetized; and when we had got a little distance away, I turned to my sister, and whispered to her, "That man will marry me." (52)

Of course the man was Richard Francis Burton, or "Ruffian Dick" as he was known to his friends. He was finishing his second year of sick leave from the Indian army occasioned at least in part by a bout of cholera. He was thirty years old, fluent in a half-dozen languages, and an initiate into the Sufi sect of Islam. While in Boulogne he was working on the first three of what would become a lifetime production of almost fifty books. Two of the books, *Goa, and the Blue Mountains; or, Six Months of Sick Leave* (two volumes) and *Scinde; or, The Unhappy Valley* (two volumes), would be published in 1851, and two more books dealing with India would follow in 1852.

The next day both Isabel and Richard were again on the ramparts, and this time he followed them and wrote, "May I speak to you?" (53) in chalk on a wall. Isabel responded by writing, "No; mother will be angry" (53), which she was when she found the chalked messages. They were eventually introduced through cousins of her father, the introduction taking place on the ramparts, beginning an agonizing period of longing during which Isabel "would invent any excuse . . . to watch him, if he were not looking. If I could catch the sound of his deep voice, it seemed to me so soft and sweet that I remained spellbound, as when I hear gypsy music. I never lost an opportunity of seeing him, when I could not be seen; and as I used to turn red and pale, hot and cold, dizzy and faint, sick and trembling, and my knees used to nearly give way under me, my mother sent for the doctor" (53).

Her mother interpreted these symptoms as indicative of a digestive disorder together with migraines and hustled her off to a doctor who cooperatively supplied pills that she destroyed dutifully in the fire.

Richard, in what must have been a masculine fog, was seemingly unaware of this attention. Further, he was engaged in a flirtation with someone else and Isabel despaired at the chance of "an ugly schoolgirl" (54) derailing that romance. Nonetheless, as time passed she read all of his books and lost none of the intensity of her focus. She wore a note that he had written her next to her heart and she permanently retired a sash and gloves that Richard had touched.

Eventually the two years in Boulogne came to an end and the family was bundled onto a steamer. Isabel, after good-byes to Caroline of the fisherwomen and other friends, decided against seeing Richard one last time as it would only bring more pain. So at midnight the steamer eased from the pier at Boulogne and set her course for England. While her family went below and to bed, Isabel stayed on deck to watch the lights that held her dreams sink into the night, while Richard began preparations for his pilgrimage to Mecca. It would be four years before they met again.

Her mother launched an intensified campaign to find a husband for Isabel, but Isabel was having no part of it. Her vision now had flesh and form and she would settle for nothing less. The "insignificant beings" (65) that were thrust at her were rejected defiantly.

I could not live like a vegetable in the country . . . with a good and portly husband (I detest fat men!) with a broadbrimmed hat and a large stomach. And I should not like to marry a country squire, nor a doctor, nor a lawyer (I hear the parchment's crackle now), nor a parson, nor a clerk in a London office. God help me! A dry crust, privations, pain, danger for him I love would be better. Let me go with the husband of my choice to battle, nurse him in his tent, follow him under the fire of ten thousand muskets. I would be his companion through hardship and trouble, nurse him if wounded, work for him in his tent, prepare his meals when faint, his bed when weary, and be his guardian angel of comfort—a felicity too exquisite for words! There is something in some women that seems born for the knapsack. (66)

At least in appearances, the relationship between Isabel and Richard was rather one-sided at this point. He was the most important person in her life, while it was far from certain that he would even remember her. Before he began his venture to Mecca, he visited England but failed to contact her, and afterward he was off to Bombay to rejoin his regiment and spend much of his time writing the first two of three volumes that would describe the adventure. Even then he did not return to England, but planned and launched an expedition into Somaliland that thrust him alone into Harar, another forbidden city. Isabel was reduced to comforting herself with the idea that if she and Richard were never to marry, "God will cause us to meet in the next world; we cannot be parted; we belong to one another" (68); a thought reminiscent of Jelaluddin Rumi's "Lovers don't finally meet somewhere. They're in each other all along."[10]

Richard survived Harar and returned to Aden to plan a return expedition that did not fare as well. The expedition's camp, housing forty-two men including four English officers, was attacked by Somali tribesmen, killing one of the officers and severely wounding two others. Burton was one of the wounded, taking the spear to the jaw mentioned earlier. English newspapers reported the disaster and Isabel agonized as to whether Richard would recover.

He returned to London to recuperate—again without contacting Isabel. The Crimean War was then under way, so after his wounds had healed, he gathered letters of introduction and made his way through France and the Mediterranean to Constantinople, and on to Balaklava in the Crimea. There he secured a commission in a cavalry unit known as Beatson's Horse, made up of Turkish irregulars. The unit, which Burton called the "Bashi-Bazouks" (rotten heads), was stationed at Gallipoli, the peninsula south of Constantinople that would be the scene of Allied disaster in World War I. To Burton's disappointment, the Bashi-Bazouks never saw combat, and he eventually returned to London, partly because he was required to testify in a trial that his commander, General Beatson, had sought against his enemies for defamation of character.

During the time that Burton had been in the Crimea and Turkey, Isabel had tried repeatedly to persuade Florence Nightingale to let her become a nurse and join her at Scutari near Constantinople. She was rejected as too young and inexperienced. Failing that, she formed an organization of women to help clothe and feed the destitute families of soldiers who had gone to the Crimea. As painful as the separation from Richard was, the net effect may have been that Isabel gained time to mature. She said of her volunteer activity that "I know now the misery of London . . ."[11] and "misery" was an understatement as London teemed with desperately poor living in slums of unimaginable squalor. Curiously, in June 1856, she ran into Hagar Burton again—this time at the races at Ascot. Hagar's first question was "Are you Daisy Burton yet?" (81). "Would to God I were!" Isabel replied. And Hagar's face lit up. "Patience! It is just coming." She waved her hand, for at that moment she was rudely thrust from the carriage. Isabel never saw her again, but within two months she was engaged to Richard.

One fine day in August I was walking in the Botannical Gardens with my sister. Richard was there. We immediately stopped and shook hands, and asked each other a thousand questions of the four intervening years; and all the old Boulogne memories and feelings returned to me. He asked me if I came to the gardens often. I said "Oh yes, we always come and read and study here from eleven to one, because it is so much nicer than studying in the hot room in this season." "That is quite right," he said. "What are you studying?" I held up the book I had with me that day, an old friend, Disraeli's *Tancred*, the book of my heart and taste, which he explained to me. We were in the gardens about an hour, and when I had to leave he gave me a peculiar look, as he did at Boulogne. I hardly looked at him, yet I felt it, and had to turn away.

Next morning we went to the Botannical Gardens again. When we got there, he was there too, alone, composing some poetry to show to Monckton Milnes on some pet subject. He came forward and said laughingly, "You won't chalk up 'Mother will be angry' as you did when you were at Boulogne, when I used to want to speak to you." So we walked and talked over old times and people and things in general.

About the third day his manner gradually altered towards me; we had begun to know each other, and what might have been an ideal love before was now a reality. This went on for a fortnight. I trod on air.

At the end of a fortnight he stole his arm around my waist, and laid his cheek against mine and asked me, "Could you do anything so sickly as to give up civilization? And if I can get the Consulate of Damascus, will you marry me and go live there?" He said "Do not give me an answer now, because it will mean a very serious step for you—no less than giving up your people and all that you are used to, and living the sort of life that Lady Hester Stanhope led. I see the capabilities in you, but you must think it over." I was long silent from emotion; it was just as if the moon had tumbled down and said, "You have cried for me for so long that I have come." But he, who did not know of my long love, thought I was thinking worldly thoughts, and said, "Forgive me; I ought not to have asked so much." At last I found my voice and said, "I do not want to think it over—I have been thinking it for over six years, ever since I first saw you at Boulogne, I have prayed for you every morning and night, I have followed all your career minutely, I have read every word you ever wrote, and I would rather have a crust and a tent with you than be queen of all the world; and so I say now, 'Yes, yes, YES!'" I would have suffered six years more for such a day, such a moment as this. All past sorrow was forgotten in it. All that has been written or said on the subject of the first kiss is trash compared to the reality. Men might as well undertake to describe Eternity. (84)

This description of the realization of her dreams underlines what, in reality, had been their fragility and near hopelessness. There was no relationship, merely an acquaintance that was almost forgotten by Burton, yet Isabel fashioned the dream and then let it guide her through six years of disappointment and despair. Three weeks earlier, Isabel appeared to be an extreme case of naiveté who should be pitied; one week later, she had begun to realize her dreams. It is tempting to believe that Rumi is right and that Isabel both sensed that reality and possessed the determination to make it happen.

The ordeal was not over. Richard began to visit her house and spend time with her family but as a new expedition was near at hand, they decided not to announce their engagement until he returned.

The expedition, possibly the most dangerous of his career, was to search for the sources of the Nile and would take over two and one-half years, risking both his physical and mental health in the process.

Burton feared farewells and consequently slipped away, with Isabel believing that they would see each other the next day. That evening she went to the theater. At 10:30 she thought she saw Richard across the theater and smiled and waved him over to the box. As minutes passed and he did not appear, she began to have a strange feeling and found herself in the back of the box with tears streaming. Later in a fitful sleep she dreamed that he held her and told her that he was leaving. The next morning a letter was delivered to her sister Blanche that enclosed a second letter for Isabel. He had left his lodgings at 10:30 and sailed from Southampton at 2 a.m. when she had seen him in her room. Such mysterious events would occur and reoccur in Isabel's life, partly because she believed in them and possibly because she needed them.

For a woman who kept her courage through six years of uncertainty, one might think that thirty-two months would be a relative cakewalk, but this was no longer hypothetical—he loved her, they were going to be married, and these months were clearly a loss. He apparently wrote only four letters during the period, although this was expected because of the nature of the journey and also because they knew that the letters would be opened and read before Isabel saw them. In what may have been the worst possible remedy for her situation, she joined her sister and her new husband on a honeymoon tour of Italy. In the course of the trip, in addition to a natural envy, Isabel also acquired several suitors whom she quickly refused. She did some mountain climbing, learned to ride astride, and became a powerful swimmer. She would row far out into a lake, undress, swim, then re-dress for the trip back to shore. She also began to acquire some travel skills, including the ability to deal with officious customs officials, skills that would bear substantial fruit in the not-too-distant future. Still, the separation was an ordeal and Isabel was beset with doubts—at one point reconsidering the possibility of life in a convent.

Then, on May 21, 1859, Richard returned to London. The next day Isabel, unaware of his return, went to visit a friend and when told of her absence, decided to wait for her return. Minutes later the doorbell rang and another visitor was asked to wait. As that person climbed the stairs, Isabel heard a voice saying, "I want Miss Arundell's address." And the voice was from her dreams: "The door opened, I turned around . . . I beheld Richard! For an instant we both stood dazed. . . . We rushed into each other's arms. . . . Richard called a cab, and he put me in and told the man to drive about—anywhere" (149).

The expedition had left Richard in poor physical condition. He had suffered through twenty-one fevers and had been partially paralyzed and partially blinded. According to Isabel, he looked like a skeleton and she longed to stay with him and nurse him. They were determined to proceed with the marriage but when they broached the subject to Isabel's parents, Mrs. Arundell was rigidly opposed.

Her mother's opposition is not surprising. Apart from resembling a skeleton, Richard's fortunes were in serious decline. He'd fallen out with Speke, his partner in the recent expedition, and Speke had returned to London before him, effectively garnering all the credit for the expedition's success; he was out of favor with the Royal Geographic Society, the government, the War Office, and the Indian army; his finances were insufficient to support a wife comfortably;

not only was he not a Catholic, he was thought to be an agnostic; and he had amply demonstrated that he was an inveterate wanderer. There were rumors about his sexual interests and habits. All in all, Mrs. Arundell probably felt that she had a reasonably solid case. Richard, on the other hand, possessed the unqualified love of a woman who had loved him since they first met almost ten years before.

But Mrs. Arundell was unyielding. Richard had enough and suggested elopement, but Isabel hoped for the approval of her family and resisted the idea. Then one day in April 1860 came the now familiar feeling that Richard was gone, and it was followed later by a note. Richard was gone—he was on his way to Salt Lake City and would return in nine months. He wanted Isabel to choose between him and her mother. If she was unable to oppose her mother, he would return to India and see her no more.

At first Isabel was overwhelmed and took to her bed in an emotional collapse, but then she rallied and launched an all-out campaign to reach her objective: moving to a farm and beginning a training program in which she learned to accomplish domestic tasks without servants and outdoor tasks such as grooming horses and milking cows. If she was going to marry a poor man she would be ready. On her return to London, she asked a friend to teach her to fence and she enlarged her reading so that she would be prepared to discuss things with Richard. She felt she was ready for the expeditions she had dreamed about. All that was left was for Isabel to make her feelings and intentions clear to her mother, and she did. Her mother still said "Never!" (159). So on Tuesday, January 22, 1861, Isabel left her house, changed at a friend's house, and she and Richard were married in the Bavarian Catholic Church on Warwick Street. The next seven months were among the happiest in Isabel's life.

After the wedding ceremony and breakfast with friends, the couple retired to Richard's rooms in St. James, where they set up housekeeping. Isabel's mother thought that she was visiting in the country until one of Isabel's aunts heard that Isabel had been seen entering lodgings on St. James and felt it was her duty to report this. Mrs. Arundell telegraphed her husband, who was away staying with friends. He wired back, "She is married to Dick Burton, and thank God for it" (173). To her mother's credit, she hastened to summon the couple, held a dinner to welcome Richard into the family, and, depending on the reporter, either became partially reconciled or grew to like Richard a great deal and treat him as a son.

As happy as these months were, this was not the life that Isabel had longed for and she bent her efforts toward acquiring a position for Richard in the Foreign Office. The result was an appointment as consul in Fernando Po on the west coast of Africa. This wasn't what Isabel was hoping for either because the climate was so unhealthful that she would be unable to accompany him—the post was known as the "Foreign Office grave." It was a beginning, though, and Richard left in August.

He returned on leave after eighteen months, and at the conclusion of the leave, Isabel accompanied him as far as Tenerife in the Canary Islands on the return voyage. This was the real beginning of the life that she had imagined, and a wild beginning it was. They left Liverpool in January on the African steamship *Spartan* and sailed directly into a major storm. A quartermaster fell over the side and was lost, bulkheads gave way, the ship took on water, and in Isabel's words, "At first I had been frightened that I should die, but now I was only frightened that I shouldn't" (188). After a week at sea, the weather calmed and two days later they dropped anchor off Funchal on the island of Madeira. After two days of exploring and climbing the lush green hills of Madeira, they set sail for Tenerife.

They stayed on Tenerife a little over a month, and the experience was near idyllic for Isabel. Positive and upbeat, she made the best of whatever conditions they encountered and, in fact, showed considerable talent in converting the most unlikely conditions and quarters into a snug nest for the two of them. As usual, they had to climb the highest peak available and in this case they had to camp out. Isabel was equal to the task: "In less than an hour our beds were made comfortable, and composed of railway-rugs, coats, and cloaks. There were two roaring fires, and tea and coffee; and spread about were spirits, wine, fowls, bread, butter, hard eggs, and sausages. We could have spent a week there comfortably" (214). The time passed too quickly and Richard soon departed for Fernando Po, leaving Isabel to make her way back to England.

Isabel proved to be a hardy and intrepid traveler. On virtually all of their trips together there were adventures and hardships as well as outright danger: filthy, unheated, insecure lodgings, complete with fleas; rock climbs, narrow paths edging sheer drops, and once in Brazil being lowered by a basket and fragile chain hundreds of feet into the depths of a mine. And it was not only alongside Richard that Isabel took these risks. She did not hesitate to strike out on her own with a pistol stuck into her belt, a rifle at her side. Her courage would occasionally slip, and once in very nonprimative Lisbon she and Richard were given a suite of rooms in "the best-looking hotel in the place." The furnishings were "gorgeous" with yellow satin and "magnificent" yellow curtains but there were holes in the wall crowded with cockroaches and they had spread over the curtains— some up to three inches in length. Isabel jumped onto a chair and screamed. Richard was unsympathetic and observed, "I suppose you think you look very pretty and interesting standing on that chair and howling at those innocent creatures" (232). Though her fear of crawling creatures was almost a phobia, she gingerly got down from the chair, took a basin of water and a slipper, and spent two hours knocking the cockroaches into the basin. She said that it cured her and she never again feared vermin or reptiles. Later they changed rooms and the original rooms were occupied by Lord and Lady Lytton. She said that "to my infinite delight" she heard the same screams coming from the same room.

The conquering of this phobia was timely for in 1864 Richard was transferred to the consulate at Santos in Brazil and they lived there together until June 1867, when Isabel managed to secure for Richard the post of consul of Damascus, the realization of both of their dreams. The land of Tancred awaited them.

13

REALIZING THE DREAM

Richard acted as "point" for the Burtons. When the time came to travel, Richard would pack lightly and depart to reconnoiter, leaving Isabel to settle their accounts and arrange for the packing and shipment of the bulk of their belongings. This became the legendary pay, pack, and follow of Richard's blunt communications. So in the summer of 1869, Richard departed for Damascus and Isabel remained in England acting as Richard's agent, packing and preparing herself. She became familiar with the detail and operation of tube wells with which Richard was hoping to produce water in the desert. She learned to remove and replace wheels and axles, and to fieldstrip, clean, and reassemble her own rifles and pistols.

This was the heart, the core of her dream. She was heading east to the Orient, to the deserts, to the land of Tancred highlighted with tints of romance and adventure. So on December 16, 1869, she parted tearfully from her family and boarded a train at Victoria Station bound for Dover, where an unusually violent storm delayed her departure, then Calais, Paris, train to Marseilles, and a steamer to Alexandria. On Christmas morning her dream became life as she set her foot on Eastern soil. The next morning she boarded the Russian ship *Ceres* bound for Beirut. She had been disappointed with Alexandria and was not impressed with Jaffa, but Beirut was lovely, with deep blue bay and azure skies framing the town of red-tiled roofs, some creeping up the lower hills, surrounded by dark green pine forests and with the snow-topped Lebanon range as a backdrop.

She took a room in a small hotel and called on the consul-general, who invited her to lunch and as a bonus showed her how to smoke her first nargileh (water pipe). That night she tried to sleep but the moment was too wrought with anticipation: "Tomorrow I was to realize the dream of my life. . . . As soon as you cross the Lebanon Range you quit an old life for a new life, you forsake the new world and make acquaintance with the old world, you relapse into a purely oriental and primitive phase of existence."[1]

The next morning, accompanied by her English maid, her large pet St. Bernard, and a guard lent by the consul-general, she left by carriage. The journey took two days for a total of fifteen days from London.

Winter may be the least flattering of Damascene seasons and arriving on a winter evening may aggravate that effect. Given Isabel's emotional expectations, her first reaction almost had to be a letdown, and it was. Soon though, she arrived at Demetri's, the only hotel in Damascus, for a warm reunion with Richard. They were soon deep into a discussion of plans for their new life in Damascus.

They took a house in an area known as Salahiya about a quarter of an hour outside of Damascus. It was located high on a hill with desert and a mountain known as Camomile Mountain in the background. The scent of chamomile marked their village, even though their house faced apricot orchards and they had their own gardens behind. In the apricot orchards they had a stable for twelve horses with a room attached for grooms. In one of the gardens, lush with roses and jasmine, they created an arbor by lifting vines and the branches of orange and lemon trees, supporting them on a framework so that no sunlight could penetrate the foliage. They furnished it with a divan and would sit on cool summer evenings overlooking the rushing waters of the river. Nearby, arranged around a courtyard containing a fountain amid orange, lemon, and jasmine trees, was the house itself. Open to the courtyard was an oriental reception room known as the *liwan*, while to the right was a dining room and to the left a sitting room. The rest of the downstairs was taken by servants and offices, while their private rooms were upstairs on two sides of the courtyard and the other two sides formed a terrace that overlooked both Damascus and the desert; there they would retreat on summer evenings with friends and nargileh, reclining on mats and carpets, savoring the joys of cool breezes and conversation.

Isabel's lifelong passion for animals expressed itself in Salahiya in what could be described as a petting zoo. Besides the horses, there were three milk goats, a camel, a snow-white donkey, turkeys, geese, ducks, guinea fowl, pigeons, five dogs that she had brought with her from England, a Kurdish puppy, a Persian cat, a lamb, and a baby panther. The menagerie grew as she encountered starving and otherwise abused animals on her journeys around Damascus. But the menagerie was not entirely peaceful. "My greatest difficulty was to prevent them from eating one another."[2]

Her days quickly settled into a pleasant mélange of attending to the business of the household, exploring Damascus, learning Arabic, riding, and hunting. On Wednesdays she opened her house in a reception where visitors were welcome throughout the day. Because Muslim women could not be entertained in the same room as men, Isabel solved the problem by using two reception rooms and sharing her time between the men and the women. On Saturdays she dragooned a doctor into holding a clinic for the poor of her village, with herself as the nurse. Normally she assumed the role of doctor rather than nurse and did not hesitate to prescribe medication where she felt it was appropriate. Moreover, she had developed a theory that because of the hot climate it was necessary to administer four times the normal dose to achieve the desired effect. Richard felt sure that a murder charge would be the inevitable result, but Isabel was convinced that given "some natural instinct about medicine," some good books, and experience, medicine was not all that difficult. No deaths were known to have occurred.[3]

With only thirty Europeans and three English in the Damascene expatriate community, it is not surprising that Isabel soon met and became friends with Jane Digby. Although there was a twenty-four-year difference in their ages, their class and backgrounds were similar, and Kew Gardens (the botanical gardens where Richard and Isabel found one another again after Richard's return from Crimea), as well as Mortlake, where Isabel had lived with an aunt and where she and Richard would soon purchase a cemetery plot, are but a short walk from Roehampton where Jane had lived with Lord Ellenborough. Isabel said that Jane's eyes would fill with tears as they talked about England and old times. On some evenings in the hot weather, Richard, Isabel, Jane, and Emir Abd el Khader would take their dinner on the rooftop terrace and then sit on cushions, smoke their nargilehs, and talk far into the night.

> I shall never forget the scene on the housetop, backed as it was by the sublime mountain, a strip of sand between it and us, and on the other three sides was the view over Damascus and beyond the desert. It was all wild, romantic, and solemn; and sometimes we would pause in our conversation to listen to the sounds around us: the last call to prayer on the minaret-top, the soughing of the wind through the mountain-gorges, and the noise of the water-wheel in the neighboring orchard.[4]

For her part, Isabel thought Jane a "romantic and picturesque personality: one might say she was Lady Hester Stanhope's successor."[5] She felt that they had become great friends and claimed that Jane had dictated to her the whole of her biography—although Jane later denied this.

Years of longing and fantasizing behind them, Isabel and Richard threw themselves into their "Eastern" life; weddings, funerals, circumcisions, no invitation was refused. As she became more comfortable with the social conventions, she found herself asked, as the highest ranking guest, to hold the boy in her arms as the circumcision was performed. Nor was their social life limited to Damascus but extended to the villages and sheikhs within two to three days' ride.

When traveling with Richard, Isabel frequently dressed as a boy and pretended to be his son. She acted as the head groom and saw that the horses were groomed, fed, watered, and saddled. They were in their saddles at dawn and rode till near sunset with a break during the worst heat of the day. If they were camped near tents or villages,

Richard would receive the sheikhs with nargileh and sherbet while Isabel tended the horses. Later she would join Richard and sit "at a respectful distance and in a respectful attitude."[6]

While Isabel began by limiting herself to short trips, Richard did not and was often gone for days at a time. Because they lived a fifteen-minute ride from the gates of Damascus and the area was considered unsafe at night, it was agreed that Isabel would confine her visits to the daylight hours. But after three months of this voluntary confinement, Isabel rebelled. She notified the head of the police that she intended to dine out when she pleased and return at all hours so that he should see to it that she was never attacked or molested. She gave him a present and then emphasized her point by showing him her pistol and explaining that she planned to "shoot the first man who comes within five yards of me or my horse."[7] She still took an escort of four of her servants, but she warned them that the first man who ran away, she would shoot from behind. She was no longer confined.

Isabel was not only armed, she usually carried two revolvers, and she knew how to use them. Once when Richard was attacked and vastly outnumbered by a crowd of Greeks in Nazareth, she had rushed to his defense brandishing her two revolvers. He waved her back and she retreated reluctantly, silently marking twelve Greeks who would die if they killed Richard. An important part of being armed is to know when not to draw your weapon, and this is particularly important in the precisely calculated etiquette of the Arab *ghazu*, or raid. A distant cloud of dust in the desert resolves into a band of armed men riding full tilt directly at the line hastily formed by your party. The attackers, lances vibrating over their heads, skid recklessly to a stop, scanning the faces of their potential victims for any sign of fear or any move to fight. A drawn pistol at the wrong moment could launch a disaster. If one were to kill an opponent, even in battle, it would likely set the stage for a cycle of blood revenge that could only be satisfied by more death or by the payment of "blood money." Isabel understood these constraints and had the discipline to control both her fear and her actions.

The first long journey was to Palmyra, and it seems to have been entirely at Richard's instigation, although Isabel was fully aware of Zenobia, and in her book *The Inner Life of Syria, Palestine, and the Holy Land* she describes Zenobia as "the great Queen of the East, who ruled Palmyra in its days of splendour (A.D. 267). She was an extraordinary woman, full of wisdom and heroic courage."[8] In addition to the desire to explore, Richard wanted to break the hold of the el Mesrab tribe on travel to Palmyra by showing that an escort was unnecessary. Isabel had described the system of escorts as a form of blackmail. The el Mesrab was, of course, the tribe of Jane Digby's husband Medjuel, and Richard's success would mean a significant loss of tribal income. This point does not appear to have been discussed by the Burtons and el Mesrabs, and their friendship continued to flourish.

When the trip began, the party consisted of the Burtons, the Russian consul, a French traveler, and servants. Isabel was dressed in "yellow button boots and gaiters, an English riding-habit with the long ends of the skirt tucked in to look like their Eastern baggy trousers, an Eastern belt with revolver, dagger, and cartridges. My hair was all tucked up under the tarbash, and I wore one of the Bedawin veils to the waist, only showing a bit of face."[9]

She had brought two of her stallions. "The first stallion would be good for travelling and fighting, and the second for bolting, if needful."[10] They were accompanied to the city gates by an official and a large cavalcade. After the requisite hot and tiring passage, complete with sandstorm, threatened but not actually attacked by bedouin, they sighted the sunlit ruins of Palmyra rising from the desert. The people of Palmyra, led by their sheikh, came out to greet them and were so obviously poor and ragged that Isabel wondered, "What have the descendants of the great Zenobia done to come to this?"[11] The ruins were another matter, and they spent five days exploring them. At one point Isabel writes that what was once a magnificent gateway is now buried in sand and "a muleteer is singing upon that noble perch, unconscious of anything grand, and wonders what I am staring at."[12]

Because Isabel was attired as a male, she felt that she had the freedom to explore without restriction. She assumed the role of Richard's son and acted accordingly, being respectful of "her father," being silent in his presence, and running to hold his stirrup as he dismounted. On the occasions when she entered harems, the women would run away screaming and laughing.

It may be that Isabel was a little complacent about her disguise, as it is difficult to believe that the bedouin were convinced that a thirty-nine-year-old woman was actually a boy or even a young man. It is more likely that they simply accepted Isabel and Richard's behavior as further evidence of the strangeness of the Franks (as Westerners were called): that it was the way some husbands expected their wives to behave in that inexplicable culture. However, it is not too hard to imagine Richard's perpetrating that image in what amounted to a cultural hoax. The bedouin politely went along.

For all her egotism and pretense, Isabel was still a very tough and competent traveler. On one occasion when they were trying to deter some bedouin from what might become a ghazu, they staged a shooting competition in which Isabel handily hit an orange on the end of a lance some seventy yards distant. She rode and endured hardship as one of the party, neither asking nor being given any special allowance. During the return from Palmyra,

> [o]n the second day we rode from dawn to sunset, with the driving wind and the sand in our faces, filling eyes, ears, nose, and mouth. I felt so cold, tired, and disheartened, that as I sat in my saddle and rode along I cried for about two hours, and Richard and the others laughed at me. Whilst I was crying we saw a body of mounted bedawin dodging about in the mountains. So I dried my eyes, and rode as hard as I could pelt until we reached Kary-atyn at sunset; but I had to be lifted off my horse and could not stand for some minutes.[13]

They learned later that bedouin had followed them during their entire journey, to what purpose they were unsure.

Other travels took them to Baalbek, where they camped in the central court of the ruins, and then over the Lebanon range to camp under the cedars. On one trip, Isabel stayed in Beirut recovering from illness while Richard went on to Sidon and Tyre. Isabel regretted that she was unable to visit Hester's grave, which was then still at Dar Djoun; Richard, however, did find the grave and made some effort to restore it. On a later journey they explored the Holy Land, visiting what were, even then, standard tourist sites. They explored Jerusalem in detail, visited Lazarus's tomb in Bethany, swam in the Dead Sea, saw Bethlehem and Nazareth, and made their way back north through Safed and on to Damascus. It was at the beginning of that trip, in Beirut, that Isabel first encountered Cook's tourists. She noted that they swarmed over the town like locusts (there were about 180 of them) and that the Beirutis said that "[t]hese are no travelers; these are Cookii."[14] She did not realize that she was being granted a glimpse of the future.

The Burtons had spent a total of almost twenty months in Damascus. On August 16, 1871, the dream was over when Richard was relieved of his duties in Damascus.

They continued to travel widely, and even when Isabel arranged for him to become consul in Trieste, Richard's restlessness required him to pay his vice-consul to assume his duties during his frequent absences. Despite the extensive travel, more than half of Richard's fifty-three books were written after he left Damascus. At least five of the books, based on translations, dealt with sexual behavior and at that time were considered to be pornographic.

Richard had an intense interest, scholarly and otherwise, in sexual behavior. Early in his career, in the Indian army, his commander, Sir Charles Napier, asked him to investigate pederasty in Karachi. Richard donned native dress and with a friend found and personally investigated three brothels in which boys and eunuchs were prostituted. His report, fully detailed and intended only for Sir Charles, was somehow forwarded to headquarters and irreparably damaged his career in the Indian army. Later, in the terminal essay appended to *The Arabian Nights*, he used some of the information he had gained in Karachi. While the text of *The Arabian Nights* is mildly erotic, both *The Perfumed Garden* from Arabic and *The Kama Sutra* from Hindi are highly erotic. Both of the latter include very specific suggestions on how a man can give sexual pleasure to a woman. Isabel could have appreciated Richard's exposure to these ideas, but she did not, and this led to actions that are criticized to this day.

For some years prior to his death on October 20, 1890, Richard had been working on a book based on his translation of *The Perfumed Garden*, and he had promised Isabel that this would be his last book on the subject. He was writing the last page of the manuscript on the day that he died. After his death, Isabel locked herself in a room with all of his diaries and manuscripts and ended up burning both his private diaries and the just completed manuscript of *The Perfumed Garden*. There was a great outcry at the time, and her reputation is tarnished to this day by what appears to be a prudish destruction of a book that Richard and others thought would be his greatest work. Isabel was a very religious woman, a committed Catholic, and anxious about Richard's overly flexible approach to religion. She had taken steps to ensure that he would die as a Catholic and he had acquiesced, but now that he was gone she feared the burden that having such a clearly pornographic work in print would have on his soul and its encounter with his maker. So she burned it page by page. While she discussed the burning of *The Perfumed Garden*, she said nothing about the burning of the diaries and it is unlikely that we'll ever know what they contained.

Richard's remains were returned to England aboard the Cunard steamer *Palmyra*, and Isabel arranged for a mausoleum to be built on their plot in the Catholic cemetery next to St. Mary Magdalene church in Mortlake. The mausoleum is shaped as a tent some eighteen feet high, constructed of dark Forest of Dean stone, and lined with white Carrara marble. The inside of the tomb provided room for two vaults side by side along with a small altar, and Richard was interred on one side in a Catholic ceremony. Isabel moved to a small house in Mortlake where she could be close to Richard and where she died on March 21, 1896.

An iron ladder is embedded in the stone on the back of the mausoleum so that one may climb to a small window and view the inside. There are two vaults now, side by side. Hagar Burton was right after all.

PART FIVE

GERTRUDE MARGARET LOWTHIAN BELL
1868–1926

My brothers, you have heard what this woman has to say to us.
She is only a woman, but she is a mighty and valiant one. Now
we all know that Allah has made all women inferior to men. But
if the women of the Anglez are like her, the men must be like
lions in strength and valor. We had better make peace with them.
—FAHAD BEY, in Wallach, *Desert Queen*

Figure 5. *Gertrude Bell Standing Outside Her Tent*. Babylon, 1909, K218, The Gertrude Bell Archive, Newcastle University.

14

GERTRUDE'S WORLD

Daniel Deronda—Theodore Herzl— Edward VII—Gavrilo Princep

Progress must have seemed painfully slow to women. By the mid-nineteenth century, writing was still a man's profession, and women, well, we have discussed that. To Mary Ann Evans the solution was straightforward if not simple; she would publish under the name of George Eliot—and she did: *Scenes of Clerical Life* (1858), *Adam Bede* (1859), *The Mill on the Floss* (1860), *Silas Marner* (1861), and *Middlemarch* (1871–72). In 1866, she met a Jewish scholar named Emanuel Deutsch, who was working as a cataloger at the British Library in the British Museum and soon was tutoring Mary Ann in Hebrew. In 1869, Deutsch traveled to Palestine and, surprised by the emotions the visit released in him, returned to London consumed with the idea of a National Home for the Jewish people in Palestine. Shortly after his return, he became ill with a painful form of cancer that several surgeries were unable to relieve, and while he continued his work at the British Museum, he severed relations with most of his friends in order to retreat and deal with the pain alone. Mary Ann was an exception and continued to visit him during his illness until he died in 1873.

At the time of his death, she was working on a new novel titled *Daniel Deronda*, and the unfortunate Deutsch became a model for the character Mordecai, who was also a great scholar and also dying. The book is a fictional presentation of Zionism that precedes and prepares for the work of Theodore Herzl and eventually the State of Israel.

159

The title character Daniel Deronda is an exceptionally moral man who even manages to complete his college education at Cambridge with no close encounters of the immoral kind. His parentage is unknown and he has been raised as an English gentleman by a kindly man of the gentry. While rowing on the Thames, he happens upon a young woman who is attempting to drown herself and saves her, and she turns out to be a Jewish singer named Mirah Lapidoth who has escaped from Prague, leaving behind a manipulative father. Her mother and brother, whose fates are unknown, are presumed dead, and Daniel takes Mirah to live with a family of his friends and admirers. With unusual strokes of luck, Daniel finds Mordecai (Deutsch), who turns out to be Mirah's lost brother. Mordecai and Daniel become soul brothers, and while Daniel learns deeply from Mordecai, Mordecai sees Daniel as the one who will carry on his work and vision. Daniel then learns that he is also a Jew, raised as an English gentleman after he was abandoned by his Jewish mother, who had rejected Judaism. Now he undertakes his quest with additional purpose and authority.

> The idea that I am possessed with is that of restoring a political existence to my people, making them a nation again, giving them a national center, such as the English has, though they too are scattered over the face of the globe. That is a task which presents itself to me as a duty; I am resolved to begin it, however feebly, I am resolved to devote my life to it. At the least, I may awaken a movement in other minds, such as has been awakened in my own.[1]

Daniel Deronda was George Eliot's last novel but it had a deep and lasting effect. It was enthusiastically received by Jews and was translated into German, Russian, and Hebrew. She mentions her delight at the many letters she received thanking her for the book, and while she was far from the first to promote or endorse the idea of what came to be known as Zionism, she added substance and thrust to the idea. There were many, including prime movers in the enterprise, who were persuaded by George Eliot. The milieu into which *Daniel Deronda* was published was marked by anti-Semitism that was widespread, especially in Russia, virulent and growing. It was an era of nationalism, and Jews were politically powerless. The book had an equally important impact on the non-Jewish British public. The highly sympathetic portrayal of Jews and their political situation contributed to the conditioning of the British public and prepared the way for subsequent events such as the Balfour Declaration.

WE HAVE NO REASON TO BELIEVE that Theodore Herzl actually read *Daniel Deronda*, but we know that he knew about the book and its theme. We do not know that he had read Disraeli's *Tancred* either, but we do know that he chose "Tancred" as his *nom de combat*. So in this young journalist it is likely that there were at least two literary influences reinforcing the thinking that he described as "an eruption from his subconscious," that the Jews must build a nation-state.

The idea was not new, but Herzl clearly qualifies as the "Father of Zionism." He published a pamphlet entitled *Der Judenstaat* (the Jewish State), where he outlines the nature of "the Jewish problem" and lays out the solution. He went on to organize the First Zionist Congress, which was held in Basel, Switzerland, in 1897. In his diary he wrote, "If I were to sum up the congress in a word—which I shall take care not to publish—it would be this: At Basle I founded the Jewish State."[2] Herzl died on July 3, 1904; the next day his remains were flown to Palestine and interred on top of a ridge facing Jerusalem—Mount Herzl.

When the State of Israel was established in 1947, David Ben Gurion signed the documents sitting in front of a large portrait of Theodore Herzl. There should have been at least a small portrait of George Eliot holding a copy of *Daniel Deronda*, given that she and her book had helped to form the Zionist enterprise. Gertrude Bell's work in the Middle East took place in a context partially structured by the Zionist enterprise, while Freya Stark would deal with Zionism directly.

ALBERT EDWARD was born in Buckingham Palace in 1841, a Victorian to the bone; he was the eldest son of Queen Victoria. Of course he became the Prince of Wales and was in an ideal position to observe the entire era; in fact, he was in that ideal position as heir apparent longer than anyone in British history, although Prince Charles is now coming into a position to challenge that record. Albert Edward could have read about Hester and Jane or known Isabel and possibly even Gertrude but there is no reason to think that he did. Charming and outgoing, he tended to come up short academically and was a disappointment to his parents, who were diligent in making him aware of his shortcomings. His father, Prince Albert, the Prince Consort, died two weeks after visiting his son at Cambridge to chastise him for an episode, reported in the newspapers, in which the actress Nellie Clifden had been hidden in his tent by fellow officers. The death was owing to typhoid and had nothing to do with the visit to "Bertie." Still, his mother blamed his father's death on Bertie and did so for the rest of her life.

When Victoria died in 1901, Bertie began his reign as King Edward VII and presided over the accelerating decline of the British Empire: a decline with such complex causes and momentum that even a king with a mighty intellect would have been unable to reverse it. Still, when he ascended to the throne and became emperor of India as well as king, the British Empire was the largest in both territory and population that the world had ever seen. Britain had digested the fruits of the Industrial Revolution; its navy ruled the seas, and Britain as the largest exporter of manufactured goods accounted for 25 percent of world trade.

But the slide that had begun is apparent only in retrospect, and British hubris remained at a peak. Sir Edward Elgar had begun composing his *Pomp and Circumstance Marches*, and out of the first of these came part of what became the *Coronation Ode* celebrating King Edward VII's coronation and even later became the *Land of Hope and Glory*, a wildly popular evocation of the British psyche that is second only to *God Save the Queen* as a national anthem. The extroverted king ably represented Britain into the twentieth century and adeptly kept a series of mistresses including Jennie Jerome (married to Lord Randolph Churchill), mother of Winston Churchill.

The world, however, was beginning to seethe with the fires of nationalism and needed only the efforts of an unemployed, tubercular teenager to erupt into disaster. The teenager was Gavrilo Princep, a Serbian born in Bosnia, son of a postman, who had been recruited by the Black Hand society along with two other young men to assassinate Archduke Franz Ferdinand, the heir to the throne of the Austro-Hungarian Empire and a man they considered to be an enemy of the Serbian people.

Archduke Ferdinand was to visit Sarajevo, and the three young men had crossed the border into Bosnia and joined up with six other men who had been recruited there. Black Hand supplied them with weapons, bombs, and cyanide capsules to take if they were captured, and they were spaced out along the route that Archduke Ferdinand's motorcade was to follow. The first assassin along the route lost his nerve and let the opportunity pass; the second, his vision obstructed, threw the bomb too late and it exploded under the second car, wounding several, and as the motorcade sped away, Gavrilo assumed that the deed was done and decided to have a sandwich. Archduke Ferdinand, after a decidedly awkward reception at the city hall, decided that he wanted to visit the wounded at the hospital, and he and his wife, Duchess Sophie of Hohenberg, set off in a motorcade along the same route taken earlier. General Potiorek, who was riding with the royal couple, had ordered that the motorcade take an altered route, and when the driver turned into Franz Joseph Street, he realized that his orders were not being followed. The driver stopped and began backing up to resume the correct route. Gavrilo, having finished his sandwich, was startled to see the car with the royal couple pass and, as he stood, begin to back up right in front of him. From five feet he began shooting into the automobile and hit Sophie in the stomach and the archduke in the neck. Sophie died almost immediately and the archduke soon thereafter. Gavrilo was seized, beaten severely, and arrested. He was convicted, saved from the death penalty by his age at the time of the assassination, and sentenced to serve twenty years in prison. He died four years later from tuberculosis.

Austria-Hungary attacked Serbia as a direct consequence of the assassination and the other nations were drawn in by a web of treaties and alliances. Thus began World War I, which would take over 15 million military and civilian lives and plant the seeds that would flower as World War II.

Perhaps more important, the war shattered illusions of the growth and perfectibility of man.

15

BRIGHT AND BRAVE

There are no elements of financial deprivation in the story of Gertrude Bell; her grandfather was Sir Isaac Lowthian Bell, ironmaster, colliery owner, scientist, and creator of a massive fortune that nourished the family past Gertrude's lifetime. Her father, Sir Hugh Bell, was Sir Lowthian's eldest son.

This is not to say that Gertrude was extravagant. She gave every indication of one who was careful with her money, but she also traveled extensively on what were clearly expensive trips without an earned income to bear the cost. So though Gertrude was born into the same degree of wealth as Hester Stanhope, her life was largely devoid of the financial limitations and anxieties that had burdened Hester.

Gertrude Margaret Lowthian Bell (she usually did not use the name Margaret) was born on July 14, 1868, at Washington Hall, County Durham, home of her grandfather. Her mother was Mary Shield, the daughter of John Shield of Newcastle-on-Tyne.

Three years later at the birth of her brother Maurice, the family was living in a new home they called Red Barns, which they had built at Redcar on the Yorkshire coast. The house, now bounded by a residential neighborhood and a railroad cut, still possesses the veneer of a stately home, but this quickly evaporates in its current life as a boys boarding school become hotel with a neighborhood pub on the ground floor. The hotel rooms are in the structure that must have been the children's wing when Gertrude was a child. The main part of the house now provides housing to some of the hotel staff, but remains largely unchanged from its wealthier days with rich woodwork on the walls of the living room and entry and on the ceiling over the main staircase. The garden, now unkempt but with railway cut hidden, still provides a hint of its former glory. Beyond the railway is a large public park that in Gertrude's day was part of the estate.

They had been in the house less than a year when Maurice was born on March 29, 1871. Mary, who had been described as frail, never recovered from the effort and died of pneumonia at age twenty-seven.

While her father grieved, Gertrude and Maurice were delivered to the care of Hugh's sister Ada and then to a series of governesses. This continued even after Hugh's remarriage five years later to Florence Olliffe, a friend of his sisters Maisie and Ada. The adventurous Gertrude was apparently a challenge, not the least of which was to separate her and her brother from the ocean. On one occasion, a German lady named Miss Klug returned from the beach exhausted and empty-handed, to complain that when she called them to go in, they had run behind a boat and then had dodged from one side to the other as she had tried to apprehend them until she finally gave up and returned for reinforcements.

Maurice was the prototype for unnumbered Arab guides, body-guards, cooks, muleteers, and camel drivers as Gertrude honed her leadership skills. Having guided him to the top of a nine-foot wall, she ordered him to jump as she did, and while she usually landed on her feet, her brother rarely did. On another occasion she led Maurice in climbing to the top of the greenhouse. While she was successful in making it to the top and down the opposite side, Maurice fell through the glass.

Gertrude's lack of fear of heights was fostered by her father. Her stepsister Elsa tells of one summer when they were adding to Red Barns and Gertrude was following progress on the project by climbing all over the scaffolding and unfinished walls. She says that her mother told of her horror at seeing Hugh climbing a ladder to an upper floor with a two- and a three-year-old each tucked under an arm. These two happened to be Gertrude's stepsister Elsa and stepbrother Hugo, but it illustrates her father's attitude, and while climbing is a reasonably common childhood adventure, in Gertrude's case it foreshadowed a career as a renowned alpine mountaineer.

In spite of her daring nature, Gertrude was an obedient child, close to her stepmother and extremely close to her father. Her parents, for their part, were unusually liberal, and while it was not customary for girls to be sent off to school, Gertrude was enrolled at Queens College in Harley Street, London, a girl's boarding secondary school whose president, Camilla Croudace, had been a friend of her mother. She was a good student in general, but outstanding at history, and history became a key that would open the way to higher education.

It was not common for women to attend university in the late nineteenth century, but her history lecturer at Queens College was so impressed with Gertrude's intelligence and aptitude for history that he strongly urged her parents to allow her to go to Oxford and, with some trepidation, they did. She arrived at Lady Margaret Hall, Oxford, in May 1886 and began what was to be a richly successful university career.

There were only two colleges for women at Oxford and both had opened in 1879. Restrictions on female undergraduates were severe; they provided, for example, that one girl could not walk the streets alone and that when a group attended lectures, they must be accompanied by a chaperone and even then must be seated at a safe distance from the men. Gertrude, in her second year, writes to her stepmother apologetically that she has met and strolled with Horace Marshall, a student at Trinity who had also been her close friend and companion since they were toddlers. Other than this occasion, there is no record of an unchaperoned outing with a male acquaintance.

Janet Hogarth, a contemporary at Lady Margaret and the sister of Dr. David Hogarth, the archaeologist who later exerted a pivotal influence on Gertrude's life, wrote in 1926,

> Gertrude Lowthian Bell, the most brilliant student we ever had
> at Lady Margaret Hall, or indeed I think at any of the women's

colleges. . . . I need only recall the bright promise of her college days, when the vivid, rather untidy auburn-haired girl of seventeen first came amongst us and took our hearts by storm with her brilliant talk and her youthful confidence in herself and her belongings. She had the most engaging way of saying "Well you know, my father says so and so" as a final opinion on every subject under discussion. . . .

She threw herself with untiring energy into every phase of college life, she swam, she rowed, she played tennis, and hockey, she acted, she danced, she spoke in debates; she kept up with modern literature, and told us tales of modern authors, most of whom were her childhood friends. Yet all the time she put in seven hours of solid work, and at the end of two years she won as brilliant a First Class in the School of Modern History as has ever been won at Oxford.[1]

A part of the final history examination was an oral examination described as the viva voce. Janet Hogarth recalls that she showed no trace of nervousness, and when Professor S. R. Gardiner, a famous historian of the times of James I and Charles I, asked her a question, Gertrude replied, "I am afraid I must differ from your estimate of Charles I."[2] Professor Gardiner was so disconcerted that he asked the examiner next to him to continue the examination.

Gertrude's stepmother's sister was married to Sir Frank Lascelles, a diplomat, and shortly after Gertrude left Oxford the Lascelles invited her to spend the winter with them in Bucharest, Romania, where Sir Frank was then a minister. This was Gertrude's second trip abroad, the first having been a summer holiday spent with a German family during her years at Oxford; this, however, was her first exposure to the world of diplomacy and to living in an expatriate community. So at the age of twenty, her father traveled with her to Paris, where they were met by Billy Lascelles, the son of Frank and Mary Lascelles, who escorted her on to Bucharest. Billy Lascelles was the same age as Gertrude and they engaged in a low-grade flirtation for several years, with the relationship blossoming into an engagement at one point, but this dissolved, leaving a long-term friendship that provided companionship in the exploration of at least four countries.

With her lively interest in people, the diplomatic social scene provided a smorgasbord of new experiences. Among those she met were two who would become chancellors of Germany and Austria, and a Mr. Hardinge, who became Lord Hardinge of Penshurst, viceroy of India, and who, in 1916, would send Gertrude to begin her career in Mesopotamia.

Before returning to England, Gertrude traveled with the Lascelles to Constantinople for her first, brief exposure to the East. There, she and Billy explored and she gathered first impressions as a base for what would become a vast store of knowledge.

For some reason, she began learning Persian and set herself the task of translating a text. One might think that she was doing this in preparation for a trip to Persia with the Lascelles, but such a trip was almost a year and a half off and Frank Lascelles would not take up his post as minister in Tehran for almost a year. It is likely that this was simply an enthusiasm, much like Latin, German, the social conditions of industrial workers in northern England, and other subjects with which Gertrude occupied her formidable and restless intellect. It also may be that Persia had come to represent the epitome of the exotic East that had already gained a foothold in Gertrude's heart.

In April 1892, Gertrude, her Aunt Mary, and her cousin Florence, sixteen, left England to join Frank Lascelles in his new post in Tehran. They stopped in Constantinople, and Gertrude and Florence explored the city with their two maids. The enchantment of the East quickly reasserted its hold, with Gertrude writing, "I feel that I could stand from now till next week at the end of the Galata Bridge and watch the people pass and never be bored for one moment. And the streets are so exciting, even to the names over the shops."[3]

From Constantinople they embarked on the most adventurous travel Gertrude had yet experienced. On a small and dirty steam launch, they coasted the Black Sea shore of Turkey to Batumi at the eastern extreme; then they took the train to Tiflis, which is now Tbilisi, Georgia. At one pass the grade was so steep that four engines were required, two in front pulling with two behind pushing. At Baku on the Caspian Sea, they took a boat to the coast of Persia near

Resht, a smaller boat upriver to Enzelli, a carriage five miles to Resht, then a caravan of victorias (four-wheeled carriages), and finally by horse and mule to Tehran, arriving one month after they left London.

> We arrived on Saturday in the Garden of Eden with a very comfortable house built in the middle of it and your letter waiting for me inside. You can't think how lovely it all is—outside trees and trees and trees making a thick shade from our house to the garden walls, beneath them a froth of pink monthly roses, climbing masses of briers, yellow and white and scarlet, beds of dark red cabbage roses and hedges of great golden blooms. It's like the Beast's garden, a perfect nightmare of roses. In the middle are three deep tanks with weeping willows hanging over them from which run a network of tiny water channels which the ten Zoroastrians who are the gardeners open and shut most cunningly, sluicing the flowerbeds with water. Inside a big rambling house, long, long passages with liveried people in every corner who rise and bow their heads as we pass, big rooms opening one out of the other, two dining rooms, two drawing rooms, Uncle Frank's study and bedroom, two rooms for Auntie Mary, a billiard room and countless little sitting rooms and cupboards; two long stone passages opening at each end with chanceries kitchens etc. in them. Florence and I are upstairs; I have a beautiful big room, cool and dark; three narrow windows opening onto the garden, the tops of the trees rustling against them and nodding in, and such a sweet smell of roses. In the evening the nightingales sing and never stop; it's delicious.
>
> Now the other people who live in our paradise are these . . . Mr. Cadogan, tall and red and very thin, agreeable, intelligent, a great tennis player, a great billiard player, an enthusiast about Bezique, devoted to riding though he can't ride in the least I'm told, smart, clean, well-dressed, looking upon us as his special property to be looked after and amused. I like him.[4]

There are five or six others who live in "our paradise," but Mr. Cadogan is clearly the critical element; his name appears in almost every letter, as in:

But Mr. Cadogan is the real treasure; it certainly is unexpected and undeserved to have come all the way to Tehran and to find someone so delightful at the end. Florence and I like him immensely; he rides with us, he arranges plans for us, he brings his dogs to call on us, he plays with our kittens—we have two Persian kittens, angels!—he shows us lovely things from the bazaars, he is always there when we want him and never when we don't. I think Auntie Mary will like him too in time, she began with a prejudice against him which is gradually wearing away.[5]

With his energy and determination, we find Mr. Cadogan giving Gertrude a translation of Omar Khayyam, sitting with her as they review the shah's troops, playing Bezique, playing tennis, riding, exploring the bazaars, watching races, hosting a tea party, hawking, and reading Catullus under the trees beside a small stream.

While most of Gertrude's time seemed to be engaged in entertainment and flirtation, there are hints of her future traveling style. She continued her study of Persian (Farsi) and progressed to the point that she and Mr. Cadogan were translating some of the love poetry of the Persian poet Saadi. She spent most of her time with the British expatriate community, but did manage to meet some of the Persians and on occasion her letters conveyed detailed cultural observations. Still, there is nothing approaching the degree to which Gertrude came to understand and become a part of the lives of the Arabs in later years.

Her parents should have anticipated the likely outcome of the developing relationship with Mr. Cadogan, but it must still have been a shock when she wrote to her father on July 30, 1892, to tell him that she was engaged. The response would have been gentle but from Gertrude's letters it is clear that the engagement was not encouraged. It may be that they asked only a delay that would allow Gertrude to reconsider away from the romance of the East, but whatever their response, Gertrude's reaction is ambivalent.

By the end of October 1892 she was back in London, and nine months later Henry Cadogan died from pneumonia in Persia.

It is too easy to criticize with the hindsight of one hundred years, but it is safe to observe that if Gertrude's parents had not dragged their heels on Mr. Cadogan, you would be reading a significantly different book today.

On her return trip from Persia, she was escorted and placed in the charge of Gerald Lascelles, who was younger than she. Apparently it never occurred to anyone that she might travel alone, and, of course, if she was to travel with Gerald, as a man he would be in charge. In the light of the way she spent the rest of her life, this is laughable.

16

FROM MOUNTAINS TO MOHAMMED

The next five years were an interlude from the East and a time of healing. There was travel of course: Algiers, Switzerland, Germany, Italy, and a six-month around-the-world voyage with brother Maurice. During these years she published a travel book on her travels in Persia, *Safar Nameh, Persian Pictures* in 1894, and in 1897 *Poems from the Divan of Hafiz*, a translation of the fourteenth-century Persian poet. H. V. F. Winstone, in his biography of Gertrude, notes that A. J. Arberry, a Quranic scholar, said of her translations, "Though some twenty hands have put Hafiz into English, her rendering remains the best!"[1] He said this in 1947. Winstone also notes that she began her translations a mere two years after she began learning Farsi.

In August 1897 the family had gone to La Grave in the Dauphine Alps in France, and Gertrude had traversed the Breche de la Meije, a pass of more than ten thousand feet, with two guides; slept at the refuge; came down over the Col du Clot des Cavales; and returned to the village pleased with herself and with a newly acquired goal to climb the Meije (13,081 feet). In the summer of 1899 she set out to accomplish that goal.

She hiked for two hours to the Refuge de l'Alpe and spent the night with her two guides and two German climbers. They left the Refuge at 4:30 a.m. and reached the top of the Col du Clot des Cavales at 8:10 a.m. That night she slept on straw on a shelf with a cloak for a pillow, "packed tight as herrings" between an Englishman, the two Germans, and one of the guides; the other guide and a porter lay on the ground beneath them.[2] Shortly after 12 a.m. they arose, and Gertrude went down to the river and washed—it was a clear, starry

night, but the moon had not risen, so at 1:00 they started off with a
lantern until the moon was up and they reached the snow.

At 1:30 we reached the glacier and all put on our ropes. . . . It
wasn't really cold, though there was an icy little breath of wind
down from the Brèche. This was the first time I had put on the
rope. . . . We had about three hours up very nice rock, a long
chimney first and then most pleasant climbing. Then we rested
again for a few minutes. . . . I had been in high feather for it was
so easy, but ere long my hopes were dashed! We had about two
hours and a half of awfully difficult rock, very solid fortunately,
but perfectly fearful. There were two places which Mathon and
Marius literally pulled me up like a parcel. I didn't a bit mind
where it was steep up, but round corners where the rope couldn't
help me! . . . And it was absolutely sheer down. The first half-hour
I gave myself up for lost. It didn't seem possible that I could get up
all that wall without ever making a slip. You see, I had practically
never been on a rock before. However, I didn't let on and presently
it began to seem quite natural to be hanging by my eyelids over
an abyss. . . . Just before reaching the top we passed over the Pas
du Chat, the difficulty of which is much exaggerated. . . . It was
not till I was over it that Mathon told me that it was the dreaded
place. We were now at the foot of the Pyramide Duhamel and we
went on till we came in sight of the Glacier Carré, where we sat
down on a cornice, . . . At 8:45 we got to the top between the Pic
du Glacier Carré and the Grand Pic de la Meije and saw over the
other side for the first time. We left at 9 and reached the summit at
10:10, the rock being quite easy except one place called the Cheval
Rouge. It is a red flat stone, almost perpendicular, some 15 feet
high, up which you swarm as best you may with your feet against
the Meije, on a very pointed crest. I sat there while Marius and
Mathon went on and then followed them up an overhanging rock
of twenty feet or more. The rope came in most handy! We stayed
on the summit until 11. It was gorgeous, quite cloudless. . . . I went
to sleep for half-an-hour. It's a very long way up but it's a longer
way down—unless you take the way Mathon's axe took. The cord
by which it was tied to his wrist broke on the Cheval Rouge and

it disappeared into space. There's a baddish place going down the Grand Pic. The guides fastened a double rope to an iron bolt and let Mr. Turner and me down onto a tiny ledge on which we sat and surveyed the Aiguille d'Arve with La Grave in the foreground. Then was a very nasty bit without the double rope—how anyone gets down those places I can't imagine. However, they do. Then we crossed the Brèche and found ourselves at the foot of the first dent. Here comes the worst place on the whole Meije. I sat on the Brèche and looked down onto the Châteleret on one side and La Grave on the other. . . . Then Mathon vanished, carrying a very long rope, and I waited. . . . Presently I felt a little tug on the rope. "Allez Mademoiselle," said Marius from behind and off I went. There were two little lumps to hold on to on an overhanging rock and there was La Grave beneath and there was me in mid-air and Mathon round the corner holding the rope tight, but the rope was sideways of course—that's my general impression of those ten minutes. Added to which I thought at the time how very well I was climbing and how odd it was that I should not be afraid. The worst was over then, and the most tedious part was all to come. . . . at last we found ourselves on the Glacier du Tabuchet and with thankfulness I put on my skirt again. . . . When I got in I found everyone in the Hotel on the doorstep waiting for me and M. Juge let off crackers, to my great surprise.[3]

She climbed another peak on this trip, tackled several more in the Swiss Alps in the summer of 1900, and in late August 1901 met with her guides Ulrich and Heinrich Fuhrer to try for more peaks. The venture was ultimately successful, with Gertrude reporting to her father that she had added seven new peaks to her list. "One of them first class and four very good."[4] On one of them, the Klein Engelhorn, they reached a point where they were stymied on an "awfully steep slope under overhanging place."[5] First Ulrich climbed on Heinrich's shoulders to try to reach a hold and was unsuccessful. Then Gertrude climbed on Heinrich and Ulrich on her and Ulrich tried to work his hands up the rock—but it still was not enough. So she lifted herself and he "fingered up the rock as high as he could" and lifted his foot from her shoulder, and as he did this, she raised her hand and straightened an arm, providing a "ledge."[6]

> He called out, "I don't feel at all safe, if you move we are all killed." I said, "All right, I can stand here for a week," and up he went by my shoulder and my hand. It was just high enough. Once up he got into a fine safe place and it was now my turn. I was on Heinrich's shoulder still with one foot and one on the rock. Ulrich could not help me because he hadn't got my rope . . . It was pretty hard work, but I got up. Now we had to get Heinrich up. He had a rope round his waist and my rope to hold, but no shoulder, but he could not manage it. The fact was, I think, that he lost his nerve, anyhow, he declared that he could not get up, not with 50 ropes, and there was nothing to do but to leave him. (125)

Later, Ulrich told her that when he was standing on her shoulders and told her that he did not feel safe, if she had said that she did not feel safe, he would have fallen and they would all have gone over. Gertrude replied, "I thought I was falling when I spoke" (126).

In July 1902 she was again in Switzerland, this time to challenge the Finsteraarhorn. She and her guides had chosen to attempt the then unclimbed northeast face with a vertical height from glacier to summit of three thousand feet.

The entire adventure was a difficult one: early on she was hit by a boulder and knocked down the slope "till I managed to part company with it on a tiny ledge" (140). She was able to get to her feet without being pulled up by the rope, which turned out to be very fortunate, for the rope had been half severed by the rock. Later it began to snow, but they felt that they had a chance to make the summit, so they pressed on and tried three routes, but failed, and by then the snow was falling faster, driven by a strong wind. So they turned back and within half an hour the clouds had closed in so that they could only get a glimpse of the mountain on either side. Snow fell faster and covered the rocks, but they pushed on till at 8 p.m., a thunderstorm started raging; lightning began striking around them. They dove down a chimney, buried their ice axe heads, and hurried away from them. They could go no further that night, so they found a crack sheltered from the wind that would allow Gertrude to sit in the back on "a very pointed bit of rock" (142), and "by doubling up I could even get my head into it" (142). Ulrich sat on her feet to keep them warm and Heinrich sat just below him; both men put their feet in their knapsacks. And thus they spent the night. Gertrude noted that at first the thunderstorm was exciting, to the point that they tied themselves onto the rock above lest "as Ulrich philosophically said one of us should be struck and fall out" (143). The strikes were almost continuous, and "The rocks were all crackling around us and fizzing like damp wood which is just beginning to burn. . . . It's a curious exciting sound rather exhilarating—and as there was no further precaution possible I enjoyed the extraordinary magnificence of the storm with a free mind; it was worth seeing" (143). The next morning as they continued to fight their way down, they were descending a chimney when they came to an overhang where Heinrich fell but was stopped by Gertrude, who was holding the rope. Then Gertrude tried it with Ulrich holding the rope, and she too fell. Finally Ulrich, held by both Gertrude and Heinrich, climbed down to the place they had both fallen, calling for advice all the way, and then fell just as they did. Just below this point, Gertrude and Ulrich ended up on a place where there was not enough room for both of them to stand and Ulrich was very insecure and unable to hold her. Heinrich was below them on the edge of a couloir, also very insecure. Her rope was fixed below her and of no use, the rock was too difficult, and the distance too great for her to negotiate, so she dropped her axe down to Heinrich and told him that all she could do was fall—and she did. Heinrich had not secured himself and they both tumbled down the couloir, which was "as steep as snow could lie" (145). Ulrich, having heard her say she was going to fall, stuck the pointed end of his ice axe into a crack above and somehow managed to hold all three of them. Gertrude said that this was the one time she thought that they would not get down alive. The ordeal was still not over because by eight that night they were still at the top of the glacier and had to stop. "It was now quite dark, the snow had turned into pouring rain and we sank 6 inches into the soft glacier with every step" (145). They were soaked and not a single match would light, even after they made a tent of Gertrude's skirt and tried to light a match under it. They tried to go on, but Heinrich sank into a soft spot almost up to his neck and it was only with great difficulty that they were able to pull him out. As "mists swept up over the glacier and hid everything; that was the only moment of despair" (146).

> We laid our three axes together and sat on them side by side. Ulrich and I put our feet into a sack but Heinrich refused to use the other and gave it to me to lie on. My shoulders ached and ached. I insisted on all our eating something even the smallest scrap, and then I put a wet pocket handkerchief over my face to keep the rain from beating on it and went to sleep. It sounds incredible but I think we all slept more or less and woke up to the horrible discomfort and went to sleep again. I consoled myself by thinking of Maurice in S. Africa and how he had slept out in the pouring rain and been none the worse. (146)

The *Alpine Journal* for November 1926 ran the following "In Memoriam":

> I do not know when Miss Bell commenced her mountaineering career. It was, however, in the first years of this century that her ascents attracted attention, and about the period 1901–1903 there was no more prominent lady mountaineer. Everything that she undertook, physical or mental, was accomplished so superlatively well, that it would have indeed been strange if she had not shown on a mountain as she did in the hunting-field or in the desert. Her strength, incredible in that slim frame, her endurance, above all her courage, were so great that even to this day her guide and companion Ulrich Fuhrer—and there could be few more competent judges—speaks with an admiration of her that amounts to veneration. He told the writer some years ago, that of all the amateurs,

men or women, that he had traveled with, he had seen but very few to surpass her in technical skill and none to equal her in coolness, bravery and judgement.

Fuhrer's generous tribute on what was probably the most terrible adventure in the lives of all those concerned. . . . "You who have made the climb will perhaps be able to correctly appreciate our work. But the honor belongs to Miss Bell. Had she not been full of courage and determination, we must have perished. She was the one who insisted on our eating from time to time. . . ." The scene was high up on the then unclimbed N.E. face of the Finsteraarhorn, when the party was caught in a blizzard on that difficult and exposed face and were out for fifty-seven hours, of which fifty-three were spent on the rope. "Retreat under such conditions, and retreating safely, was a tremendous performance which does credit to all. The date was July 31 to August 2, 1902; the occasion was a defeat greater than many a victory. When the freezing wind beats you almost to the ground, when the blizzard nearly blinds you, half paralyzing your senses. . . . when the cold is so intense that the snow freezes on you as it falls, clothing you in a sheet of ice, till life becomes insupportable. . . ." Then, indeed, was Miss Bell preeminent.

The Lauteraarhorn-Schreckhorn traverse was probably Miss Bell's most important first ascent, July 24, 1902. It is related that she and her guides, meeting on the ridge another lady with her guides making the same ascent from the opposite direction, were not greeted with enthusiasm. In the seasons 1901–1902 Miss Bell was the first to explore systematically the Engelhorner group, making with Fuhrer many new routes and several first ascents. . . . [Signed] W.A.B. Coolidge.

The notes contain the following, all relating to the different Engelhorner and all new routes or first ascents:

Similistock, August 30, 1901

King's Peak

Gerard's Peak, August 31, 1901

Vorderspitze

Gertrude's Peak

Ulrich's Peak, September 3, 1901

Mittelspitze

Klein Engelhorn

Gemsenspitze, September 7, 1901

Urbachthaler Engelhorn

Klein Similistock, July 8, 1902

For the reasons stated above, it is difficult to name her other expeditions in the Alps, but a well-known climber has stated that his most vivid recollection of an ascent of Mont Blanc was the effort to follow Miss Bell.

Such, briefly and inadequately rendered, are some of the Alpine qualifications for her who must ever be regarded as one of the greatest women of all time. —E.L.S. (149)

Even in the mountaineering years, Gertrude continued her study of Arabic, and by February 1900 she was able to read the story of Aladdin without a dictionary. In November 1899, after her climb of the Meije, she traveled to Jerusalem and was met by the German consul and his family; together they explored the area around Jerusalem. Two months later, in March 1900, she set out alone for Moab (now Jordan).

She rode out of Jerusalem, chatting with first one bedouin traveler and then another. Some of them tried to persuade her that Moab was dangerous and she would be safer if they accompanied her. She had sent her cook and two muleteers on ahead, two hours before her own departure, and she met her guide Tarif coming up to join her about half way to Jericho. Tarif had traveled from his home in Salt in what is now Jordan and his horse was tired, so Gertrude left him to follow at his own pace. By the time the cook, Hanna, arrived with the tents, it was too late to make camp, so she spent the night in the Jordan Hotel. There must have been something to the tales the bedouin were telling about Moab, for the next morning when she visited the mudir of Jericho he sent a guide to Madaba to make arrangements for an escort. Hanna was waiting with the mules at the Jordan Bridge, and they crossed the river and wound their way through the Ghor (the Jordan plain) "full of tamarisks in full white flower and willows in the newest of leaf . . . It was the most unforgettable sight—sheets and sheets of varied and exquisite colour—purple, white, yellow, and the brightest blue . . . and fields of scarlet ranunculus" (67).

They made their way pleasantly, joined for a time by two Christians from Bethlehem, gathering an occasional wild plant, stalking wood pigeons unsuccessfully, and admiring the passing scene. They camped at a place called Ayan Musa (springs of Moses) below Mount Nebo, where Moses is said to have been shown the Promised Land. They bought a hen and *laban* (sour milk) from the local Arabs, and Hanna prepared a meal of rice and olive oil soup, Irish stew, and raisins. She notes that the women are unveiled and that "[t]hey wear a blue cotton gown 6 yards long which is gathered up and bound round their heads and their waists and falls to their feet. Their faces, from the mouth down, are tattooed with indigo and their hair hangs down in two long plaits on either side" (69).

She reached Madaba and called at the Government House to see what arrangements the Jericho mudir's letter had elicited. A representative of the Madaba mudir, who was away, came to see her and inform her that no soldiers were available. She invited him into her tent and offered him cigarettes and coffee and then "determined to wait till the coffee and cigarettes had begun to work" (70). In the ensuing conversation they touched upon the subject of photography, and the effendi revealed that his great desire was to be photographed with his soldiers. Gertrude offered to take his picture and send him copies. The next day she started off with her soldier, "a big handsome cheerful Circassian mounted on a strong white horse" (71).

They rode out on a day trip to Qasr al Mushatta. After four hours of riding, they approached the ruins that Gertrude attributed to the Persians but that are now considered to have been built by the Umayyad Khalif Walid II in 743–44. Today the ruins are on the grounds of the Queen Alia International Airport, a few miles outside the suburbs of Amman, Jordan. On the return trip they were accosted twice by apparently hostile men of the Beni Sakr tribe who grudgingly backed off at the sight of the soldier.

The next day they set out on the King's Highway bound for Kerak and Petra. Then, as today, there were two routes south from

Amman and Madaba. There is a mostly flat desert route that paral-
lels the Hijaz Railway for much of the distance and is now called
the Desert Highway. This, presumably, is the road that the Israelites
were forced to take when they were refused passage through Moab
to the Promised Land. Alternatively, there is a rugged and steep route
that frequently clings to the side of mountains overlooking precipitous and magnificent views of the wadis below, with more mountains
of Moab in the distance. Gertrude chose the latter, and at least the
first campsite sounds idyllic:

> Oh, my camp is too lovely to-night! I am in a great field of yellow
> daisies by the edge of a rushing stream full of fish and edged with
> oleanders which are just coming out. (I have a bunch of them in my
> tent.) On either side rise the great walls of the valley and protect
> me from every breath of wind. I have just been having a swim in
> the river under the oleander bushes and Tarif has shot me a par-
> tridge for dinner. . . . There is a very pretty white bloom flower-
> ing. Mashallah! Oh, the nice sound of water and frogs and a little
> screaming owl! (72)

On the next day they reached Kerak, which sits on the top of a
steep hill together with a massive crusader fort. From the top of the
walls it is possible to see the Judean Hills to the west, in the direction
of Masada and Hebron. After some exploration of the fort, coffee,
and conversation with local women, Gertrude ordered the departure
for Wadi Musa, the town outside Petra.

One access to Petra is through a narrow chasm over a mile long
called the Siq. In Gertrude's day a small stream ran down the center,
around and over remnants of pavement. Not too many years ago,
a flash flood roared down the Siq, trapping and drowning twenty-
three tourists; since then a dam has been built that diverts all water
flow away from the path. There are patches of oleander in cracks
in the high walls and in the narrow ravines penetrating the walls
that squeeze the path. As the Siq opens into the great valley that is
the heart of Petra, there is a grand scene that has been described by

travelers through the centuries. Particularly in the early morning, the Siq itself is deeply shadowed by the high walls of the gorge, so as the traveler comes in sight of the end of the passage she suddenly finds her forward view framed by the chasm walls and glowing with the brightly lit façade of a tomb carved in the red rock wall some thirty to forty yards beyond the opening. This tomb is called the Khazneh (treasury), and lit by the rising sun it has a bright rose glow. Scenes in the movie *Indiana Jones and the Last Crusade* were shot here.

From this tomb on, the walls of the valley are lined with tombs carved in the rock walls with façades that make them appear as temples. Not far beyond the Khazneh, the valley widens into what would pass for a town square with an amphitheater carved into the rock to the left and a row of façades high up the wall a short distance to the right. Beyond this, the valley opens up into a huge basin with more façades and a variety of ruins in the interior. Gertrude and her party spent four days exploring, then riding and climbing to the top of Mount Hor, on top of which is a tomb alleged to be Aaron's. "I have never seen anything like these gorges; the cliffs rise 1000 ft. on either side, broken into the most incredible shapes and coloured: —red, yellow, blue, white, great patterns over them more lovely than any mosaic" (76).

One of Gertrude's muleteers was a Druse she described as "a great big, handsome creature, gentle and quiet and extremely abstemious" (79). This was the same sect that Hester Stanhope had lived among many years before, and they are still found in Israel, Lebanon, and Syria. In Gertrude's time they were concentrated in the Hauran, which lies in the southern part of Syria. The muleteer, Mohammed, told her a great deal about his people and their life, other than their religious practices, which were still secret, to the end that Gertrude was very anxious to visit them and determined to do so as early as possible.

Three weeks after her return to Jerusalem in April 1900, she set off again, this time for the Druse Mountains. She was accompanied part of the way by friends, but after reaching Deraa in what is now Syria, they parted ways and she proceeded east with her muleteers

Muhammad and Yakoub, and Hanna, the cook. An innovation on this journey was a masculine saddle.

> [T]he chief comfort of this journey is my masculine saddle, both to me and to my horse. Never, never again will I travel on anything else; I haven't known real ease in riding till now. Till I speak the people think I'm a man and address me as Effendim! You mustn't think I haven't got a most elegant and decent divided skirt, however, but as all men wear skirts of sorts too, that doesn't serve to distinguish me. (84)

On reaching Bosra, at the edge of Druse country, she became enmeshed in a test of wills with Turkish authorities: "Salkhad! There is nothing there at all, and the road is very dangerous. It cannot happen. It must happen" (87). With neither side conceding, she rose at two one morning, packed quietly (she was camped just outside the city walls), and stole away into the darkness, heading not for Salkhad where they expected her to go but to Areh farther north. After several false turns, they were well on their way and the muleteers began to sing. White-turbaned peasants working in the vineyards stopped to salute them as they passed, and Gertrude was filled with joy at having eluded the Turks.

As she was predisposed, the Druse enchanted her; they were kind, cultivated, civilized, and beautiful. She was taken to meet Yahya Beg, the leader of the Druse, and when she entered, he was seated on a carpet with others, eating out of a large plate. He motioned her into the circle, and she joined them, using thin slabs of bread as utensils. The food was laban and a mixture of beans and meat. The beg gave her his protection wherever she might choose to go and she photographed him standing on his verandah.

Though her initial contact was usually with men, she normally made it a point to observe and comment on the life of the women. In the village of Habran, higher in the hills, she noted, "The women are very shy; they don't unveil even to me, but they let me photograph them. They appear to spend most of their leisure time mending their mud roofs, but the men treat them with great respect and affection even when they are muddy up to their elbows. Isn't this all too wonderful?" (93).

After almost a week of enjoying the country, its ruins, and its people, Gertrude reluctantly left the mountains of the Druse and started for Damascus.

Four days in Damascus, then she was off to Palmyra and the residual aura of Queen Zenobia. With an escort of three soldiers, her muleteers, and her cook, she left through the northeast gate of the city and rode three hours through gardens, orchards, and vineyards fed by running water, on a road shaded by walnut trees. After a lunch by the edge of a clear running stream, they moved into a changing landscape, barren and desiccated, and then on into the desert. Her Arabic was improving daily, enough now to carry on enjoyable conversations with the soldiers, who were bright and possessed *dam khafeef* (light blood—a sense of humor). The hours passed pleasantly, although the fierce heat of the desert now became a burden balanced by bitter cold at night. She saw mirages appearing to be vast sheets of water in the distance, which retreated as they advanced. She added a guide to their party because the last two days of ten to twelve hours' travel would be waterless, and before that having a sufficient supply of water would depend on locating known springs along the way. They began to travel at night to spare both the animals and themselves the intense heat of the day, and it was necessary for the guide to locate from memory such springs as did exist. On one occasion, they reached a spring, and Gertrude "drank the clear, cold water, closing her eyes to avoid seeing the weeds and creatures swimming in it."[7]

Early in the trip she noted that her chief impression of the desert was its silence, "It is like the silence of mountain tops, but more intense, for there you know the sound of wind and far away water and falling ice and stones; there is sort of the echo of sound there, you know it Father. But here nothing."[8]

For all its hardships, the trip was a pleasant one for Gertrude. She tells of one incident in which she fell from her horse:

Yesterday I fell off. I was still sitting sideways in my saddle with a map in one hand and a parasol in the other when suddenly my horse began to trot. I hadn't even got the reins in my hands, so I jumped off, much to the amusement of my soldiers. They are a good lot, my soldiers, more amusing than I expected. I thought it would be rather tame after my recent experiences, but I'm enjoying it very much. This sort of life grows upon one. The tedious things become less tedious and the amusing, more amusing, especially as Arabic grows. (105)

She had made a rudimentary sleeping bag: "an enormous muslin bag in which I sleep and which protects me from all biting animals down to sand flies. I'm very proud of this contrivance, but if we have a *ghazu* of Arabs I shall certainly be the last to fly, and my flight will be as one who runs a sack race" (105). On some occasions she put on extra clothes, wrapped herself in a blanket and a cape, and slept on the ground without the protection of a tent.

Then Palmyra: "At length we stood on the end of the col and looked over Palmyra. I wonder if the wide world presents a more singular landscape. It is a mass of columns, ranged into long avenues, grouped into temples, lying broken on the sand or pointing one long solitary finger to Heaven. . . . And beyond all is the desert, sand and white stretches of salt and sand again, with the dust clouds whirling over it and the Euphrates five days away. It looks like the white skeleton of a town, standing knee deep in the blown sand" (108). They explored Palmyra, and then days later as they were leaving, just at dawn, Gertrude looked back and "Palmyra looked like a beautiful ghost in the pale stormy light" (109).

On the return trip to Damascus, she spent some time riding a camel and comments that after riding a horse for a long stretch it is a relief "to feel the long comfy swing and the wide soft saddle of a camel beneath you" (112). It was also on this trip that she committed a cultural faux pas and recovered from it.

A large tribe of Arabs had arrived and set up camp near hers, and their sheikh came to call on her. Later, she returned the visit, was seated on carpets and cushions in his tent, and was plied with coffee while seated in a circle of tribesmen. One of the men began to play a *rubaba*, a single-stringed instrument, and sing:

> The murmur of the rubaba ran through it all—weird and sad and beautiful in its way. All the silent people sat around looking at me, unkempt, half-naked, their keffiyehs drawn up over their faces, nothing alive in them but their eyes, and across the smoldering fire of camel's dung, the singer bent his head over the rubaba or looked up at me as he sent the wailing line of his song out into the dark. Sometimes one would come into the open tent (the front is never closed) and standing on the edge of the circle, he greeted the Sheikh with a "Ya Muhammad!" his hand lifted to his forehead and the company with "Peace be upon you," to which we all answered "And upon you peace!" Then the circle spread out a little wider to make room for the new comer. (113)

Finally she got up, said her good-bye, and left the tent, only to be told by her soldiers that she had given great offense. They had killed and were preparing dinner, and she should have stayed. They added that because he was a great sheikh, she also should have given him a present. She went to her tent, thought it over, and sent one of the soldiers back with a pistol as a gift and the message that she had not known that he was planning to do her such an honor and would he accept this present. He replied that he was only doing his duty and would she rejoin them. She did, and the waiting continued with more Arabs dropping in until the circle stretched all around the large tent. Eventually, at 9:30, a black slave came and poured water over their hands.

> And at last dinner—four or five men bearing in an enormous dish heaped up with rice and the meat of a whole sheep. This was put down on the ground before me, and I and some ten others sat round it and ate with our fingers, a black slave standing behind us with a glass which he filled with water as each guest required it. The food was pretty nasty, saltless and very tough—but it was 9:30! They eat

extraordinarily little, and I was still hungry when the first circle got up to make place for the second. More hand-washing, with soap this time, and I bowed myself out and retired to bisquits and bed. It was rather an expensive dinner, but the experience was worth the pistol. (114)

With regard to what the Arabs eat, she had noted earlier that when traveling they ate surprisingly little, nothing but bread, dates, milk, and coffee, and little enough of that. This may help to account for the trim physical condition in which Gertrude kept herself throughout her life.

She rode through Ma'lula and noted that it was one of three places where the old Syrian language is still spoken. Today it is among the few places where Aramaic, the language that Jesus spoke, is still spoken. And then she returned to Damascus.

During the following month she visited Baalbek, camped among the cedars on the slopes of Mount Lebanon, visited Beirut, returned to Jerusalem, and then on to England. She took with her cones from the cedars of Lebanon, some of which are growing in England today. All of Gertrude's trips until now were, in retrospect, preparation for the real expeditions that she would soon undertake.

17

JOYOUS JOURNEYS

Gertrude's writing is suffused with such enthusiasm and joy that it is easy to lose sight of the difficulties and challenges she faced. The trips from Jerusalem were far from easy and bore their share of danger, but did not compare to the journeys in Mesopotamia and northern Arabia in either difficulty or danger. The latter trips leap over the line that divides travel from exploration.

The first of these began on February 10, 1911, from Dumayr, a town northeast of Damascus. Her journey would actually take her southeast, but once again she was misleading the authorities, who were under the impression that she was headed for Palmyra in the company of four *zaptiahs*, Turkish police officers. In fact, her caravan consisted of fifteen, including Fattuh her cook and caravan master Ali, a desert postman who would be their guide, an old sheikh from Kubeisa who was returning home, four camel men, and seven merchants who were going across the Euphrates to buy sheep. She began the journey riding her mare, but when they were well into the desert, she mounted a riding camel.

> She is the most charming of animals. You ride a camel with only a halter which you mostly tie loosely round the peak of your saddle. A tap with your camel switch on one side of her neck or the other tells her the direction you want her to go, a touch with your heels sends her on, but when you wish her to sit down you have to hit her lightly and often on the neck saying at the same time: "Kh Kh Kh Kh," that's as near as I can spell it. The big soft saddle, the "shedad," is so easy and comfortable that you never tire. You loll

189

about and eat your lunch and observe the landscape through your
glasses: you might almost sleep.[1]

She has a knack for idyllic description, as when she describes
their camp on the third night: "The name of the place is Aitha, there
is a full moon and it is absolutely still except for the sound of the
pounding of coffee beans in the tents of my traveling companions.
I could desire nothing pleasanter" (270). Or, their departure on the
sixth morning:

> We were off at five this morning in bitter frost. Can you picture the
> singular beauty of these moonlit departures! the frail Arab tents
> falling one by one, leaving the camp fires blazing into the night;
> the dark masses of the kneeling camels; the shrouded figures bind-
> ing up the loads, shaking the ice from the water skins, or crouched
> over the hearth for a moment's warmth before mounting. "Yal-
> lah, yallah, oh children!" cries the old sheikh, knocking the ashes
> out of his nargileh. "Are we ready?" So we set out across the dim
> wilderness, Sheikh Muhammad leading on his white dulul [riding
> camel]. The sky ahead reddens and fades, the moon pales and in
> sudden splendour the sun rushes up over the rim of the world. (273)

And then an interesting remark: "To see with the eyes is good,
but while I wonder and rejoice to look upon this primeval existence,
it does not seem to be a new thing; it is familiar, it is a part of inherited memory" (273).

There was little doubt that Gertrude was in command. Nine
days into their march, they encountered sleet and generally inclem-
ent weather, and on the following day when Gertrude and the merchants were ready to start, the sheikh and her camel drivers were
still in their tent, sitting over the coffee fire. Gertrude simply pulled
out their tent pegs and brought the tent down on their heads, to the
delight of the rest of her caravan. They continued south into what
is now Iraq, passing to the west of Baghdad through Kubeisa where
the old sheikh left them. They stopped at the Castle of Ukhaidir
where Gertrude had stopped before, and she made corrections to her

previous plan of the site in addition to measurements for the preparation of an elevation. She then cut directly across the desert to An Najaf in order to find rumored ruins and draw plans. It being March and the rainy season, much of this travel was in the rain or under the threat of rain. While this might seem a pleasant condition in a desert, it actually raised additional difficulties such as flooded, dangerous, if not impassable wadis. In certain low-lying or marshy areas, the surface is composed of soil described as *sabkha*. Sabkha is sandy when dry, but when wet it becomes a glutinous paste that is slippery and difficult, if not impossible, to walk on. Camels in particular are unable to keep their footing under these conditions. A caravan could become trapped and unable to move—a particularly difficult situation if it was also out of rations. While her caravan slipped and slid, they did not become trapped and eventually made their way to the road connecting Karbala and An Najaf, the most important shrines to Shia Muslims and the focus of an annual pilgrimage. Gertrude noted that this was the first day, March 5, 1911, she had spent on a road since leaving Damascus on February 7. They made their way to An Najaf and then reversed their direction to Babylon, where she lunched on top of the Tower of Babel, and proceeded to Baghdad, where they spent almost a week, with Gertrude being entertained by the consul and his wife. After that they headed north to Bakuba with the ultimate destination of Diyarbekir in the mountains of what is now eastern Turkey.

Throughout this portion of the journey, she stopped at every ruin, mapped and/or photographed its various aspects, and pushed on. At Qasr-e-Shirin, which is across the border in Persia, she worked on Sassanian palaces in spite of bullets fired at her party and earnest warnings about thieves. Gertrude says that she was skeptical concerning the thieves, but there was no doubt about the bullets, "and it is almost as annoying to be shot by accident as on purpose" (295). On at least two occasions, the caravan was forced to hazard the crossing of flooded rivers, which they managed without serious loss.

Near the end of the journey, she took a slight detour to visit Carchemish in the hope of finding the archaeologist David Hogarth, her friend and the brother of her college classmate Janet Hogarth. Hogarth had left, but she met there a young man named T. E. Lawrence who was working on the excavations. Their lives would entwine in the years to come. She was back in England by June 1911.

Two and one-half years later, in December 1913, Gertrude was in Damascus planning a trip to Arabia. The initial destination was to be Hail in Central Arabia, the capital of Ibn Rashid, who with the support of the Ottomans had been suppressing the Saudi state, although this was about to change with the advent of Abd al-Aziz ibn Saud. Gertrude had longed to make this trip for years, and her friends and other sources in Damascus were telling her that because the tribes were at peace, this was the ideal time to attempt a journey into Arabia; the fall rains had been good, there should be ample water and grass. Some idea of the economics of her travel is given in the letters to her mother and father concerning this trip. She asks her father for an extra £400 and details her expenses for the trip: 17 camels at £13 each including "their gear," £50 for food, £50 for gifts, £80 cash, and £200 for a letter of credit to be drawn at Hail. "I am practically using all my next year's income for this journey, but if I sit very quiet and write the book of it the year after I don't see why I shouldn't be able to pay it all back. And the book ought to be worth something if I get to Nejd and beyond" (254). "Beyond" refers to the Persian Gulf, which she felt she had a good chance of reaching. But whether Hail or the Gulf, this journey carried with it substantial risk and uncertainty, and she prepared her parents carefully, telling them when they might hear from her, alternative communications channels, whom to contact if news of her was "greatly overdue," and to "remember always that I love you more than words can say, you and Mother" (310).

As with most of her adventures, this trip lacked the blessing of the authorities, and she started out looking over her shoulder. The beginning was more difficult owing to the absence of Fattuh, who had contracted typhoid. Gertrude had to instruct and supervise the unpacking and pitching of her tent, which was English and unfamiliar to the Arabs; cooking; repacking; and the general organization and progress of the caravan. But soon the men learned and the days became agreeably routine. Gertrude slipped gratefully into the familiarity of the desert, where "silence and solitude fall round you like an impenetrable veil; there is no reality but the long hours of riding, shivering in the morning and drowsy in the afternoon, the bustle of getting into camp, the talk round Muhammad's coffee fire after dinner, profounder sleep than civilization contrives, and then the road again" (314).

Gertrude spent her time mapping the areas they traversed and drawing plans of the ruins they found. The first dangerous encounter, with Arabs of the Jebel Druse, was escaped only because at the last minute the attackers recognized her camel herder. No one was hurt, their possessions were returned, and a man was assigned to travel with them to prevent a recurrence. This was standard procedure in the desert, where the likelihood of encountering hostile tribes was great. They had begun the journey with a representative of the Ghiyatah who would vouch for them with that tribe. They planned to pick up a member of the Beni Hassan, who are enemies of the Ghiyatah, as soon as they were able to find one. As it happened, the next encounter was with Ottoman officialdom.

They had worked their way into the eastern desert of what is now Jordan. Gertrude had drawn a plan of the fort at al Azraq (T. E. Lawrence, by then Lawrence of Arabia, would later spend a winter in this fort), and another plan of a nearby Umayyad pleasure palace. At the same time she was working her way closer to the railway, hoping to locate Fattuh as well as her mail. She found both, and shortly thereafter she was located by a detachment of soldiers and a police officer who told her that they had been looking for her ever since she had left Damascus. He ransacked their baggage, confiscated their weapons, and posted men around her tent. The nearest higher authority was in Salt, and two days later she found him in Amman on his way to see her; with his help she was able to sort things out.

Gertrude encountered and became friends with several sheikhs of the Howaitat, a major tribe of northern Arabia. She spent three days with one, Muhammad Abu Tayyi, searching out ruins and enjoying the hospitality of his tribe. She describes her evenings:

> Of an evening we sat in his big tent—he is an important person, you understand—and I listened to the tales and the songs of the desert, the exploits of Audah (Muhammad's brother), who is one of the most famous raiders of these days, and the romantic adventures of the princes of Nejd. Muhammad sat beside me on the rugs which were spread upon the clean soft sand, his great figure wrapped in a sheepskin cloak, and sometimes he puffed at his narghileh and listened to the talk and sometimes he joined in, his black eyes flashing in question and answer. I watched it all and found much to look at. And then, long after dark, the "nagas," the camel mothers, would come home with their calves and crouch down in the sand outside the open tent. Muhammad got up, drew his robes about him, and went out into the night with a huge wooden bowl, which he brought back to me full to the brim of camel's milk, a most delectable drink. And I fancy that when you have drunk the milk of the naga over the campfire of Abu Tayyi you are baptized of the desert and there is no other salvation for you. (333)

After much discussion, they decided to proceed straight through the desert from their current position, which was near the northern border of what is now Saudi Arabia. This course took them directly into the great sand desert—the An Nafud. Looking at a map of Saudi Arabia, the Nafud is a large blank space in the northwest, below which stretching to the southeast is the second major sand desert, the Najd, and below that to the south and southeast, the huge expanse of the Ar Rub' Al Khali, the Empty Quarter. This course carried the obvious risk of insufficient water and fodder for the camels, but it minimized the risks of *ghazus*, or raids. The winter rains had been good so the pools were full and occasional bushes were spouting green in the sand: "I never tire of looking at the red gold landscape and wondering at its amazing desolation. I like marching on through it and sometimes I wonder whether there is anywhere that I am at all anxious to reach" (335). On February 25, 1914, they rode into

Hail, seventy-one days after leaving Damascus on December 16, and thus began a strange interlude during which Gertrude was virtually a prisoner.

It seems that the amir was away on a raiding trip and left his uncle Ibrahim in charge at Hail. When Gertrude arrived, she was given a diplomatic welcome, installed in a large house, but told that she was not to leave the house without Ibrahim's permission: for her own protection, of course. At this point she had exhausted her money and needed to draw on her letter of credit in order to continue her journey. This was not possible, they replied, because the letter of credit had been made out by the amir's agent to the amir's treasurer, who was traveling with the amir. Given that the amir was not due to return for at least a month, Gertrude resolved to leave with such funds as she had plus those derived from the sale of the weakest camels. Then she was told that she could not leave without the amir's permission. From sources in the town she heard that general opinion held that the whole affair was being manipulated by Fatima, the amir's grandmother. Gertrude said later that it was all like a story from the Arabian Nights, and that this was even more accurate when she was invited to the palace by the women: "The women in their Indian brocades and jewels, the slaves and eunuchs, and the great columned rooms, the children heavy with jewels—there was nothing but me myself which did not belong to medieval Asia. We sat on the floor and drank tea and ate fruits—vide, as I say, the Arabian Nights passim" (345).

She continued declaring her intentions to leave and her requests for a *rafiq* from the tribe to accompany them. The answer continued to be that nothing could be done without the permission of the amir. Finally Gertrude marched into the men's tent and "spoke my mind to Said without any Oriental paraphrases and having done so, I rose abruptly and left them sitting—a thing which is only done by great sheikhs you understand" (345). She had also discussed her problems with Turkiyyeh, a female slave of the amir's brother Muhammad, and Turkiyyeh later told her that she had explained the entire situation to Fatima. Whatever the cause, dramatic change followed, for

that evening Said appeared with "£200 in a bag and full permission to go where and when I liked. The *rafiq* was ready" (346). She
responded that she wished to see the town and the palace by daylight
and would leave the following day. She had previously investigated
and learned that the road south was not possible that year, so after
exploring and photographing the town, they set out for Baghdad.
They rode across the Nafud to the Euphrates at An Najaf. The trip
was both dry and more fraught with tensions as they endured several
close calls that they dodged with the presence of a series of rafiqs. In
one encounter, a tribe tried to bribe the rafiq to abandon Gertrude's
caravan so that they could attack it. Fortunately, he refused the offer.
After several weeks in Baghdad, she trimmed the size of her caravan,
lightened their loads, and drove through the now hot desert in a
series of long marches. By the 30th of April they were in Damascus.

On April 14, 1927, the president of the Royal Geographic Society, Dr. David Hogarth, had this to say about Gertrude's journey to
Hail:

> Her journey was a pioneer venture which not only put on the map a
> line of wells, before unplaced or unknown but also cast much new
> light on the history of the Syrian desert frontiers under Roman,
> Palmyrene, and Umayyad domination. . . . But perhaps the most
> valuable result consists in the mass of information that she accumu-
> lated about the tribal elements ranging between the Hejaz railway
> on the one flank and the Sirhan and Nefud on the other, particu-
> larly about the Howaitat group, of which Lawrence, relying on her
> reports, made signal use in the Arab campaigns of 1917 and 1918.
>
> Her stay in Hayil was fruitful of political information espe-
> cially concerning both the recent history and the actual state of
> the Rashid house, and also its actual and probable relations with
> the rival power of the Ibn Sauds. Her information proved of great
> value during the war, when Hayil had ranged itself with the enemy
> and was menacing our Euphratean flank. . . .
>
> The jaded traveller, writing in April 1914 her diary and letters
> at Bagdad, had no suspicion that, in little more than a year, the
> knowledge and experience acquired during the past four months

would become of national value. Nor could she foresee that, even after the war, Northern Nejd would return to the obscurity from which she had rescued it. Up to this year of grace, 1927, her visit to Hayil, thirteen years ago, remains the last that has been put on scientific record by a European traveller. (353)

Gertrude spent the summer of 1914 in England, and when the war started she began her contribution by making speeches about the war that were enthusiastically received. By November she was in Boulogne organizing the office and procedures for tracing the missing and wounded. Her success in this effort led to her recall to London to organize the office there, which she did.

The next year, in November, she was sent to Cairo at the request of Dr. David Hogarth, who felt that her knowledge of the tribes of northern Arabia would be invaluable: particularly to Colonel T. E. Lawrence, who was engaged in the Revolt in the Desert.

Six weeks later, Gertrude scrambled to board a troop ship at Port Suez bound for India, where she was to work with the government of India concerning coordination between their operations and those of the Arab Bureau in Cairo.

These early years of the war, and even the trip to Hail, overlaid an intense romance that was probably the last of her life. Now in her forties, she fell in love with Colonel Charles Hotham Montagu ("Dick") Doughty-Wylie, whom she had first met in 1907 when he was vice-consul at Konia in what is now Turkey. The colonel was a renowned and heavily decorated soldier whose stint in the diplomatic corps was intended to allow him to recover from a series of wounds. The colonel was also married. Well-documented as Gertrude's life is, with detailed letters to her parents and friends, her diaries, and her own published works, this relationship, as might be expected, is not clear. About the time of Gertrude's journey to Hail, he and his wife traveled to Albania on an assignment to the International Boundary Commission. He wrote that he was going to destroy her letters, which he apparently did, leaving understanding to depend on his letters to Gertrude and a few of Gertrude's letters to him and to a friend. All of the relevant letters in the Bell family's hands were with-held until after the death of Colonel Doughty-Wylie's wife in 1960, and thus do not appear in any of the volumes of published letters. Nonetheless, from the available evidence, it is clear that Gertrude was deeply in love, and at one point wrote,

> I can't sleep—I can't sleep. It's one in the morning of Sunday. I've tried to sleep, every night it becomes less and less possible. You, and you, and you are between me and any rest; but out of your arms there is no rest. Life, you called me and fire. I flame and am consumed. Dick, it's not possible to live like this. When it's all over you must take your own. You must venture—is it I who must breathe courage into you, my soldier? Before all the world, claim me and hold me for ever and ever. That's the only way it can be done. No: I don't permit an ultimatum; whatever you wish I shall do. But it will come to the same in the end. Do you think I can hide the blaze of that fire across half the world? Or share you with any other?[2]

And again:

> I won't write to you like this anymore. Take this letter and lay it somewhere near your heart that the truth of it may bore itself into you through the long months of war. I've finished. If you love me, take me this way—if you only desire me for an hour, then have that hour, and I will have it and meet the bill . . . and if you die, wait for me—I'm not afraid of that other crossing; I will come to you.[3]

This last caused him some anguish and he urged her, "don't do anything so unworthy of so free and brave a spirit. One must walk along the road to the end of it."[4] The question of the extent of their physical relationship seems to be answered in the following:

> Was it perhaps some subtle spirit of foreknowledge that kept us apart in London? As I go now I am sorry and glad, but on the whole glad—the risk to you was too great—the risk to your body,

and to your peace of mind and pride of soul . . . I must stop. Now, as I write, I know also that you will do nothing to yourself. Peace be upon you; for you have still the garden and the trees to walk under, where there is nothing but peace and understanding.[5]

On April 29, 1915, Colonel Doughty-Wylie lay dead on the beach below the cliffs and hills of Gallipoli. He had led his Australian troops on an assault of the Turkish fort at Hill 141 and was shot in the head just as the Turks ran away and his troops cheered him in victory. Fortunately, Gertrude was in England at the time of his death and could look to her family for emotional support. It was on November 19, 1915, almost seven months after Dick Doughty-Wylie's death, that she boarded the SS *Arabia*, a troopship bound for Cairo.

18

CREATING IRAQ

Gertrude was sailing into a period of her life in which she would influence world events. In spite of, or perhaps because of the turmoil and pain of her personal life, she would immerse herself in the building of the modern Middle East. She has been described as the most powerful woman in the world during these years.

As she arrived in Egypt, the last of the troops had been withdrawn from Gallipoli; the Sykes-Picot agreement had delineated the division of Mesopotamia, Syria, and Palestine between France and England; and Lieutenant General Sir Archibald Murray, in command of the Mediterranean Expeditionary Force based in Egypt, was pushing for an Arab Movement to be led by Sharif Hussein of Mecca.

Gertrude had been recruited by the Arab Bureau, a newly established intelligence organization headquartered in Cairo. Her friends David Hogarth and T. E. Lawrence were on the staff, and for Gertrude it was a homecoming. She immediately set to work, using intelligence files and her own vast knowledge, compiling a book on the sheikhs and tribes of Mesopotamia.

Her social life began to reinflate with old and new friends, and in letters to her stepmother she wonders "if you sent me out a purple evening chiffon gown . . . also a new white skirt" and "Could you possibly send out to me the blue shot silk gown with a little coat and its own hat trimmed with feathers? . . . I should like too the purple satin day gown with a cape . . . and a mauve parasol."[1]

Her life in Cairo was put on hold when she was invited to India by the viceroy, Lord Hardinge, whom she had first met in 1888 on her trip to visit the Lascelles in Bucharest. This was not a social invitation but an assignment to build coordination and cooperation between the Foreign Office of the British Government of India and the Arab Bureau and to determine how best they might cooperate in intelligence work. As a consequence she was sent back, not to Cairo but to Basrah in Mesopotamia (Iraq) as an unofficial liaison between Cairo Intelligence and Indian Intelligence.

She was the only woman assigned to Indian Expeditionary Force D and as such she stepped into a puddle of testosterone-fueled resentment at her presence. For the most part, the resentment was expressed in adolescent shunning and ridicule that Gertrude ignored with aplomb as she took on additional duties: briefing officers of the Expeditionary Force on tribes and terrain, and becoming editor of the *Gazetteer of Arabia*, an intelligence survey. She did encounter serious and growing hostility from A. T. Wilson, a deputy and soon to become her chief. In fairness to Mr. Wilson, Gertrude did have a habit of ignoring the chain of command and corresponding directly with her friends who also happened to be senior officials in the government. Still, instead of confronting Gertrude directly, he fueled his own resentment and resorted to carping and petty tactics such as refusing to take meals with her.

By the time Gertrude had reached India, the armies of the Indian Expeditionary Force were facing a disaster second only to Gallipoli. In an attempt to march on Baghdad they had slogged through marshes and swamps to confront a large Turkish force with unexpected fighting ability and had been forced to retreat into the town of Kut al Amara, where they were surrounded and came under siege. Without food or ammunition to break out on their own, numerous relief forces were sent to rescue them only to be confronted by superior forces and forced to abandon their effort. On one ignominious occasion T. E. Lawrence was sent to attempt to bribe the Turkish commander into freeing the besieged troops, but he was refused. General C. V. F. Townshend (who we last saw as a lieutenant colonel in the Omdurman campaign) surrendered thirteen thousand Indian troops, who were marched off to a likely death. Some twenty thousand more had been killed during the campaign and the subsequent attempts at relief.

By 1916 a new commander, Lieutenant General Sir Stanley Maude, had planned, built a force, and launched a fresh campaign to take Baghdad. It was taken in March 1917, and Sir Percy Cox, who at that time was still chief political officer, moved his headquarters from Basrah to Baghdad. Gertrude, who had been named oriental secretary and was thus responsible for intelligence, followed shortly after. At about this time, her book on the tribes was published as *The Arab of Mesopotamia*; it provided an essential guide to both British military and government.

During this period, Gertrude frequently expressed feelings of satisfaction and even happiness. She felt at home. In Mesopotamia she had close friends around her, both British and Arab. She missed her family and friends in England, especially her father, but it was here that she belonged. She arrived in Baghdad in April 1917, and though she had been assigned housing by the British authorities, she decided to find a place of her own. Close to the Political Office, she discovered three summer houses in a rose garden owned by an old Arab friend. She rented the property immediately and began making arrangements to add a kitchen, bath, and other amenities. She hired a cook and other household staff and began settling into Baghdad life amid masses of roses.

Her day began with an early ride into the countryside, a bath, breakfast, and to the office by nine. A bowl of sour curds for lunch, tea with Sir Percy at four, work till around seven, and then dinner and to bed by nine or so. Her work days were filled with Arab visitors: old friends coming by to say hello and strangers anxious to meet the legendary Al Khatun (the lady; she was also known as *umm al mumineen*, or mother of the faithful). With each visitor she was able to catch up on the latest situation in the towns and villages and with the tribes and, of course, add this information to her intelligence reports. Her papers and reports were highly regarded by the British government in Whitehall and clearly prepared the ground for the critical steps that were to follow.

In 1916, the Arab Revolt began under Sharif Hussein ibn Ali, the emir of Mecca. The Arab forces were led by Emir Faisal, Hussein's son, and they were joined by a slight blond-haired captain detailed from Military Intelligence in Cairo, T. E. Lawrence. Armed and financed by the British and motivated by promises of an Arab state, the forces under Faisal and Lawrence pursued a largely guerilla-type campaign, harassing Ottoman forces and destroying bridges and track on the Hijaz railway. A signal victory was achieved and immortalized in the film *Lawrence of Arabia* when after a legendary ride through the desert they attacked and seized the Ottoman fort at Aqaba in what is now Jordan. They then battled in parallel with General Sir Edmund Allenby, who was leading British forces in a campaign from Jerusalem to Damascus. In a political gesture Allenby allowed Faisal to enter Damascus first, to the cheers or the disregard of the local population, depending on which version of the event that you choose to believe. Janet Wallach in *Desert Queen* notes that David Hogarth gave Gertrude much of the credit for the Arab Revolt because she had provided the information about the tribes that T. E. Lawrence depended on in the Arab campaigns of 1917 and 1918.

The net effect of the Arab Revolt was that the Arabs did have an influence on the outcome of the war and had earned themselves a place at the Peace Conference, which was convened in Paris in 1919. Among the delegations meeting to consider peace terms, the League of Nations, and the division of geographic spoils was a team of distinguished lobbyists consisting of Emir Faisal, Gertrude, and now Colonel T. E. Lawrence among others who argued forcefully in the Arab cause. Then, for Gertrude, it was back to Baghdad and the process of building a state.

In March 1921, Winston Churchill convened a meeting in Cairo of the majority of British Middle East authorities with the objective of resolving a direction for British policy in the region. Gertrude was in the delegation, again along with T. E. Lawrence. A famous picture was taken on this occasion that shows Churchill, a group of men, and one woman mounted on camels with the Sphinx and pyramids in the background. The woman mounted on a camel next to Churchill is, of course, Gertrude. Before the picture was taken, Churchill had slid off of the camel. The others urged him to sit on a horse, but he struggled back onto the camel and said, "I arrived on a camel, and I shall leave on a camel."[2]

The substance of the conference was somewhat more difficult than the camel. In the urgency of fighting the war, Britain had made promises, some of them conflicting, that she now had to make good. Sir Henry McMahon, the British Resident in Cairo, had promised Sharif Hussein an Arab state in Mesopotamia. Mark Sykes and Georges Picot had negotiated the Sykes-Picot agreement that divided the Middle East between France and Great Britain; France would be the Mandatory Power for what is now Syria and Lebanon, while Britain would be the Mandatory Power for Mesopotamia and Palestine. Finally, in a clear echo of *Daniel Deronda*, the British foreign secretary Sir Arthur Balfour had written a letter to Lord Rothschild as a leader of the Jewish Community that stated, "His Majesty's Government view with favour the establishment in Palestine of a national home for the Jewish people, and will use their best endeavours to facilitate the achievement of this object, it being clearly understood that nothing shall be done which may prejudice the civil and religious rights of existing non-Jewish communities in Palestine, or the rights and political status enjoyed by Jews in any other country."[3]

The conference had been carefully planned and its results pre-arranged to provide Britain's answer to its dilemma; Prince Faisal would become king of Mesopotamia, now to be called Iraq, and his brother Abdullah would become king of a section of Palestine that would now be called Transjordan. The debates and discussion had been concluded before the conference. Gertrude had drawn the boundaries of the new state of Iraq, and T. E. Lawrence had argued that the ethnic and religious structure of the area was such that a single state would not work—three states would be necessary. Nonetheless, one state it was and Britain's problem was to secure the people's acceptance of Faisal as their king.

Gertrude had lobbied hard both for an Iraq and for Faisal. Now she took the lead in persuading her Arab friends to accept him, and assuming success, she began drafting Iraq's new constitution. At Faisal's coronation Gertrude was quietly in the background, but as he settled into the job Gertrude was at his side. She was adviser, confidante, and frequent companion. There were picnics, swimming trips, dinners, and hours of private conversation. Gertrude seemed to be infatuated with Faisal, and there have been suggestions that their relationship was more than what was apparent. Possible of course but nothing I have found supports that possibility.

Gradually, her access to Faisal and her influence dwindled. She became curator of antiquities and devoted her considerable energies to the creation of a national museum.

On July 11, 1926, Gertrude took her usual swim, asked her maid Marie to call her at six the following morning, and went to bed. She died in the early hours of July 12. It has been said that her death was a suicide and there is some evidence of depression. She told her father, for example, that she felt that she was carrying on an existence. She used a barbiturate named Dial to help her sleep and kept a supply by her bedside. Some suggest that she deliberately took an overdose. On the other hand, it is easy to accidentally overdose on barbiturates, as little more than twice the normal dose can be deadly. Because the drug has an intoxicating effect, it is also not unusual for someone to forget how much they have taken and accidentally overdose. We will likely never know, but I choose to believe that her overdose was accidental.

She was buried in the British Cemetery in Baghdad.

PART SIX

FREYA MADELINE STARK
1893–1993

And then the wonder happened! Camels appeared on our left
hand: first a few here and there, then more and more, till the
whole herd came browsing along, five hundred or more. . . .
I can't tell you what a wonderful sight it was: as if one were
suddenly in the very morning of the world among the people of
Abraham or Jacob. . . . I never imagined that my first sight of
the desert would come with such a shock of beauty and enslave
me right away.

> —FREYA STARK in a letter to Penelope Ker, in
> Caroline Moorehead, *Over the Rim of the
> World: Selected Letters of Freya Stark*

Figure 6. Herbert Olivier, *Dame Freya Madeline Stark*.
Oil on canvas, 1923. © National Portrait Gallery, London, with permission of Jasper Olivier.

19

FREYA'S WORLD

Arabs and Jews—Travelers Health

Howard M. Sachar in *A History of Israel: From the Rise of Zionism to Our Time* describes a missed opportunity for Arab-Jewish cooperation that occurred in 1913 when Arab leaders approached a Zionist representative and suggested a united front against the Turks. The initiative failed because of a lack of commitment on both sides, but the reservations were largely tactical rather than strategic. This was simply one of the earliest among what must be hundreds of missed opportunities that might have altered the conflict that Freya saw during her lifetime: a conflict more contorted and intractable today.

In the late nineteenth and early twentieth centuries in a series of immigration waves that the Jews describe as aliyahs, tensions arose between the Arab and Jewish communities, and after the Mandate with the British as well. At the same time, nationalism was blooming around the world and the Arabs in Palestine were no exception. While violence between Arabs and Jews had been rare before the turn of the century, the combination of increased immigration, the political goals of the Zionists, and the nationalism of the Arabs began to generate episodes of violence. In 1929, there were demonstrations and riots over Jewish activities associated with their prayers at the Wailing Wall, and the outcome was more than one hundred deaths on each side. There were other instances of violence in 1928 and 1929, with more than a hundred deaths on each side. During the next six years the Jewish state became even more likely and in the years 1936 through 1939 the Arabs revolted. Over a thousand deaths resulted, and part of the result was that the Jewish community, or Yishuv, began developing organized defensive capability including a nascent army called the Haganah and a splinter group called the Irgun, who with less oversight were prone to revenge and acts of terror. Thus began a parade of violence including but not limited to: Israel's war of independence in 1948, the Suez Crisis in 1956, the Six-Day War in 1967, the October (Yom Kippur) War in 1973, a continuing variety of smaller yet no less deadly engagements, and acts of terrorism on both sides. Freya Stark would have to defend Britain's role in the evolution of the Israeli-Palestinian conflict.

FREYA HAD NUMEROUS HEALTH PROBLEMS on her travels, and she has been described as a hypochondriac, a description that is demonstrably inaccurate given their diagnoses.

Philip D. Curtin in his book *Death by Migration* suggests a hypothetical experiment:

> If several thousand human subjects could be recruited in a particular region of Europe, one part to live overseas while another stayed at home, and the health of both groups kept under careful medical observation over a period of years, with particular attention to the cause of death, we would have some hard evidence. The group at home would serve as a control from which to measure the changing health of the group overseas. The experiment should also exclude the application of modern medicine, and it should be repeated at intervals of ten years or so.[1]

He then goes on to point out that such experiments were actually performed repeatedly throughout the nineteenth century and into the twentieth. They were performed by European nations sending soldiers overseas while keeping other military units at home, and they kept and published meticulous medical records. The statistics are striking: during the period from 1860 to 1914 the mean mortality rate per thousand in France was 6.66 while in Algeria it was 21.61, more than three times as high; in Britain it was 6.01 while in British

India it was 17.20, 2.86 times as high. The leading cause of death for British troops in India was typhoid fever, followed by dysentery and diseases of the digestive system, tuberculosis, respiratory system, malaria, and cholera. By the turn of the century, things were improving; the germ theory of disease had been developed in the 1880s, and this was followed by strides in public and private hygiene. By the period 1909–13, deaths per thousand were down for all the disease categories mentioned above, but the death rate for all disease in the British troops in India was still 2.5 times that for British troops in the United Kingdom. While Curtin does not present statistics for Arab countries other than Algeria, we might expect the relative difference between the Middle East and Britain to be similar. It is safe to conclude that traveling can be dangerous to your health, in more ways than we have already described.

20

ACCEPTING THE TORCH

On July 12, 1926, when Gertrude Bell was laid to rest in the harsh soil of Iraq, Freya Madeline Stark was in London studying Arabic in preparation for a career that would lead to Baghdad and far beyond. Her life would offer an odd parallel to Gertrude's, with places and people in common. In many ways, Freya was the capstone of these improbable women.

Her father, Robert Stark, was the son of the proprietor of a furniture rental business in Torquay on the south coast of Devon. Her mother, Flora Stark, Robert's first cousin, was the daughter of an artist who had moved to Italy and married a German governess employed by a Roman family. Robert and Flora were married in 1878 and began a peripatetic life that set a pattern for Freya.

Both parents were artists, and by the time that Freya arrived on the 31st of January 1893, they were living in a studio on the Rue Denfert Rochereau in Paris. During Freya's first year "we spent ten days in the country near Paris, travelled to England (at four months), visited in Basingstoke and Torquay, and settled close to Dartmoor for the summer . . . visited in Paris, spent a first Christmas with the Genoa grandmother."[1] The wandering continued, and it is not too surprising that at almost four years "the joy of running away became conscious" and Freya set off down the road to Plymouth to find a ship and go to sea. A fortunate encounter with the postman diverted the journey as he examined her traveling kit of mackintosh, toothbrush, and one penny halfpenny, and suggested that this was not sufficient cash for such a journey—another long-term pattern for Freya—and that perhaps they should return home for more cash and a fresh start. Freya remembers "a warm pleasantness in the holding of his comfortable hand, and a tiresome amount of surprise shown by a group on the lawn" (37). This fascination with ships and the sea was a motif with Freya. In the girls' bedroom at Ford Park, the last house owned by the family in Devonshire, her mother decorated the toy cupboards and bedsteads with whatever the little girls requested. Freya asked for sailing ships "so that I might look at them from my pillow and think of myself sailing far away; and I spent many early mornings before Fräulein called us, looking at the little white triangles doubling a cape round which I could not see" (51).

Freya was a difficult child, or "naughty" as such a child was described in that era. Her behavior suffered also by comparison with that of her sister, Vera, one year younger, who was somewhat passive although almost as stubborn as Freya. Vera is reported to have sat in a chair for twelve hours rather than apologize for some transgression. Freya, on the other hand, when made to sit in a corner for tearing strips of wallpaper off the wall, saw no reason to stay and wandered away until her father sat and held her—comforting Freya with the thought that at least "they were both in the corner together" (38). On another occasion when her mother whipped her for trying to hit her with an umbrella, Freya "went round among her [mother's] friends and discussed the matter, leaning up to the drawing-room chairs and murmuring, 'My mama beats me' in an irritating way" (38).

The only source on her childhood years is the first volume of her autobiography *Traveller's Prelude* in which she portrays her childhood as warm and affectionate, yet leaves the impression that her account is carefully edited. Robert and Flora's marriage was troubled, and Robert's absences eventually graduated to permanent separation and his emigration to Canada. She describes her mother as remote and notes her mother's readiness to dump the girls on others while she devoted her care and attention to strangers. The picture that emerges is of the two children wandering alone or accompanied by a governess in pursuit of their adventures. When their father appears it is different. Walks are no longer solitary and his imagination and gentle hands guide their activities. They sleep out on mattresses under the trees, listen to stories about "trackless forests and Siberian wolves" (48), are bribed to walk alone in the woods at dusk, and are introduced to the wonder of toads, salamanders, moorhens, and fallow deer. When cousins moved nearby and ended the girls' solitude, Freya responded by becoming "a most insufferable bully" (48). She had conceived the idea of building the *Argo* (the ship sailed by Jason in search of the Golden Fleece) in a nearby wood, and because it was her idea, she became captain and made the others walk behind her wherever they went. The cousins registered their complaint with her father, and he suggested that it was time for a mutiny by the crew as they were, after all, bigger than the captain and outnumbered her four to one. Nevertheless they did not.

> My father would take us to visit the peasants shut up in their stables for warmth . . . I have never known anyone with less "class-consciousness" . . . he never thought of people except as individuals, and had the same manner exactly towards all. He was completely truthful; I never heard even the smallest complimentary lie from his lips—and I think he gave to both Vera and me a feeling of almost physical discomfort in the face of any lie, which lasted throughout life. Appearances meant nothing at all to him . . . (71)

Freya's idealization of her father lasted throughout her life although it was probably assisted by the seven-thousand-mile separation that followed his emigration to British Columbia.

The family continued to move frequently in what seemed to be a contest of the parents' personalities. A house in Devonshire on the edge of Dartmoor was followed by a rented villa in Farnham while a house was built nearby at Upper Hale, Surrey; this, in turn, was followed by a new house near Chagford at the edge of Dartmoor, and then both were left as they returned to Italy. This wandering left Freya with a yearning for a stable home that transmuted many years later to a feeling that her center, as Freya called it, did not move no matter where the rest of her might wander. This center was attached to Asolo, just north of Venice, Italy, in later years, but three years in her English homes between the ages of five and eight had also left some roots in Devonshire on Dartmoor.

It is one thing to look for first causes that, once embedded in a person's psyche, might later incline them toward travel. It is another to ferret out those influences that would lead someone east or, more specifically, to the Arab world. Books, of course, are a possibility. Freya, with large quantities of solitude, began reading early and read widely throughout her life. Hans Christian Andersen's *Little Mermaid*, Joan of Arc, King Arthur, the Mowgli stories, *The Arabian Nights*, the *Greek Tales*, Sir Patrick Spens's *The Inchcape Rock*, *The Nut-Brown Maid*, and *Count Arnoldos* were followed in later years by George Sand's *Consuelo*, Darwin's *Life*, *Voyage of the Beagle*, and *Origin of the Species*, and by Peacock, Fanny Burney, Spenser, Browning, Hazlitt, Milton, Jane Austen, Gibbon, Cowper, Crabbe, Pope, *Don Juan*, eight volumes of Lockhart's *Scott*, Borrow's *Romany Rye*, Lavengro, Dante, Horace Walpole, Mme de Sevigne, Montaigne, Balzac, and Trollope. Still later, after the interest in Arabia had begun to flower, she read Charles M. Doughty, Philby's *Arabia Deserta*, and T. E. Lawrence, and prior to each trip she read intensively in the literature relevant to that adventure. Did she read Balzac's *Lily of the Valley* and if so, was she intrigued by Jane Digby's fictional counterpart? Possibly. In the meantime Freya was forced to deal with a friend of her mother whom she found distinctly unromantic.

Count Mario di Roascio was twenty-three in the summer of 1901 when he came to stay with Flora and the girls during their summer in Belluno in northwest Italy. "A short, bouncy, dictatorial young man" (61), the girls disliked him on sight, and when their mother persuaded them to accompany him on walks, carefully led him along rocky streambeds on their favorite ledges. He asked never to be sent out with them again. By the next summer they were living in Dronero, the home of the count. It was to become the hub of their lives for the next sixteen years and the count himself the source of much unhappiness.

In her autobiography Freya acknowledges that it is hard to write about the family's relationship with the count without making it sound as if her mother was having an affair with him. She was convinced that this was not the case, but she is right about the difficulty. At the least, Mario exerted a strange domination of Flora and through her of the entire household. He owned a carpet factory, and Flora became heavily involved in that operation: working up to twelve hours a day and ultimately investing in the company as well. While this association provided one anchor for the relationship, there must have been more, for Mario seems to have been omnipresent, dominating everything, even joining the family on holidays. That would not necessarily have been a problem for the girls except for the fact that his arrogance led him to try to subjugate everyone around him and thus he was able to spoil many an outing. At some point Mario's romantic attention shifted to Freya, who, although sixteen, remained mostly unaware of the significance of his behavior. After over a year of what must have been a frustrating courtship, Mario, while on a long walk with the girls, asked if they would "like us always to be like this—together?" This was overly subtle for Freya, who replied, "No, I think once a week would be enough" (104). That evening as she undressed for bed, it dawned on her that she had rejected a proposal. Less than four years later, in 1913, Mario married Vera.

It was in Mario's new factory just before her thirteenth birthday that Freya came close to disaster. On a tour of the new factory, her long hair was caught up by a whirling shaft, and she was snatched up into the air and spun around the shaft. Mario wrenched her free, but by then half of her scalp had been torn away and her eyelid had to be stitched back into place. After skin grafts and four months in the hospital in Turin, Freya was healed, but with scars that guaranteed self-consciousness and spoiled "such looks as I might have had" (86).

In the early years in Dronero, the girls were sent to the Convent of the Sacred Heart for an hour every day to learn French, and two hours a week they learned sewing and embroidery. Little else was done for their education until the fall of 1911 when, at eighteen, Freya went to London to prepare for matriculation at Bedford College. In the fall of 1912 she entered the college as a day student, studying first for a degree in English literature, shifting later to history. Her study was ultimately interrupted by the war and never resumed. The experience, however, was a happy one and helped to rub off some of the "foreign" demeanor that Freya had acquired in Italy. She also formed a friendship with Professor W. P. Ker that would last for the rest of his life and assert an influence on her throughout hers. It was Ker who introduced her to Matthew Arnold's poem about the Oxus in *Sohrab and Rustum* that lived in his voice in her memory:

> But the majestic river floated on,
> Out of the mist and hum of that low land,
> Into the frosty starlight, and there moved,
> Rejoicing, through the hushed Chorasmian waste,
> Under the solitary moon . . . [2]

Under the looming clouds of the First World War, Freya decided not to go on with her education and to learn nursing instead. With the assistance of a friend she was employed by the Clinic of St. Ursula in Bologna. This was a bit on the daring side as nursing was then a less than respectable profession; all but one of the other nurses at St. Ursula were women of the streets and carried on both professions. While the physicians treated Freya with respect and even gallantry, the nurses were jealous and treated her badly until she challenged them directly and asked them what the problem was. She then went on to explain her feelings about the war and what it meant to all of them—this solved the problem and the other nurses were kind to her from that point on. She did well in nursing, even administering anesthesia during surgeries. As Italy drew nearer to the war, Italian ladies rushed to the hospital and as some of them were from upper strata of Bolognese society, the respectability of nursing was established.

In the fall of 1916, Freya was in England working as a censor in a building near the Strand. She read some 150 letters a day, most of them dull, but she found the suspicious ones quite interesting and felt that the work helped to prepare her for her role in the Second World War by developing "a sort of sixth sense for what people are really meaning."[3] She was anxious to get back to nursing, afraid that the war would end before she could get into it, and finally entered training at a hospital in Highgate. She was accepted into the Trevelyan Ambulance Unit stationed in Italy largely because of her fluency in Italian and knowledge of Italian hospitals.

In late July 1917, she left England to join her unit near Udine, close to the eastern border of Italy north of Trieste, and after a short visit in Dronero reported to her unit on the 3rd of September 1917. The hospital was located at Villa Trento, a short drive from Udine and close to the fighting: close enough to see clouds of gas over the distant trenches during the day and the flicker of artillery fire at night. The wounded were brought by ambulance from collection points near the front, and the load on the staff was determined by the situation on the battlefield. The living conditions for the staff were on the primitive side—Freya estimated that she had one bath in two months—but there was a camaraderie among the staff that helped them cope with both horrors and difficulties. Freya discovered that "I had a magnetic sort of hand and could soothe pain by massaging gently." Consequently, she had no free time at all (182).

An Austrian offensive began and an Italian retreat followed, with shelling drawing nearer to the hospital, causing the house to sway and quake. As the only British unit, they were the last hospital left to function, but eventually they were forced to evacuate as well. Freya and six other nurses were launched into the chaos of a slow retreat along the packed roads. After three nights they made it to a train that was then bombed by a German aircraft with blessedly poor aim, and finally reached Padua late in the fourth night. The unit reassembled, and while the staff had gotten out safely, they had lost all of their equipment and stores and the hospital was disbanded. The unit less the English nurses planned to reconstitute at another hospital. Freya tried to join them but was considered too young and went instead, after a visit in Dronero, to a hospital in Turin.

AFTER THE WAR, Freya's father bought her a small cabin with a two-and-one-half-acre flower farm on the Italian Riviera near the Franco-Italian frontier. Part of the motivation was to get Flora away from Dronero, leaving some possibility of happiness to Vera in her marriage to Mario. Remodeling the house, named L'Arma after an old name for the land, aggravated the chronic financial problems of Freya and her mother and left her susceptible to an inducement to smuggle.

Bernard d'Hendecourt, a connoisseur, came to visit L'Arma, was attracted to one of their paintings, and offered a thousand pounds for it and an extra one hundred pounds to Freya if she could get it across the border. Freya put the painting in a cart, placed a friend who was leaving together with her bags on top, and proceeded through four frontier posts while chatting with a guard. She found that she "enjoyed smuggling for its own sake" and felt that it came naturally to her (263). Her father, who disapproved of this pastime, would become an unwitting smuggler when Freya would slip parcels of coffee beans in his pocket and then watch him innocently cross the barriers.

There was a thrill, perhaps a little fear, and at least a touch of youthful thoughtlessness in these forays into crime, but in mountain climbing, another similarity with Gertrude Bell, she had a real and rational fear of tenuous perches on high places, and used climbing as an opportunity to continue her program of defeating fear. Here she differed from Gertrude in that Gertrude did not seem to experience a great deal of fear in mountain climbing. In fact, in general, I suspect that the women in this book, including Freya, felt less fear than others. While dictionaries include fearlessness as a form of courage, I would define courage more narrowly as the trait that enables one to act in spite of fear and thus to defeat fear itself. So Freya in mountain climbing certainly showed courage. And Gertrude? Well, there are dozens of adjectives, but "intrepid" fits.

Freya's first rope climb was before the war on an outing with W. P. Ker, the professor she had met at Bedford College who had become a good friend and mentor. The first occasion was thrilling; "the happiness was almost frightening" (135). The second climb was with Vera and with Mario, who with typically supreme but unjustified confidence jumped on what he thought to be earth but was really ice and almost yanked both Vera and Freya off of a six-inch ledge. The women clung to the rock until the guides could rescue Mario. On a second occasion the same day a rock fall passed over them on an ice slope and Mario decided to give up climbing, making Vera give it up as well (135–37).

In 1923, while again climbing with W. P. Ker, they had reached about nine thousand feet and were preparing to rope up when Ker cried out, collapsed, and died. Freya sat with him for seven hours waiting for villagers to arrive with a ladder to carry him down. He was buried in the cemetery where guides are buried under the ridge of Monte Rosa. The year before, Ker had climbed the Matterhorn and had written Freya "that he had felt me nearer to him than ever before" (288). Freya decided to confront her grief by climbing there as well. With a guide and a porter she proceeded to Zermatt, spent the night, and then walked up to a hut on the mountain and slept till midnight. With snow lit by an early moon, they began a five-hour climb on hard rock. "The top of the Matterhorn is a long thin ridge, about fifteen minutes, one side rock, one snow, but very narrow . . . on either side you look down, Switzerland right and Italy left." Freya wanted to crawl on all fours, but the guide insisted that she walk and so "I just walked along" (288–89). Courage.

IN 1926, after a miscarriage, Vera became ill with blood poisoning. During this last struggle Vera thanked Freya for the two years of happiness with Mario that had followed Flora's removal to L'Arma. She died on September 23, one of Freya's "two great sorrows," which she described many years later as "still as harsh as ever and will be as long as I can feel" (325). At the same time, Vera's death cast off one of the last mooring lines that held Freya to the West.

Five years before, Freya had begun the study of Arabic in a strenuous twice-weekly regime that involved an hour's walk from L'Arma to Ventimiglia, half an hour by train to San Remo, and then a walk to a monastery where an "old white-bearded Capuchin" who had spent thirty years in Beirut gave her lessons (276). The choice of Arabic was certainly unusual and seems to have been viewed as an

eccentricity by her friends. Years later she said she had been motivated by the looming importance of oil and its presence in the Arab
world, but in her autobiography she says that she cannot remember
what actually started her in that direction. Jane Fletcher Geniesse,
in *Passionate Nomad: The Life of Freya Stark*, points to the 1920s
in San Remo where the victorious Allies divided the spoils of the
fallen Ottoman Empire as an influence. I think at least part of the
reason goes back to *The Arabian Nights* and the little white sail-
boats painted on her bedroom cupboards. Whatever the seeds, the
study of Arabic was part of a plan that would lead to her liberation.
She read everything she could find about travelers, particularly those
who had traveled in the Middle East, including Charles Montagu
Doughty's *Travels in Arabia Deserta*, and works by and about Isabel
and Sir Richard Francis Burton. She must have listened to Verdi's
Jerusalem, Il Corsaro, Othello, and *Aida* with a particular thrill and
longing. She set financial goals in terms of income levels that would
take care of Flora and allow her to begin her adventure. She was
far from an astute investor and had recently lost almost everything
on Mexican Eagle Oil. Still, when a friend told her that Canadian
Grand Trunk Railways would soon go up, she scraped together all
the money she could muster, went to Barclays Bank in Monte Carlo,
and bought shares. A bank manager tried to dissuade her because
the railroad was engaged in a lawsuit and everything depended on
the outcome. She watched the share prices until they began to drop
and then resolved not to look again for a fortnight. When she did
check the prices, they were rising and when they had risen 43 percent
she sold. When she arrived at the bank, two managers came out to
congratulate her. It seems that because of her seemingly unshake-
able confidence, the entire bank staff had invested in the stock as
well. With this gamble, her annual income reached the target level of
£300, and the year after Vera's death, at age thirty-four, she finally
cast off the remaining lines.

21

ASSASSINS AND INCENSE

On November 18, 1927, Freya boarded the SS *Abbazia* in Venice and sailed for Beirut. For Freya, having read and dreamed and prepared for this moment, the small vessel with five other passengers and a cargo of cement, sugar, oil, matches, figs, almonds, and soap was the dirt, steel, and sweat equivalent of a lateen-rigged Arab dhow. An aura of adventure and mystery lay like a fine mist over the ship, with the fresh smell of open sea, the rushing sound of the bow wave, and the pilot's boat disappearing into the black obscurity of night at sea. New land appeared with each new day and even the names were magical: Corfu, Ionian Sea, Ithaca, Corinth, Salamis, Cyclades, Sporades, and finally Rhodes. Almost 116 years after Lady Hester Stanhope was shipwrecked on the coast of Rhodes, Freya explored the island, had tea with the governor's lady, and boarded a new ship, the SS *Diana*, bound for Beirut. The parade of romantic names continued, with the *Diana* calling at Larnaca and Alexandretta. On a side trip to Antioch, she was finally able to use her Arabic, which she found to be "adequate."[1] Then Tripoli, where the men unloading the ship wore baggy trousers and red-tasseled tarbushes, and looked "just like Sinbad the Sailor as I met him in the picture-book on my ninth birthday. Herbert gave him to me, and is probably responsible for my being here" (22).

After three weeks they reached Beirut, and Freya made her way up the winding roads to Brumana, a mountain village thirteen miles northeast of Beirut. She moved in with Mademoiselle Rose Audi, who lived alone with a maid in "a little square stone house with white-washed rooms, very clean and full of plants in pots" (23).

Freya was something of a mystery to the other British in Brumana. They did not understand why she would want to study Arabic, and when she was asked, she told them it was for pleasure. While
this was true, it sounded so implausible to the other expatriates that
they decided she was trying to deceive them. She must be a spy or a
novelist. The Syrians, however, were delighted to find someone who
was simply interested in them with no desire to convert or educate.
Eventually she concluded that she did not like missions and missionaries because they shared so little of the local life—they created and
lived in little Englands outside of England. Because Freya preferred
the Syrians, she was considered eccentric at best.

THERE ARE TWO FORMS OF ARABIC: classical and colloquial.
Classical Arabic is the same across the Arab world and is what is
found in most written forms of the language, in newspapers and the
Quran for example. While virtually all Arabs would understand spoken classical, they would speak the colloquial unique to their area,
and these versions can be significantly different. Someone speaking
Moroccan Arabic would not easily be understood by a person familiar only with Gulf Arabic. Freya had studied classical, and the colloquial language of Syria was a major challenge. In her first month,
she estimated that she understood about one word in a hundred in
a conversation: "I have reached the interesting stage when I can ask
my way and not possibly understand the answer" (31). Nevertheless,
Salehmy, her teacher, was impressed and spread word of her brilliant Arabic and unprecedented intelligence. Freya discounted this as
owing to a low feminine standard.

Her days were filled with Arabic grammar, visits to neighbors
with Mademoiselle Audi, and long walks through the countryside.
Her clothes were apparently a hit with the Syrian community. "I have
never been anywhere where it is more fun to have clothes: everyone is
so interested in them, and if I put on a fresh hat on Sunday mornings,
it is with the agreeable certainty that it is going to give pleasure to
the whole congregation" (53). The long walks alone were a different
story. They were considered peculiar by the British community and

dangerous by the Syrians. Freya, of course, did not see the danger, and her only real problem turned out to be choosing among the fifteen different ways to say good-bye and thank you. She could not help feeling conspicuous when in what she thought to be absolute solitude she suddenly heard the voices of woodcutters calling out the news of a solitary female wanderer. While she carried her lunch, it was unnecessary as everyone that she met would offer food and it would be impolite not to accept it. She described one occasion when a man she encountered pulled dried figs wrapped in bread from "somewhere in the region of his tummy, inside his big red sash— inside everything he had on, I rather suspect" (49). Because it was all wrapped up in a clean white handkerchief, she ate it, found it delicious, and gave him chocolate in return.

Cold was a constant feature of life in Brumana during her stay. She discovered that a high window in Mademoiselle Audi's sitting room had no glass and owing to a shortage of wood they lit a fire only in the evening. Freya wore her fur coat constantly and still said that the only time she was warm was at the end of the night in her bed or when the sun shone for a few hours into her room. On some days she simply surrendered and spent the day in bed.

In spite of the discomfort, the East had already gripped her imagination. She puzzled over its fascination and concluded that it was the "genuine original roughness of life, . . . the feeling that life is not merely primitive but genuinely wild" (30). She recognized that Brumana was not the Orient but only a semi-European fringe, and yet she was still enchanted and felt that she wanted to plunge deeper into this world and spend years coming to understand it.

When planning for the trip to Brumana, Freya had arranged to meet a friend, Venetia Buddicom, and travel together through the Hauran area of Syria. Venetia's family owned a villa and kept a yacht in Bordighera, a town not far from La Mortola where Freya's flower farm L'Arma was located. They had been introduced in 1923 when Freya was thirty by Viva Jeyes, a family friend, and they quickly became good friends. Venetia seems to have introduced Freya to adventure travel when she suggested and they undertook a mule trek into Andorra, followed by a walk into Spain. The trip was a success and the two friends agreed to further trips, particularly to the Middle East. While Freya was spending the winter in Brumana, Venetia was staying with a cousin in India. They planned to meet in Beirut in May.

In the meantime, Freya traveled to Damascus, took a room in the home of a family in the Muslim quarter, and proceeded to come down with dysentery. This illness foreshadowed many of Freya's travels, and while this was a relatively mild case, there were to be many more virulent future cases, as well as other illnesses that were more serious, even life-threatening. Her vulnerability to illness came in part from her fascination with and her sensitivity to the culture, the very reasons for her popularity and success with Arabs. Hospitality and generosity are highly regarded in the Arab culture, and food and drink are important features of both: so important that to refuse either is likely to offend the host, while to accept brings the risk of illness. Freya, by throwing herself wholeheartedly into the society and virtually never refusing hospitality, raised the risk to a near certainty.

She objected to and avoided hotels because their Europeanized atmosphere interfered with her experience of the culture. On the other hand, living with a family as she did resulted in an almost total loss of privacy. Her room had seven windows, which made dressing and undressing tricky. On top of that, because the family rarely undressed, they felt that the bedroom had no particular privacy requirement. In fact, the family thought that Freya's illness was because of her strange habit of undressing at night. Her landlady would bring visitors straight to Freya's room, forcing her to grab whatever was at hand to be presentable.

As she recovered, Freya began walking around Damascus building her strength for the coming adventure and continuing her introduction to Arab culture. She thrilled to the muezzins' calls to prayer as they seemed to echo from minaret to minaret across the city. The *suq*, or bazaar, was straight from the pages of the *Arabian Nights*: a maze of covered alleyways lined with small, open shops and merchants perched among their goods fingering their prayer beads, drinking tea and idly observing the transactions of their neighbors. Buying a dressing gown was "pure Romance": "You sit on the ledge of a little shop and the merchant spreads his wares: an audience gathers, and advises: the money-changer comes along to help. Then you bargain. You are told that the thought of profit does not enter with One whose face is like the Moon: whereupon you offer half. Then the diplomatic merchant says that he knows you are 'a daughter of the Arabs': and who could refuse him anything after that" (107).

Though Damascus is on the edge of the desert, Freya had not seen the desert till one day in April when she persuaded some Muslim friends to visit it with her. As they left Damascus the trees stopped, the land became barren, villages were collections of bare baked-mud walls resting on the slope of small hills, and finally there were no more villages as the road disappeared into hard sand and sparse low brush.

> The country looked white like chalk here, all gentle lines and traveling shadows; and, half lost in the distance, a glimmer of snow from Hermon, and the Damascus hills.
>
> And then the wonder happened! Camels appeared on our left hand: first a few here and there, then more and more, till the whole herd came browsing along, five hundred or more. I got out and went among them to photograph. The two Beduin leaders, dressed gorgeously, perched high up and swinging slowly with the movement of their beasts, shouted out to me, but the Beduin Arabic is beyond me. I can't tell you what a wonderful sight it was: as if one were suddenly in the morning of the world among the people of Abraham or Jacob. The great gentle creatures came browsing and moving and pausing, rolling gently over the landscape like a brown wave just a little browner than the desert that carried it. Their huge legs rose up all around me like columns; the foals were frisking about: the herdsmen rode here and there. I stood in a kind of ecstasy among them. It seemed as if they were not so much moving as flowing along, with something indescribably fresh and peaceful and free about it all, . . . I never imagined that my first sight of the desert would come with such a shock of beauty and enslave me right away. (109)

Venetia arrived in Brumana on May 3rd and on the 5th they took a taxi to Damascus, spending the night in Baalbek on the way. Freya had arranged a Druse guide and muleteer after the first guide recommended, a Christian, had refused, saying that he would be killed. Najm, the guide, and his small nephew had started earlier with three donkeys and the women's luggage, and they arranged to meet beyond Damascus in order to avoid alerting the authorities. Their plan was to head south through an area of the old Roman frontier described by Gertrude Bell in *The Desert and the Sown,* on into Transjordan and then Palestine. The Syrian portion of the trip appears to have been exceptionally risky as the area was closed and under martial law following a series of armed attacks on the French military. Had the French authorities known, they would never have let them go.

Regardless of the risk, the only problems they encountered were of a nonthreatening nature: after six hours on a donkey, Freya found it difficult to sit anywhere, privacy and solitude were out of the question when they were anywhere near a village, avoiding hospitality was simply not possible, and fleas.

In the village of Sawara al Kebir, they had planned to rest through the afternoon and go on, but they were begged to stay. After dinner, guests began to drop in until eventually there was a circle of twenty, all men. The aunt who ruled the family they were staying with came out and sat with them so they would not be uncomfortable. An instrument was brought in and the son of the house played while others sang. Three men got up and danced the *Dabki*—holding hands and twisting from side to side as they progressed in a formal pattern of steps, and later a man came in and played the pipes for them. Finally the men left, and at that point the women came in anxious to talk. The atmosphere was so cordial that the aunt suggested that Freya might want to marry the son of the house though Freya was under the impression that the son had not been consulted.

Things continued in a positive vein for two more days until they reached the village of Shahba, encountered the French military, and were placed under arrest. They were not permitted to return to the house where they were staying and thus were without their luggage.

The French officers installed them in a vacated bedroom and loaned them pajamas and clothes. Freya and Venetia took it all lightheartedly, acting as if they were guests and grateful for the French hospitality. Freya was convinced that they thought she was a spy and Venetia an innocent dupe. It is more likely that the French officers found the two women to be an interesting diversion. They were taken horseback riding in the hills and visited a bedouin camp, enjoyed a sightseeing tour of Shahba, and traveled by car to a remote village where they were guests at a wedding. Two days later, they were on their way again.

By the end of the trip Freya "came back with a feeling, dim but insistent, that the whole of my future must be rearranged."[2] Venetia and Freya traveled as far as Venice and then went to their separate homes. They had planned another trip but Venetia broke her neck in an accident, and though she recovered, the trip was not to be.

Freya journeyed to Canada and spent the winter of 1928–29 in British Columbia with her father. In September 1928, her first article, on the Syrian trip, was accepted by the *Cornhill*. She then wrote an article on Canada that was accepted by the same publication in April 1929. The idea of a new career as a writer must have taken root about this time, for in May 1929 she wrote to her father describing a new project: "I also have a good subject for the winter, if only it hasn't been exhaustively done already, and that is to combine a sort of history with travel notes to the fortresses of the Assassins, who were the followers of the Old Man of the Mountains, and had a series of castles between Aleppo and the Persian Borders."[3]

The word *assassin* is taken from the Arabic term *hashashin*, or hashish-eaters, and the name Assassins refers to an Islamic sect of the eleventh to thirteenth century that considered the murder of its enemies a religious duty. The leader of the sect, Hasan ibn al Sabbah, captured the mountaintop fortress of Alamut near Kazvin, Iran, and according to a legend passed along by Marco Polo, created a beautiful garden accessible only through the fortress that was used to prepare young men to carry out their duties as assassins. While under the influence of hashish, they were tended by beautiful young women and assured that this was a sample of the heavenly life that they were promised should they die in executing their duties. I have often wondered if the young men really bought this idea, or simply went along with what must have seemed to be amazing good fortune. By the end of the eleventh century, Hassan commanded a network of fortresses in Persia and Iraq. By the beginning of the twelfth the Assassins had expanded to Syria, and the grand master there was Rashid al Din al Sinan, known in Arabic as Sheikh al Jebel or the Mountain Chief, but known by the crusaders as the "Old Man of the Mountain." Their power ended as the Persian fortresses were captured one by one by the Mongols, with Alamut falling in 1256. The Syrian castles were taken by the Mameluke sultan Baybars I and placed under Mameluke governors.

Thus in October 1929, Freya proceeded to Baghdad to immerse herself in local culture, polish her Arabic, and prepare for her journey to Persia in search of the Assassins. She found a room with the family of a shoemaker with four big windows and a wide balcony overlooking the Tigris. Her Arabic studies included individual lessons with a tutor and sitting in a classroom with Iraqi schoolgirls. The local British community was suspicious as usual; they simply could not grasp that someone would desire to learn Arabic for pleasure. This disbelief was aggravated when Freya began to study Persian in Arabic. In addition they resented Freya's preference for the company of Iraqis. She was told "that one can't be friends with natives and British both."[4] Another woman asked if she did not think that she was lowering the prestige of British womanhood by sitting in the classroom with Iraqi schoolgirls. Freya exacerbated the situation by accepting an invitation for her and a friend to visit the chief sheikh of the bedouin Shammar tribe in the desert. This was the same tribe that had held Gertrude Bell at Hail fifteen years earlier in February 1914. The British men were unanimously opposed to the idea, and it was with difficulty that she found a woman to go with her. It turned out to be a delightful experience: "We have a big tent to ourselves with white mattresses and purple cushions spread in it, and all the tents of the Sheikh's family and slaves spread around, with horses, donkeys, camels, and small foals and children all out enjoying the short delicious season. I can't tell you what a scene of peace and loveliness it is: the women sit out with their tents open on the sunny or shady side according to the time of day, and show us their old barbaric jewels and magic beads."[5]

In April 1930, Freya left Baghdad on the journey into Persia that would establish her reputation as both an explorer/traveler and a writer. After making her way to Qazvin, northwest of Tehran, by car, she engaged a *charvardar,* or muleteer, named Aziz, who told her that he would "be like my mother."[6] With the two charvardars Ismail and The Refuge of Allah, whom Aziz brought with him, she set out to the Rock of Alamut in the land of the Assassins. This trip lasted only ten days, and during the next year, while in England, she wrote an article for the *Cornhill* describing the trip, did further research on the Assassins, and received instruction on surveying from the Royal Geographic Society. In August 1931, she again set out from Qazvin. Three days later she became ill with malaria and dysentery and was laid up for a week while the malaria subsided. When they went on, Freya spent much of her time identifying and measuring mountains and other geographic features in this previously unsurveyed portion of northwest Persia. When she reached Tehran, she delivered her notes to the military attaché at the British Legation, who passed them on to the War Office, where they were eventually incorporated into a Royal Air Force map in 1932. This data, apparently very thorough, added a scientific dimension to her adventures and subsequent reputation. Leaving Tehran, she headed for Luristan, a dangerous area where stealing was an art form. While she had little difficulty with the Lurs themselves, she was detained by the police and expelled from the country. A year later she again traveled to Luristan. This time she was searching for a treasure said to be hidden in a cave, and while she was able to locate the area of the cave, she never found the cave itself. Her search was cut short by the police, who took her into custody and again escorted her to the Iraqi border. When she reached Baghdad, she found that her friends had been anxious over her safety because of a rumor that six men had been sent after her with orders to see to it that she did not return. According to a later rumor, the men had been intercepted by one of the tribes and tortured into admitting their mission, and had returned to Baghdad.

During the winter of 1931–32 in Baghdad, Freya worked as a freelance journalist. Although it was becoming apparent to her that writing was to be her vocation, it was also a matter of necessity, as her dividends had been more than halved by current economic conditions. In January 1932, she was offered a position with the *Baghdad Times* writing stories based on material from the incoming news wire, and for extra income, she continued to write pieces having to do with the people and places she encountered. As many of these pieces were accompanied by photographs, Freya became skilled at photography, especially at taking surreptitious shots from loose folds of the black *abaya* she wore over her clothes. Her articles were published in the *Illustrated London News*, the Royal Geographic Society's *Journal*, the *Contemporary Review*, and the *Cornhill*, and they were subsequently incorporated into the book *Baghdad Sketches*, which was originally published by Freya at her own expense. Later, after her second book, it was published by John Murray in London.

Freya left Iraq in March 1933. Reaching Asolo, she was told that the Royal Geographic Society was about to award her the Back Memorial Prize for her journeys in Luristan. The award was made in June 1933, and in October 1934 she was awarded The Sir Richard Burton Medal by The Royal Asiatic Society of Great Britain and Ireland. The latter medal is awarded to the person chosen to deliver the Richard Burton Memorial Lecture and is a triennial award. Freya was only the fourth person and the first woman to receive the honor.

For Freya, public speaking was a significant downside of fame; she was sick with fear before each speech, and years later when she was on lecture tours, she bemoaned the fact that she could not get over the feeling of panic before speeches and had spent an entire lecture tour of North America in a state of nausea. Nevertheless she continued to speak and learned that frightened, panicked, or not, she could speak very and sometimes exceptionally well.

Also in 1933, Freya met John Grey Murray, a young man of twenty-two who was working his way up in the publishing firm of John Murray. His timing was excellent, as he arranged to edit and publish what became *The Valleys of the Assassins*, a book that was very successful, becoming a classic and remaining in print for many years thereafter. The two became lifelong friends, and John Murray eventually published more than twenty of Freya's books.

By the time *The Valley of the Assassins* was published, Freya was well into preparing for her next adventure. The world had discovered an explorer, and an explorer she would be. She decided that her next objective would be on the southern end of the great incense road, in reality a cobweb of routes beginning on the south coast of Arabia in Yemen, where frankincense and myrrh were both harvested as well as unloaded from incoming ships and carried north. As they drew away from the Hadhramaut, the routes joined and proceeded north through Mecca, Medina, and Petra and then fanned out again to reach Baghdad, Damascus, and the coast of the Mediterranean.

She did her usual extensive preparatory study, poring through manuscripts in the British Museum, talking with scholars, and reading classical authors and early geographers. She found early Arab maps and painstakingly correlated place names with current maps.

She sailed from Venice on November 24, 1934, and after two weeks in Egypt boarded a ship in Port Tewfik and continued her journey down the Suez Canal to the Red Sea and on to Aden, where she arrived on the 19th of December. Part of her planning had been the accumulation of a substantial folio of letters of introduction: one of these was from Lady Allenby to a Frenchman resident in Aden named Antonin Besse. A self-made man, Besse had built a trading empire based in Aden and serviced by his own ships. Richly successful, he was able before he died to give an anonymous gift of a half-million pounds to finance the founding of St. Anthony's College, Oxford. Besse was staying in his home in Aden with his daughter Meryam and warmly welcomed Freya. He found her a house nearby and insisted that she take her meals with them. When she did not, he had the meal delivered to her house.

Besse was an ideal contact for Freya. He was able to provide additional letters of introduction as well as to arrange travel on his own ships. Beyond that, they found a similarity of natures and interests and became good friends. If their friendship initially lacked romantic overtones, it was not because of a lack of effort on Monsieur Besse's part. On Christmas Day M. Besse spirited Freya away from a dinner party he was hosting for his staff, leaving his daughter to carry on alone. He bundled Freya onto his launch and with his Somali chauffeur as a lookout set out to sea under a rising moon. Lying in great comfort on cushions, M. Besse with one hand on the tiller guided them past the holiday lights of Aden and round the volcano connected to the shore by a narrow isthmus. As luck would have it, M. Besse knew of a cave where they could sleep on the sand, but Freya thought she might aim at keeping some shred of reputation and the journey ended with a breathtaking trip through the waves of the headland and a smooth glide to his front door. In July of the next year (1935), Freya spent six weeks with M. Besse and his wife, Hilda, at their estate in Provence. In fact Besse picked her up in his car at Asolo and, after dropping her mother off to be with her grandchildren, continued on the long journey to the French Riviera that Freya later described as enchantment. In the middle of this visit with the Besses, Freya wrote to her friend Venetia about a "shattering crisis"[7] that she had undergone but could not write about. Certainly the crisis must have involved her relationship with the Besses, but whatever it was it seems to have been quickly resolved as the remaining letters from this period are clearly happy. The relationship became clearer in a letter she wrote to Venetia almost a year later:

> I do seem to have given and must rectify an unjust impression if I suggested he was ever morally fickle to Hilda. He gives little importance to the physical side of love, and I think he is right so long as the spiritual position is very rigidly kept in order: this he has never failed in with her, as far as I know, nor ever swerved in his devotion, and this is why they are bound to be happy and, if he had gone on caring for me, he would have been able to tell her as he had

promised—or I would. I don't think I have ever caused any woman a moment of real unhappiness—at least I would do anything to avoid that—but feeling as we did, I think it was possible to make of our love a beautiful, creative and enduring thing for all three.[8]

By the time this letter was written, the affair and the friendship with Venetia had been irreparably broken. Freya was in London awaiting the arrival of M. Besse and he failed to call on the day that she expected him. The next day, however, he appeared with his daughter Meryam and casually remarked that he had taken Venetia, whom the Besses had met some time before, to dinner and the theater. Freya was crushed—her lover and her best friend—that he would choose not to see her first after so many months. After Anton and Meryam left, she hastily packed and left London. Perhaps Anton misjudged Freya, or more likely, had calculated her precisely, but either way the affair was over, and though they would write occasionally, their love was not to endure. Sadly, Venetia and Freya were unable to repair their friendship, though they tried. All of this was in the future when Freya left Aden on Besse's steamship the *El Amin* on January 12, 1935, bound for Al Mukalla, a city in the Hadhramaut region of Yemen.

"The Land of the Presence of Death." Freya was convinced that it did not deserve the name, but the captain of the *El Amin* looked over the side at Freya sitting in a shallow draft boat, his face an ill-concealed mask of distress and pity; he had previously given her a note that said "God bless you." A delighted Freya reclined under a black umbrella and surrendered to the care of happy and enthusiastic wild men. She estimated that she was the only European within hundreds of miles in any direction but because she was not the first European to travel through the area, she considered herself a mere tourist.

After five days in the palace of the sultan of Mukalla, she met her guides and carriers:

Two wild little men of some earlier world than ours . . . They looked caged, like creatures that might beat themselves against the furniture to get out. They were both completely indigo, and the little wisp around their loins had taken on the same colour, whatever it may once have been: from it, almost at right angles, a curved dagger thrust out its handle, so that no time need be lost in drawing it. . . . They had their silver armlet over the right elbow, and a cornelian set in silver strung by a black cord around their neck by which they stop, they say, the bleeding of a wound; a strand of dark wool was tied under each knee. Their lips, like their faces, were blue with indigo, and they strolled about my room on bare dancing feet, lifting my boxes silently and gently to judge of their weight.[9]

These two, Said and Salim; Salim's ten-year-old brother Mohammed; a soldier assigned by the government of Mukalla as her escort and security; and finally two bedouin, Ahmad Ba Cort and another Said who had simply added themselves to the party became her six traveling companions. The baggage was distributed over six donkeys with one reserved for Freya to ride.

On a typical day they woke around four in the morning, were on their way by six, found a rock overhang by nine, and settled in to pass the hot hours of the day. The soldier made a bed under the overhang for Freya, while the bedouin collected firewood and made coffee. Later Said cooked a lunch of rice and powdered red pepper into which he crumbled rotted shark, added oil from a goatskin, and stirred with a stick he had found on the ground. Freya said the rotted shark made every caravan on the Hadhramaut smell as if something had died in its midst. Said filled up a plate for Freya while the others crouched over the pot and ate with their fingers. They rested till two and set out again. At around five they camped for the night. The soldier set up Freya's bed, and when supper was ready, Freya joined them around the fire. This gesture was apparently a key to Freya's relations with the bedouin. They welcomed her to their fire and told her of their previous resentment of *Nasara* (Christians) who had insisted on a separate fire and had refused to eat with them. Freya noted that she never had difficulties with "her" bedouin and always found them friendly and anxious to be of service.

In Freya's mind, her role as a tourist on this trip would end when she reached the town of Shibam and set off for Shabwa, the site of ancient Sabota on the incense routes. Unfortunately, she never made it. First she came down with measles, which the Arab women were convinced she had contracted by using scented soap. The difficulty caused by this theory was that the women steadfastly refused to let Freya bathe lest she aggravate the problem. This was when Freya discovered that she did not get much dirtier after the first two days. One woman tried incantations that included spitting on the weak and helpless patient and others were keen to try applying a hot iron to the back of the neck—a treatment that she managed to avoid. Her condition became more serious when she began having what seemed to be heart problems. She gave herself injections of Coramine (a stimulant that was once used on Hitler to counter barbiturate overdose), but she became weaker. Later it was determined that the problem was fatigue but, heart or fatigue, all thoughts of finding the lost city were gone and Freya began planning the long trek to evacuate herself to the coast. She was saved by a flight of Royal Air Force bombers bearing a doctor who had apparently been alerted by solitary messengers across the desert. She was strapped onto a stretcher, loaded into the cockpit of a Vickers Vincent, and flown to a hospital in Aden. Later she was transferred, again by stretcher, onto the SS *Orontes* to the accompaniment of the applause of the other passengers. Successful or not, her life tended toward the dramatic and she was now a famous explorer. The next year, 1936, H. St. John Philby, the famous Arabian explorer, reached Shabwa from the north with two cars and an escort of twenty armed camel men.

In the latter part of 1935 and early 1936 she wrote *The Southern Gates of Arabia* about her experiences in the Hadhramaut. It was published in May 1936 and quickly became a great success, with excellent reviews and recommendations by the Book Guild and Book Society. This success stimulated John Murray to republish *Baghdad Sketches* under their imprint in 1937. Freya basked in the attention, fretted her way through the necessary public speaking, and then departed in February 1937 to visit friends in Lebanon, Syria, Iraq, and Kuwait, where she spent much of her time with Colonel H. R. P. Dickson, the British agent, and his wife, Violet. It was Violet who as a young bride was introduced to Gertrude Bell and insulted when Gertrude refused to shake hands, saying that it was a pity that young men married and brought out such incapable young wives. In addition to being rude, it was inaccurate, as the Dicksons (both of them) were now experts on the desert with an extensive collection of diaries, reports, correspondence, books, and articles to their credit.

In June 1937, Freya returned from the Middle East and began arrangements for a more scientific expedition. Freya had met Gertrude Caton Thompson, an archaeologist and prehistorian, in November 1934. Caton Thompson was five years older than Freya, and the acquaintance remained that until Freya enhanced her credentials with the expedition to the Hadhramaut. It began to seem obvious to each of them that there was something to be gained in collaboration: Freya sought the cachet of scientific legitimacy that would accompany such an expedition with Gertrude, and Gertrude, in turn, sought the experience and contacts that Freya had built. Freya's first contribution came almost immediately when she was able, through the brother of W. P. Ker (Charles), to meet with Lord Wakefield and raise from him the entire cost of the expedition. With that they added Elinor Gordon, a geologist who had worked with Caton Thompson on previous digs in Egypt. The objective of the expedition was to look for possible links between the Sabaean culture of southern Arabia and the Zimbabwean ruins of what was then Rhodesia. In the racial climate of the times, a serious disagreement concerned the ability of Africans to have developed the Zimbabwean culture unassisted.

With the advantage of hindsight and distance, it seems apparent that while the expedition was setting out prepared to face the difficulties encountered when East meets West, it was not as well prepared to deal with the East-West conflict that existed within the team. Freya liked Arabs, admired much about their culture, and after what was by now a substantial exposure, had both adapted to it and incorporated some of it in her own behavior. Caton Thompson, with her scientific background, was rigorous and careful, and had little patience with the mores of the locals or the process of building a relationship with them. From her point of view the expedition was just short of a disaster from the beginning.

After flying into Cairo and spending time with friends in Alexandria, Freya proceeded to Suez instead of to Port Said where she was to join the ship carrying her colleagues, and only managed to make the connection by a frantic overnight journey in a taxi. For hotel reservations in Aden she had relied on Anton Besse only to find that Besse was away for two weeks. On top of this, part of the baggage, including all of the instruments, was not unloaded and went on with the ship headed for Singapore. Then, to put a fine polish on the problem, they learned that they had arrived during the Islamic holy month of Ramadan when believers fasted during the day and feasted and celebrated with their friends throughout the night; the resultant lethargy during working hours made real accomplishment negligible and launching an expedition on a predetermined schedule next to impossible.

Eventually they were on their way but feelings were bruised, confidence was lost, and there was little reserve for dealing with the problems ahead. Freya saw it as her responsibility to build a positive relationship with the local population, while Gertrude could not understand why they must be subjected to a constant stream of curious visitors. She thought it was Freya's responsibility to get rid of them.

> I find I get through much more with far less exertion than my party. It is far more useful in this climate to sit quiet and make other people do things. A little chat about their own family affairs does more to get willing and efficient helpers than all the ordering about in the world: I think Elinor Gardner still considers it a waste of time, being used only to Egyptians who can be browbeaten. The Arab has the charming attitude that anything he does is done as a kindness, so it is no good chivvying him about for it. It is a great mistake to look as if you can do everything yourself if you want people to put themselves out for you.[10]

As usual, all three women became sick at one point or another. In spite of all of this, the expedition did produce results including, incidentally, no evidence of a link between south Arabia and the Zimbabwean ruins. The women never made up their differences, and both Freya and Gertrude tried to exact some measure of revenge in their later writings.

Freya managed to salvage two major pluses from the affair. First, when they arrived in Aden the ship was met by a young British official who was assigned to assist a party of oilmen who were to look for oil in the Hadhramaut. In another example of Freya's luck, he had been reading *Baghdad Sketches* and was already primed for Freya's charm. The oilmen were firmly moved into second place as Freya accepted his help. The young man's name was Stewart Perowne and they would meet again. The second plus came at the end of the expedition when Freya decided to return to the coast by a route other than the one they had planned. She wanted to follow an ancient camel track to a point that she was convinced had been a central port for the ancient incense traffic. The 120-mile journey should take about three weeks by camel, three of which had been ordered for the next day's departure when Freya decided to inform her companions. The scientists elected to stick with the original plan, and the next day there was a less than amicable parting of the ways. Two weeks later she reached Azzan, where the local sultans, concerned that something might go wrong in these unpacified areas that would leave them with the blame, insisted that she wait until a caravan could be formed that would be accompanied by members of the sultans' families and armed guards. A caravan of twenty-seven camels with a cargo of tobacco was made up and traveled by night to the coast, where Freya secured passage on a dhow to Aden. She arrived in an elapsed time of a little over three weeks and was admitted to a hospital suffering from dengue fever. A little more than a week later she embarked on the SS *Orontes* for home and a world preparing for war.

22

WAR FROM CAIRO TO BAGHDAD

While with the caravan from Azzan to the coast, "My Old Uncle," a bedouin, pulled an eighteen-inch lizard from his loincloth and presented it to Freya as a gift, "[a] scaly-tailed creature with blue gills and a crest, like a small dragon."[1] This vulnerable creature, whose only defense was to wrap himself in his tail and pretend to be a small thorn bush, found a gap in Freya's defenses. She named him Himyar and devoted herself to his care. Because Himyar was not fond of civilization and as they sailed north was even less fond of the climate, much of Freya's care consisted of efforts to keep him warm and relaxed. Boxes, a hot-water bottle, and eventually an electric light inside a suitcase were deployed for warmth, but the only thing she found that would relax him was to stroke him under his chin. It was a doomed relationship. She was advised to leave Italy as soon as possible and did on the 27th of September 1938 through Switzerland to Paris and on to London. There are, of course, less lizard-friendly environments, but this was sufficient, and Himyar died in early January 1939. "My poor little Himyar is dead . . . I can't think or speak of him without crying . . . he and I were alike in lots of ways."[2]

Himyar's brief lifespan coincided with a rather successful year in the life of Adolf Hitler. In February 1938 he assumed personal control of Germany's armed forces and essentially completed the Nazi revolution. In March he ordered the invasion of Austria, and Austria became a province of the German Reich. In September he signed an agreement with the leaders of England, Italy, and France, allowing the German army to enter Czechoslovakia on October 1 and occupy the Sudetenland by October 10. It was on the return from this occasion that British Prime Minister Neville Chamberlain announced that he believed it was peace in our time.

Mussolini, in spite of the strange affinity between himself and Adolf Hitler, had yet to join in the Pact of Steel, but the pact was close. The war scare that had driven Freya out of Italy was just a scare, but tensions were high. Freya returned to Asolo to pack their most valuable possessions and give them to friends to be hidden. Then as Europe lurched from problem to crisis, Freya left to wander the hills and fields of Syria, examining ruins left by the Templars and the Assassins.

By September she was back in London in the Middle East Propaganda Section of the Ministry of Information. Within two weeks she was transferred to Aden at the request of Stewart Perowne to be assistant information officer.

Freya took advantage of the long trip to Aden to visit and renew contacts in the various British missions en route. In Ankara she met Sir Archibald Wavell, newly appointed as commander in chief, Middle East, a man who would become a lifelong friend and a significant influence on her life. In Cairo, where she had to wait several days for a coastal steamer to Aden, she renewed a stream of acquaintances and through one of them met Colonel Walter Cawthorn, an Australian in charge of the Middle East Intelligence Centre. The MEIC was chartered by the Committee of Imperial Defense and charged with gathering and organizing intelligence for the three service commanders in the region. By the time she left Cairo, she had been recruited to undertake an assignment in Yemen: an assignment unconnected with her duties in Aden, unapproved by her superiors in Aden, but potentially useful to General Wavell.

On June 10, 1940, Adolf Hitler's defeat of France was all but certain and this proved sufficient to lure Mussolini into the conflict. While the decision appeared to be a safe one for Italy, it posed a major threat to British forces in Egypt and the Sudan, where 9,000 British and Sudanese troops faced an Italian army of more than 200,000 men in Eritrea and Abyssinia. In the north, an even larger Italian force in Libya threatened the 36,000 British, New Zealand, and

Indian troops defending Egypt. Thus Wavell was confronting more than 500,000 enemy troops with a force of little more than 50,000. He chose to attack, conducting a series of raids and surprise attacks to harass the enemy. The Italians seemed reluctant to move, and when they did they moved slowly—six divisions moved cautiously into the western desert and after only fifty miles, less than halfway to the British positions, they stopped and built a chain of fortified camps that were too far apart to support one another. Wavell's response was to launch what was, in effect, a large-scale raid in which the British forces eased through a gap in the chain of camps and attacked the camps one by one from the rear. The tactic was stunningly successful, and by the end of the campaign the Italian army in North Africa was destroyed. Wavell, however, did not have the forces necessary to occupy the territory taken, and so Libya and the western desert were left for the German General Erwin Rommel to recontest. In Italian East Africa the result was similar, with an Italian surrender by May 19, 1941, and a total of 230,000 Italian prisoners.

When Freya arrived in Aden in November 1939, all this still lay ahead—Italy was not yet an enemy though she was not a friend. In addition to her colonization in North and East Africa, she was the dominant foreign presence, though small numerically, in the isolated kingdom of Yemen just north of Aden.

The office in Aden overlooked the harbor, and Freya lived in two small rooms over the office. Her duties involved converting the Reuter news agency releases into Standard English for subsequent translation into Arabic radio news bulletins, which were broadcast in the evenings over loudspeakers in the main square. In the swirl of prewar tension, Aden must have seemed the calm before the storm. She writes of persuading the regimental band of the 15th Punjabis to learn *The Blue Danube* waltz for the Governor's Ball. There were rides in the starlight before sunrise and lunch with the "Navy" every day at the Marina Hotel, and in the evening on the office balcony, she and Stewart enjoyed vermouth and sherry while watching ships in the harbor. The split with Anton Besse was healed to the point that Freya visited with Hilda and Anton "twice a week or so," and

Anton would take her climbing on the peaks around Aden. "Surrounding it all . . . the charm and forthrightness of the South Arabian Arabs was perhaps the chief pleasantness of our days."[3]

By February 1940, arrangements had been made for the secret portion of Freya's assignment, and she set off in a lorry with a driver, a cook, a servant, two mechanics, and a film projector hidden among her luggage. Representations of human beings are forbidden in Islam and thus the projector was a prohibited object, not to mention the canisters of films that she had brought with her from London. Also, the films were certain to be found politically offensive by the Italians and other German sympathizers. The trip took six days, often following dry riverbeds as the only roads, until they reached Sana'a, the capital of Yemen.

With the Italian presence, the news received in Yemen carried a distinct political slant. One of Freya's tasks was to counter that bias, and she did that on what she claimed was the advice of her cook. "All things in Arabia," he said, "are done by the harem; get them to wish what you wish, and you will get it."[4] Life in the harem was such that the distractions provided by the films and by Freya herself were irresistible. Of course her mechanics were not allowed into the harem itself, so Freya would set up the projector, start it, and then explain the film in Arabic while making sure that the film's volume was loud enough for the audience to enjoy the sounds of guns and bombs. After she was able to arrange the first showing, word-of-mouth advertising carried from one harem to the next in a highly successful run through the leading families of Sana'a. In all cases, she would show her films only if the imam approved, and when she showed the films in the imam's own harem she was not aware that he attended, though he could have slipped in unobserved. Nonetheless Freya's efforts were sufficiently effective to upset the Fascist community. Here in the middle of their own preserve, a middle-aged Englishwoman speaking fluent Italian and Arabic was muddying the water they had so carefully treated. Their aggravation led to a public confrontation between the head of the Italian Mission and Freya over a minor question concerning where Freya would show her films to the Italian community. Freya remained formally polite, while the little man blustered and thoughtlessly blurted the damaging quote: "We are the chief people here."[5] The result of the confrontation was that the Italians did not get to see the films and Freya had a great quote to use with all the known gossips. Also, she noticed that even strangers were beaming at her in the street.

The other dimension of Freya's assignment in Yemen is not clear. It may have been as simple as identifying the key players in the Italian community, or it may have involved the gathering and sifting of rumors and attitudes. Whatever the purpose, after two months Freya returned to Aden with a newly polished reputation as a political warrior.

Waiting for her in Aden was an invitation to become a godmother to Alan Lennox-Boyd, who would later be colonial secretary under Winston Churchill in the 1950s. The godfather was Winston Spencer Churchill. Also waiting for her, though she would not learn of it till she reached Cairo later in the summer, was the news that her mother and their close family friend Herbert Young had been arrested by the Italian authorities. Freya had fretted over the possibility that antagonizing the Italian hierarchy in Yemen might lead to retaliation against her mother and their friend, but had felt that their ages of seventy-nine and eighty-six respectively would be likely to protect them. Later she learned that the arrest had been instigated by the Italian chief of mission in Sana'a, perhaps as a warning to Freya. They spent a month in a local jail followed by a second month exiled to another village, and then through the intervention of influential Italian friends were allowed to return to Herbert Young's house in Asolo. They were restricted to three rooms on the second floor because the house had been requisitioned to house evacuees. Herbert Young died a few months after his release and Flora was allowed to leave for America, where she lived with friends until her death a year later.

In Aden, Stewart Perowne bought a sailboat, and idyllic afternoons were spent sailing around the harbor and watching fish dart through the coral. On the 10th of June 1940, England and Italy were at war, and on the 17th they learned that France had surrendered. Night air raids began, and Freya would lie on her balcony watching the explosions and return fire from a cruiser and destroyers in the harbor. On one day there were three raids of which she noted, "I am ashamed to say that it is the only thing lately that I have really enjoyed."[6] In the same letter, which was to John Grey Murray, her publisher, she assures him, "You will be glad to fight. There is a strange liberation when once you have looked into the eyes of Death and know that, beyond the natural human panic and recoil, there is nothing to fear. The earth becomes your garden and pleasure ground for ever when once you know that it is easy to leave. There are two families of mankind, those who know this and those who don't, and I am glad to think that you are among the freemen."[7]

In June a submarine was captured, and Freya's fluent Italian was employed in interrogating the prisoners. She found that among the enlisted men (all but one officer had been killed) there was little enthusiasm for the war. The experience led her to believe that careful handling of the prisoners might convert many who were opposed to the Fascists to support of the Allies. These could be formed into what was later called a Garibaldi Brigade to fight with the Allies in an invasion of the Italian mainland. She and the colonel in charge of anti-Fascist activities in Cairo wrote a pamphlet of anti-Italian propaganda that included the idea of such a force, and later she presented specific ideas on a raid on Genoa to General Wavell. His response at the time was that he did not have enough troops, but he kept the idea and later had a subordinate look into it although it was again rejected.

In July Rushbrook Williams, director of the Middle East Propaganda Section in London, suggested that Freya attend a Ministry of Information conference in Cairo in order to discuss ideas on anti-Fascist propaganda. She left aboard an ammunition ship on the first Red Sea convoy after Italy's declaration of war. In the steamy heat of July the crew was almost naked, and Freya as the only female aboard felt compelled to remain in her stifling cabin to preserve her modesty given that they were not particularly concerned about theirs.

Freya felt that the most effective propaganda was that which asked the recipients to give rather than receive. She thought that there was a natural generosity in people that made them glad to serve and sacrifice, and this in turn generated a natural affection for the people and cause being served. It was important, she argued, that those asked to serve be allowed to do so in their own way. The end result would be a people who were loyal as well as helpful. This was the foundation for Freya's idea of a pro-British network in the Middle East. The secret aspect of the network was said to have originated in Freya's study and travel in pursuit of the Assassins ten years previously.

Fluency in Arabic joined with extensive knowledge of the Arab countries was not a common qualification in Cairo, particularly among the Allied forces. Freya not only possessed these qualifications, but her prewar fame made it certain that she and her qualifications were known to the key players in Cairo and London. At the Ministry of Information conference, Freya was approached by a colonel in the British Middle East Office with the idea of a whispering campaign aimed at countering Axis propaganda. The result was the Ikhwan al Hurriyah or Brotherhood of Freedom.

The idea met with general approval, and Freya accepted with the proviso that she be allowed to return to Aden to pack and clear her affairs. The military's interest in her project is indicated by the fact that her return journey was in the nose of a Blenheim bomber.

In Aden she was met by a chill as Stewart Perowne and Harold Ingrams, the acting governor, felt betrayed by her departure. The rift was temporary, though, and was mostly healed as they put her aboard a small steamer to join a convoy up the Red Sea. This time they were attacked by air, leaving Freya impressed by the plumes of water and the beauty of the ship's guns firing at night. They made it safely to Port Sudan, and Freya left the ship to travel overland to Cairo, never to revisit the Red Sea.

The Brotherhood, born in the summer of 1940, had the full support of Sir Miles Lampson, the ambassador, and through Freya the goodwill of General Wavell and the military. It began with two students from Cairo University sitting on Freya's terrace drinking tiny cups of coffee and laying out the structure of their new society until the sun slipped behind the pyramids and the dim streetlights took charge. Each week Kemal and Muhammad came, brought friends who became new members, and quickly outgrew Freya's terrace. Soon they were meeting in separate groups across Cairo and publishing a small bulletin to coordinate the attention and discussion across the membership. By the end of 1940 there were more than 400 members and 3,000–3,500 by the end of 1941.

Freya bought "a Baby Austin with a hood like a Salvation Army bonnet, an ugly little thing,"[8] and after a few driving lessons took her place in Cairo's traffic, a feat that many would rank as one of the more impressive of her career. On an occasion at the Mena House Hotel when Freya managed to back into the hotel while trying to go forward, Sir Arthur Longmore, a friend, inquired as to why she was savaging "that innocent hotel"[9] and then sent his driver, who helped her upgrade to a larger vehicle. Apparently Freya never really mastered any automobile, for her driving seemed always to be a source of amusement. This, however, did not stop her from launching expeditions using automobiles that others would consider major adventures—her departure from Cairo would be one of those.

Wartime Cairo inspired a bright and busy social scene. Freya's nights, indeed any free time, were absorbed in a whirl of events. Women were being evacuated from Cairo and a place among the few Western women remaining created a certain responsibility. Freya told Sir Sydney Cockerell of an incident that had occurred in Aden: "P.S. A touching little episode happened at my Aden pub the other night as I sat at dinner. A rather cheerful sailor came up with outstretched hand: 'I wants to thank you, Miss, for looking like what you do. You reminds me of someone in England.' And then as I shook hands in some surprise: 'Its green fields and faces like yours we likes to think of.' I suppose I was the only woman he'd seen for quite a time."[10]

In Cairo there were evenings spent in the embassy gardens alongside the Nile with the Lampsons, an occasional overnight with them in a cottage they maintained in the desert at Fayyum, and a week at Christmas staying at the Winter Palace in Luxor. General and

Mrs. Wavell came to Freya's flat for dinner and an evening of talk that had nothing to do with the war. Freya considered her friendship with the Wavells "among the greatest fortunes of that year, or of many years."[11] Having a job at full pay left Freya more comfortable financially than she had been for some time. She was able to indulge her taste for new hats and clothes. Her hats, in particular, became a popular source of amusement and conversation, and Freya, delighted with the attention, played along. One of her hats was a blue cart-wheel decorated with a clock face on which the hands were pointing at five and seven, *cinq à sept*: a reference to the early evening hours during which a man could safely visit his mistress because her husband was using those hours to visit his. It was supposed that Freya, in her innocence, was ignorant of the significance of the design and this only added to her legend. Wearing the hat, Freya went to the zoo for a walk with a friend. At the gate she asked if an Englishman had just gone through; the guard said yes there were plenty of Englishmen in the garden, but would not an Arab do as well? Freya said that she had doubts about her hat ever since. Later, General Wavell made it a point to see Freya when passing through Baghdad, giving as his reason the need to see her new hats.

FREYA WAS SENT TO BAGHDAD for six weeks in March 1941. In April, though the situation was critically unstable, she took a chance on a quick trip to Tehran. Acting on a premonition, she left Tehran early and started back to Baghdad. With a little effort, she was able to just miss a telegram from Sir Kinnahan Cornwallis, the ambassador, telling her to stay where she was, and instead she tried to make her way back to Baghdad. She had been careful not to get a return visa to Persia so that if she managed to get back into Iraq, it would be more difficult for the Iraqis to expel her. She was able to cross the border without difficulty, but when she reached the town of Khanikin where she would catch the train, a policeman jumped onto the running board of her taxi and escorted her to the police station. A young lieutenant told her that she would be unable to travel to Baghdad because he had received a telegram telling him to stop all travelers. Did the telegram say women as well as men? Freya asked. No, it just said travelers, he replied with slightly less confidence. Well then, Freya explained, think how much difficulty detaining a woman would involve: a separate house, the necessity of employing a maid because she never stayed anywhere without a maid. The lieutenant asked her if she would rather return to Baghdad by car or train and she chose that night's train. Still under guard, she was sent to wait in the station and spent the time there shifting the guard's attitude from neutral to pro-British. By the time she boarded the train, the guard was convinced that he was protecting her rather than guarding a prisoner and they had become friends.

In Baghdad, in spite of being warned to stay away from the embassy, she insisted on being taken there and found it in a state of siege. The grounds were guarded by sandbags and barbed wire, a six-foot pile of documents was being burned in the courtyard, and the women had been evacuated two days before. Still another twenty women had been collected after the evacuation, and the total number inside the embassy grounds was 360. The women divided up a large bedroom into a dormitory with some sleeping on mattresses with no beds and others on beds with no mattresses. Freya took her mattress onto the balcony where she arranged it behind a pillar that would provide some protection from stray shots. For the most part, fire was directed against British aircraft trying to drop messages and items to the beleaguered embassy, but stray shots and the odd sniper were still a risk.

Captive life inside the compound seemed patterned after a typical film dealing with British expatriates in crisis. At 6 p.m. a bar was set up under the palm trees, although they were rationed to one drink per person. An entertainments committee was established and games were organized. The ambassador dined on blue and gold china and rotated invitations so that the whole garrison dined with him in turns. Food was purchased through the Iraqi Foreign Ministry, with whom diplomatic relations were maintained.

Freya went to work on the only locals available to her: the police and soldiers stationed on the river outside the compound. After dark one night a soldier noted that the Germans are the family of Satan and said thank God when she told them that six German planes had been shot down. "But we have burnt forty of yours," someone added as an afterthought. Freya replied that "I take refuge with God from your untruthfulness,"[12] and a general burst of laughter indicated agreement.

On another occasion, Freya was chatting with police on the river patrol when British bombers flew overhead. The men raised their guns to fire at the planes when Freya told them it was ridiculous to think they could hit anything that far away. So they laid down their guns.

The siege went on for over thirty days until June 3rd, when it was resolved by units of the Iraqi army turning against the rebels and pressure from two British battalions sent from Palestine by General Wavell.

Freya returned to Cairo but was requested by Ambassador Cornwallis to take a more permanent position in Baghdad. She would be attached to the embassy, initially as a temporary attaché, and would eventually become Second Secretary. Her assignment was to extend the Brotherhood to Iraq.

On July 18, 1941, Freya left Cairo, driving her "Standard Eight" against the urgent advice of friends who were familiar with her driving. They must have had a point, for she admitted to anxiety at the thought of hills. Having learned to drive in Cairo, she was familiar with straight and level conditions but not with hills. She did have a friend with her as far as Jerusalem, but from there she traveled alone. Before she was well out of Jerusalem the self-starter came out in her hand. A red-bearded man stopped his truck and showed her how one manages without a self-starter. Later she stalled but got a push from a group of men heading home to their village. She spent the night at stations along the pipeline that leads back across the desert into Iraq. Once she reached the edge of the desert, there were no more roads, so she followed a winding track into the low ridges and wadis. She made it into Ruba Wells, a small village with a colonel and a unit of Sikhs in residence. They wanted to provide her with a military escort, but instead she offered a lift to a Shammari tribesman who knew the way. As they arrived at one camp, the captain in charge was said to have exclaimed, "My God, it's a woman!" and later, after the tribesman had been left with relatives and she pulled in alone into an RAF base not far from Baghdad, the airmen were greatly amused because a colonel had just telegraphed asking for an armored car escort in order to cross that same desert. Freya made the trip several more times.

She now set out on the task of building the Brotherhood in Iraq, a task made more difficult by Nazi propaganda efforts. Contrary to the policy in Egypt, she received permission to set up cells in the army, and the army itself housed a strong pro-Nazi core. Nevertheless she made progress, and the Brotherhood began to grow, although it would never reach 60,000 members and endure into the 1950s as it did in Egypt. Her efforts took her to all corners of Iraq including Kurdistan, where in Kirkuk in 1943 she learned that she had been awarded the Founder's Medal of the Royal Geographic Society for her travels in Persia and southern Arabia, and for her books. Before leaving the Middle East in the spring of 1943, Freya managed to squeeze in one more adventure. Field Marshal Lord Wavell, now viceroy of India, and his wife invited Freya to visit them in New Delhi. She spent three weeks with them and then decided to drive back overland because that would be both economical and an interesting way of gathering information for a report on Persia. She bought a car, and because the field marshal insisted, she accepted a driver. The two proceeded on a three-day journey to reach the Indus, where they waited forty-eight hours while guards were posted through Baluchistan. With guards a few hundred yards from one another to protect their single car, they drove on. Freya described it as "a memory of empire in its greatness."[13] When they reached Quetta in what is now Pakistan, the driver was replaced by Johnnie Hawtrey, a friend, who thought he was taking a leave to rest. They skirted Afghanistan and after three days reached Meshed to find that the roads on to Tehran were flooded. Rather than wait weeks for the floods to subside, they backtracked six hundred miles to the frontier of Baluchistan and then turned and proceeded across two deserts to Isfahan. When they reached Tehran, Freya sold the car at a handsome profit (which became a matter of some scandal), and they arranged for a flight to Baghdad only to watch aghast as a damaged aircraft was drawn to the flight line. With three army officers they drove instead, making it to Baghdad in time for Johnnie to catch a flight to Delhi and make it back before his leave expired.

In July 1943, it was time for Freya to leave.

When the day for departure came I was sad to leave. In spite of grief, and illness growing upon me, these years had been happy in their private brightness against the stormy background. Friendships had come in overflowing measure, and some, now dead, went very deep—Cornwallis and Bishop, Wavell and Clayton. The world is not so good without them. Love, too, had come easy, but perhaps happy for that reason. It is, I think, an ungenerous heart that does not give itself in wartime, where man's mere physical hunger for women is so great.[14]

23

TO THE END OF THE ROAD

Flora Stark died in California in November 1942 while Freya was still in Baghdad. The Ministry of Information had asked her to travel to the United States on a lecture tour, but she felt that it would end the nascent Brotherhood in Iraq and she put them off for a year. Had she gone at the first request, she would not have been there in time, and this was the last of her immediate family: her sister, father, and mother were gone.

When she did leave Baghdad, it was with Stewart Perowne, driving on a somewhat roundabout trip through Syria, Lebanon, Palestine, and Transjordan to Cairo, where she then flew along the north coast of Africa to Algiers and spent ten days, during which she managed to meet and be very impressed with General Dwight Eisenhower.

In October she and five thousand troops with a few other women and children embarked on the converted liner *Aquitania* bound for Halifax, Nova Scotia. On the third or fourth day Freya had an attack of acute appendicitis and was carried off the ship on a stretcher in Halifax. Describing the event in *Dust in the Lion's Paw*, her autobiography from 1939 to 1946, she says that "my cortege appeared like the funeral of Sir John Moore at Corunna, surrounded by shadows and rain. The five thousand looked down in silence, the stretcher bearers stumbled on."[1] General Sir John Moore was, of course, Hester Stanhope's love, the loss of whom launched her on her epic journey. After a fortnight Freya was walking, and by the middle of November she was beginning her assignment.

Her task was to step into the controversy over the future of Palestine and to defend the stew of British policy that was generally unsatisfactory to the Jews or the Arabs. To the history of the McMahon-Hussain Letters, the Sykes-Picot agreement, and the Balfour Declaration, the British had added The White Paper of 1939. The latter promised a Palestinian state in ten years with governance to be shared by Jews and Arabs. In the interim, Jewish immigration was to be limited and would last only five years during which the Jewish population would have reached approximately one-third of the total population of Palestine. No further immigration would be allowed without the approval of the Arabs. This of course countered the implications of the Balfour Declaration, depending upon one's definition of "homeland" for the Jewish people. The pro-Zionists were perturbed, but the Arabs were not thrilled by the paper either. So Freya's job was to try to win the hearts and minds of influential Americans in support of Britain's management of the Mandate.

Given her intense fear of public speaking, this lecture tour drew heavily on her reserves of courage. On at least two occasions she remarked that she would much rather be doing something she really enjoyed such as fighting alongside the Italian guerillas. She lectured to students, military personnel, businessmen, and groups of influential people. She gave lectures at the War Department and to the OSS (the predecessor of the CIA). In the course of the tour she was introduced to a large sample of the day's Who's Who in America, which included such people as Elsa Maxwell, Henry Luce, Clare Booth Luce, John Gunther, and Dorothy Thompson. Her activities caught the attention of the Zionists, and questions were raised about her in both the U.S. Congress and the House of Commons. Pro-Zionists were assigned to follow her across the country and raise questions. This does not seem to have posed too big a problem for Freya, whose low tolerance for sentimental inaccuracies and whose combative nature were a potent combination. The white paper position on limiting immigration was a major target as was the idea that immigration should not take place over the objections of the inhabitants. When asked where the Jews were to go, Freya observed that there was more than enough room in the United States. By the end of June the ordeal was over and Freya returned to England, sharing the honeymoon suite in a flying-boat with the only other woman aboard.

FREYA'S FIRST AND ONLY ATTEMPT at marriage seems to have been a problem from the beginning. She and Stewart Perowne had maintained contact after she left Baghdad, and he spent three weeks in Asolo in June 1946 while on leave and again in May 1947 at the end of his assignment in Baghdad. Not the least of the problems was that Stewart was homosexual. Her friends tried to warn her, but Freya was strangely naïve, even obtuse on the subject. It was not the first time that Freya was attracted to a homosexual man, and it is difficult to accept the naiveté as real. Her upbringing with Flora was more than a little bohemian and Freya was far from an unperceptive woman. It is possible that at age fifty-four, the feeling that this might be her last opportunity overwhelmed sexual considerations. Perhaps love was still possible, certainly companionship, and there were other forms of intimacy besides intercourse. Stewart's motivation is less of a problem. His appointment in Baghdad was not renewed and his career with the Colonial Office appeared to be at an end until he received an appointment as colonial secretary in Barbados, a position second only to the ambassador. A wife was almost a necessary accoutrement of such a position and Freya, a famous woman, was something of a trophy. This may be unfair; perhaps Stewart at forty-six also felt the drumbeats of time. In either event, they were married on the 7th of October 1947 at Saint Margaret's, Westminster.

By February 1948 Stewart was in Bridgetown, Barbados, in the position of vice-governor. Freya followed and within months cracks began to appear in the marriage. At first Freya blamed Barbados and attacked the problem by lobbying for a new posting for Stewart. She was successful and Stewart was posted to Cyrenaica in what is now Libya, a far more satisfying location for both of them. Her influence in the matter is indicated by the fact that she was unofficially informed of Stewart's appointment before he was.

Still the marriage was not well. Even in Benghazi in the culture she knew and loved, she wrote John Murray her publisher, "I had an idea that my proper work was to love and be loved, but it isn't: it is just to write books, so what is the good of not doing so."[2] This idea, in turn, foreshadows the remaining forty-eight years of her life. In a March 1951 letter to Stewart: "Things are so sad and superficial between us that I have long been feeling that they cannot go on as they were and have only waited to write or speak because I could not bear you to think that any trivial cause, or want of affection, made me do it."[3] By April 1952 they were separated—more formally than usual—and by May 1952 it was over and she had taken her maiden name again.

True to her word she turned again to writing and, of course, travels. After age fifty-eight she wrote eleven more books. Some of these books were essay collections and others autobiographical, but at least five were travel books preceded by her meticulous study and planning, typically consuming two years or more, then strenuous execution including walking, riding, hiking, and sometimes travel by Jeep, which she found the most strenuous of all.

Three of her journeys and the subsequent books explored the western and southern coasts of Turkey. *Ionia: A Quest* dealt with the relatively tame northern part of these coasts; *The Lycian Shore* described a sea voyage along the coast, and *Alexander's Path* traced Alexander the Great's route through Turkey and into Syria. Freya was able to turn any trip into a strenuous adventure, but with *Alexander's Path* she outdid herself. She spent two months in Antalya, making it her base for extended sorties on Alexander's route and in one letter describes two of the days as twelve-hour days in the hills: one and a half hours by car, three and a half by Jeep, three by mule, "the rest sitting on a quilt and talking,"[4] and then up at five the next morning. Not surprisingly, at age sixty-three she begins to despond over her ability to continue strenuous travel: "I don't believe I can go on doing these escapades for very many more years. There is a very wearing span between the day's delight and the awful depression of the night when all the troubles of the flesh come upon one, food, insects, washing so difficult, and amiability to too many strangers at once in a foreign tongue. One wonders why one does it, till that glorious moment in the saddle makes it right for another day."[5]

The thought recurs in her letters, but the complaints are more about the aggravations of primitive travel and nighttime depression than the arduous physical demands. In the quote above she ties the depression to the aggravations but in other letters it is simply "awful depression,"[6] and there seems to be little question that she fought the human condition that we now call clinical depression. At least in her letters, the depression does not dominate and is quickly replaced by some aspect of the joy she finds in travel. In a letter to John Murray, her publisher, she writes,

> Don't you sometimes find that everything you see has suddenly taken on a heightened meaning as if you were looking through and into and not at things? I felt like that this evening, walking back through the last sunlight, with the hills swelling around white and dry under the thin olive trees, nearly all the flourishing houses roofless in the brightness, and the rows of dead vineyards faint like ribs in the hillsides.
>
> At six o'clock the sun went down. I rowed out and sat under the *Elfin* awning, watching a caique with its hanging lantern lit and a star above, and felt that an evening like this is worth almost any price that Fate can ask. What can one want more than to feel right *inside* the world, so much so that time seems to stop? It only lasts a short while, but it is like that glimpse in the fairy tale.[7]

Many travelers seem to be receptive to and even searching for transcendent experiences and moments in their travel, and it is the intermittent realization of such moments that keeps them traveling. Freya seems to be one of those, and perhaps this is what lured her to travel through the remaining years of her life. She describes richness, months saturated with beauty, the goodness and joy she finds in the "poor hard lives" of the people she meets,[8] a view of a distant valley that seemed to be "Romance incarnate: a happy feeling of the world being open and alive . . . a feeling of my own life being mixed up with all I saw."[9] Some of Freya's transcendent moments involved visions that were spiritual if not mystical and consistent with a spiritual thread that began to develop in her letters. In many instances she was trying to comfort her friends but they still give an insight into her faith. Her friend Pam Ruthven's husband, Pat, was killed in the battle of Tobruk in the Second World War, and in 1950 while she and Stewart were in Benghazi, she visited Tobruk "in the moonlight and the whole desert seemed alive with the young, the gay, those who will never be old. It was strangely happy" and later "as the evening fell . . . I suddenly had one of those happy times that come like a visitation, a feeling of enveloping *mercy* into which all this turmoil melted, so that one knew it cannot matter in the end."[10] She had an overriding feeling that life and death were one, that death was a union and not a separation, and while she wondered what was around the corner the prospect filled her with delight. It is clear from her letters that she was supported by a foundation of great faith.

And again:

[A] vision rather than a dream and strange because I am not worthy of visions. I had been thinking of my first love and thinking kindly though he had not deserved it; but all the sorrow had faded and only gentleness remained and from that the memory of the true deep love came (also divided it was, by time). I fell happily asleep, and the vision came—*nothing*, but only an overwhelming presence, which enveloped; it was not inside me but I in it, and I felt an incredible joy that I was it and not a self any longer . . . I was filled with a joy greater than I can tell you, knowing freedom, and that I was a part of *love*, not possessed or possessing, but intrinsically one.[11]

As age took its toll, her sexual appetites lost their hold and she told a friend that she was very happy "that going to bed with anyone is over! It seems to me to leave a lovely free world where all the essentials of affection can flourish and that terrible possessiveness is absent."[12] This loss did not impact her appreciation of men, however. In one instance she remarks on the beauty of a Greek sponge diver climbing onto the boat, whose face as he climbed aboard shifted from "hard beautiful repose to gentleness and amusement" and brought tears to her eyes.[13] When in Turkey she noted that "Turks extremely virile almost frightening but very agreeable always a man to woman feeling—must say adds a lot to the fun of life."[14] A British major named Colin Mackenzie had read the introduction to *Perseus in the Wind* and was so taken with Freya that he had been writing to her for six years. He apparently was a kindred spirit and spent his leaves traveling. He visited Freya in Asolo, and Freya found him charming and good-looking: "I would be head over heels in love if fifty years were taken off my shoulders!"[15]

Freya was a famous woman known throughout the Arab world as well as the United Kingdom. Once in Derna, a small town in what is now Libya, she went into a shop to buy needles. The old shopkeeper asked where she had learned Arabic and she told him that she studied. He asked her name and she replied, "Faraya." "Is it Faraya Stark?" he asked, and it turned out that he knew all about her.[16] In Britain she was made a Commander of Order of British Empire and the C.B.E. ribbon was pinned on her by Queen Elizabeth on the 27th of July 1953. She was now Dame Freya Stark. Years later she was invited by the Queen Mother to visit her at her castle, The Castle of Mey in Caithness on the coast of Scotland. Apparently she and the Queen Mother got along very well, and at one point Freya describes them sitting overlooking the sea: "I forgot it was the Queen as we sat there, two old women with most of our world behind us but happy in what we remember and what remains."[17] And again a year later she was visiting the Queen Mother when the "whole" Royal Family, who were cruising on the Royal Yacht *Brittania*, left the ship to visit the Queen Mother. At lunch she was seated between Prince Philip and Prince Charles, both of whom she found easy and pleasant to talk with.[18] Both are sailors, of course. Not bad for a girl who once ran away from home to find a ship and go to sea.

DAME FREYA STARK died on May 11, 1993. Not only had she seen much of the development of the modern Middle East and the fall of the British Empire, she was familiar with the lives of her predecessors.

She had written about Zenobia in *Rome on the Euphrates* and she had read widely about the other improbable women. She had visited Hester Stanhope's tomb, found Jane Digby charming, and had what seemed to be an alternating competitive and admiring attitude toward Gertrude Bell. She said that she wished she had not been two years late to see her in Baghdad.

Notes

Bibliography

Index

NOTES

INTRODUCTION

1. Abraham Rabinovich, *The Yom Kippur War: The Epic Encounter That Transformed the Middle East* (New York: Schocken Books, 2004), 269.

2. W. H. Wilkins, *The Romance of Isabel Lady Burton: The Story of Her Life*, vol. 1 (New York: Dodd Mead & Co., 1897), 21.

3. Ibid., 52.

4. Josephine Kamm, *Daughter of the Desert* (London: The Bodley Head, 1956), 114.

1. THAT WOMAN IN PALMYRA

1. Agnes Carr Vaughn, *Zenobia of Palmyra* (New York: Doubleday & Co., 1967), 216.

2. Pat Southern, *Empress Zenobia: Palmyra's Rebel Queen* (New York: Continuum US, 2008), 5.

3. Vaughn, *Zenobia of Palmyra*, 9.

4. Ibid., 91.

5. Edward Gibbon, *The Decline and Fall of the Roman Empire*, vol. 1 (N.p.: Plantagenet Publishing, 2011), chap. 11, part 2.

6. Vaughn, *Zenobia of Palmyra*, 62.

7. Southern, *Empress Zenobia*, 143.

8. Gibbon, *Decline and Fall*, chap. 11, part 3.

9. Vaughn, *Zenobia of Palmyra*, 163.

10. Ibid., 173.

11. Southern, *Empress Zenobia*, 160.

12. W. H. Wilkins, *The Romance of Isabel Lady Burton: The Story of Her Life*, vol. 1 (New York: Dodd, Mead & Co., 1897), 421.

13. Lady Bell, ed., *The Letters of Gertrude Bell*, vol. 1 (London: Ernest Benn Ltd., 1927), 108.

14. Ibid.

3. FORGED IN CONFLICT

1. Duchess of Cleveland, *The Life and Letters of Lady Hester Stanhope* (London: John Murray, 1914), 153.

2. Ibid., 155.

3. Duchess of Cleveland, *Life and Letters*, 1.

4. Ibid., 5.

5. Ibid.

6. Ibid.

7. Ibid., 4, footnote.

8. Aubrey Newman, *The Stanhopes of Chevening: A Family Biography* (London: Macmillan & Co., 1969), 170–85.

9. Ibid., 158.

10. Ibid.

11. Tresham Lever, *The House of Pitt* (London: John Murray, 1947), 304.

12. Charles Lewis Meryon, *Travels of Lady Hester Stanhope as Related by Herself in Conversations with Her Physician*, vol. 2 (London: Henry Colburn, 1846), 20.

13. Duchess of Cleveland, *Life and Letters*, 10.

14. Meryon, *Travels*, 2:25.

15. Ibid.

16. Duchess of Cleveland, *Life and Letters*, 36.

17. Ibid., 51.

4. FIRST LADY

1. Duchess of Cleveland, *Life and Letters*, 47. Parenthetical page numbers in the text in the remainder of this chapter are from this source.

2. Stanhope, *Memoirs*, 1:32.

3. Duchess of Cleveland, *Life and Letters*, 209.

4. John Watney, *Travels in Araby: The Travels of Lady Hester Stanhope* (London: Gordon and Cremonisi, 1975), 85.

5. Stanhope, *Memoirs*, 2:37.

6. Joan Haslip, *Lady Hester Stanhope: A Biography* (New York: Frederick A. Stokes, 1936), 68.

7. Ibid.

8. Virginia Childs, *Lady Hester Stanhope: Queen of the Desert* (London: Weidenfeld & Nicolson, 1990), 36.

5. ON DEALING WITH BRUTAL MEN

1. Haslip, *Lady Hester Stanhope: A Biography*, 81.

2. Watney, *Travels in Araby*, 111.

3. Childs, *Lady Hester Stanhope*, 48.

4. Ian Bruce, ed., *The Nun of Lebanon: The Love Affair of Lady Hester Stanhope and Michael Bruce* (London: Collins, 1951), 66.

5. Duchess of Cleveland, *Life and Letters*, 96.

6. Ibid., 102.

7. Childs, *Lady Hester Stanhope*, 69.

8. Ibid.

9. Ibid., 70.

10. Ibid.

11. Duchess of Cleveland, *Life and Letters*, 117.

12. Haslip, *Lady Hester Stanhope: A Biography*, 125.

13. Childs, *Lady Hester Stanhope*, 104.

14. Duchess of Cleveland, *Life and Letters*, 126. Parenthetical page numbers in the remainder of this chapter are from this source.

15. Meryon, *Travels*, 2:6.

16. Duchess of Cleveland, *Life and Letters*, 136.

17. Meryon, *Travels*, 2:74.

18. Duchess of Cleveland, *Life and Letters*, 142.

19. Ibid., 154.

20. Meryon, *Travels*, 2:176.

21. Ibid., 193.

6. A NUN IN LEBANON

1. Bruce, *Nun of Lebanon*, 212.

2. Ibid.

3. Meryon, *Travels*, 2:310.

4. Bruce, *Nun of Lebanon*, 249.

5. Ibid., 291.

6. Duchess of Cleveland, *Life and Letters*, 194–95.

7. Stanhope, *Memoirs*, 1:205.

8. Ibid., 206.

9. Duchess of Cleveland, *Life and Letters*, 217.

10. Ibid., 217.

11. Ibid., 430.

8. Everything for Love

1. E. M. Oddie, *Portrait of Ianthe: Being a Study of Jane Digby Lady Ellenborough* (London: Jonathan Cape, 1935), 33. Parenthetical page numbers in the text in the remainder of this chapter are from this source.

9. Affairs to Remember

1. Oddie, *Portrait of Ianthe*, 89.

2. Ibid., 69.

3. Mary S. Lovell, *A Scandalous Life: The Biography of Jane Digby el Mesrab* (London: Fourth Estate, 1995), 65.

4. Ibid., 100.

5. Honoré de Balzac, *Lily of the Valley*, 2nd ed. (New York: Carroll & Graf, 1997), 173.

6. Ibid., 176.

7. Margaret Fox Schmidt, *Passion's Child: The Extraordinary Life of Jane Digby* (New York: Harper & Row, 1976), 138–45.

8. Lovell, *A Scandalous Life*, 113.

9. Ibid., 127.

10. From Bandit to Bedouin

1. Oddie, *Portrait of Ianthe*, 163–71.

2. Ibid., 172.

3. Ibid., 173, chap. 13; Lovell, *A Scandalous Life*, 122, 127, 134.

4. Oddie, *Portrait of Ianthe*, 184.

5. Ibid., 182–83.

6. Schmidt, *Passion's Child*, 165–66.

7. Oddie, *Portrait of Ianthe*, 204, 206.

8. Lovell, *A Scandalous Life*, 203.

9. Oddie, *Portrait of Ianthe*, 244–45.

10. Lovell, *A Scandalous Life*, 249.

12. CREATING A DREAM

1. Isabel Burton, *The Life of Captain Sir Richd F. Burton, K.C.M.G., F.R.G.S*, vol. 1 (London: Chapman & Hall, 1893), 150; Edward Rice, *Captain Sir Richard Frances Burton* (New York: Charles Scribner's Sons, 1990), 102, 104, 108; Mary S. Lovell, *A Rage To Live: A Biography of Richard & Isabel Burton* (New York: W. W. Norton, 1998), 734, 773.

2. Richard F. Burton, *Personal Narrative of a Pilgrimage to El Medinah and Meccah*, 2nd ed., vol. 1 (London: Longman, Brown, Green, Longmans, & Roberts, 1857).

3. Jean Burton, *Sir Richard Burton's Wife* (New York: Alfred A. Knopf, 1941), 16.

4. Ibid., 17.

5. Wilkins, *Romance of Isabel Lady Burton*, 1:21.

6. Ibid.

7. Ibid.

8. Fawn M. Brodie, *The Devil Drives: A Life of Sir Richard Burton* (New York: Ballantine Books, 1967), 152.

9. Wilkins, *Romance of Isabel Lady Burton*, 1:22. Following parenthetical page numbers in the text are from this source.

10. Coleman Barks, *The Essential Rumi*, new expanded ed. (New York: HarperOne, 2004), 106.

11. Wilkins, *Romance of Isabel Lady Burton*, 1:78. Parenthetical page numbers in the remainder of this chapter are from this source.

13. REALIZING THE DREAM

1. Wilkins, *Romance of Isabel Lady Burton*, 1:369.

2. Jean Burton, *Sir Richard Burton's Wife*, 111.

3. Ibid., 113.

4. Wilkins, *Romance of Isabel Lady Burton*, 2:397.

5. Ibid., 393.

6. Jean Burton, *Sir Richard Burton's Wife*, 116.

7. Wilkins, *Romance of Isabel Lady Burton*, 2:400.

8. Isabel Burton, *The Inner Life of Syria, Palestine, and the Holy Land* (London: Kegan Paul, Trench & Co., 1884), 176.

9. Wilkins, *Romance of Isabel Lady Burton*, 2:405.

10. Ibid., 405.

11. Isabel Burton, *Inner Life*, 173.

12. Ibid., 177.

13. Wilkins, *Romance of Isabel Lady Burton*, 2:422.

14. Ibid., 469.

14. Gertrude's World

1. George Eliot, *Daniel Deronda*, vol. 2 (New York: Thomas Nelson and Sons, 1920), 615.

2. Walter Laquer, *A History of Zionism* (New York: Schocken Books, 1989), 108.

15. Bright and Brave

1. Bell, *Letters of Gertrude Bell*, 1:11.

2. Ronald Bodley and Lorna Hearst, *Gertrude Bell* (New York: Macmillan, 1940), 21.

3. Elsa Richmond, ed., *The Earlier Letters of Gertrude Bell* (New York: Liveright Publishing, 1937).

4. Ibid., 266–67.

5. Ibid., 272.

16. From Mountains to Mohammed

1. H. V. F. Winstone, *Gertrude Bell* (London: Quartet Books, 1980), 37.

2. Ibid., 68.

3. Bell, *Letters*, 1:52.

4. Winstone, *Gertrude Bell*, 73.

5. Ibid., 72.

6. Bell, *Letters*, 1:125. Parenthetical page numbers following in the text are from this source.

7. Janet Wallach, *Desert Queen: The Extraordinary Life of Gertrude Bell: Adventurer, Advisor to Kings, Ally of Lawrence of Arabia* (New York: Nan A. Talese, 1996), 55.

8. Bell, *Letters*, 1:104. Parenthetical page numbers in the remainder of this chapter are from this source.

17. Joyous Journeys

1. Bell, *Letters*, 1:251. Parenthetical page numbers in the text are from this source.

2. Winstone, *Gertrude Bell*, 155.
3. Ibid.
4. Ibid., 156.
5. Ibid., 157.

18. CREATING IRAQ

1. Bell, *Letters*, 1:361–62.
2. Wallach, *Desert Queen*, 300.
3. Anton La Guardia, *War without End: Israelis, Palestinians, and the Struggle for a Promised Land* (New York: St. Martin's Press, 2002), 110.

19. FREYA'S WORLD

1. Philip D. Curtin, *Death by Migration: Europe's Encounter with the Tropical World in the Nineteenth Century* (Cambridge, UK: Cambridge Univ. Press, 1995).

20. ACCEPTING THE TORCH

1. Freya Stark, *Traveller's Prelude* (London: John Murray, 1950), 30. Parenthetical page numbers in the remainder of this chapter are from this source.
2. Matthew Arnold, *Poetical Works of Matthew Arnold* (London: Macmillan & Co., 1907), 91.
3. Stark, *Traveller's Prelude*, 171.

21. ASSASSINS AND INCENSE

1. Freya Stark, *Letters from Syria* (London: John Murray, 1942), 19. Parenthetical page numbers in this chapter are from this source.
2. Freya Stark, *Beyond Euphrates* (London: John Murray, 1951), 7.
3. Ibid., 66.
4. Ibid., 111.
5. Freya Stark, *Baghdad Sketches* (London: John Murray, 1946), 73.
6. Freya Stark, *The Valleys of the Assassins* (London: John Murray, 1936), 203.
7. Molly Izzard, *Freya Stark: A Biography* (London: Hodder & Stoughton, 1993), 98.
8. Ibid., 104.
9. Freya Stark, *The Southern Gates of Arabia: A Journey in the Hadhramaut* (London: John Murray, 1938), 56.

10. Caroline Moorehead, *Over the Rim of the World: Freya Stark Selected Letters* (London: John Murray, 1988), 138.

22. WAR FROM CAIRO TO BAGHDAD

1. Izzard, *Freya Stark: A Biography*, 124.

2. Ibid.

3. Freya Stark, *Dust in the Lion's Paw: Autobiography 1939–1946* (New York: Harcourt, Brace & World, 1962), 14.

4. Ibid., 23.

5. Ibid., 33.

6. Caroline Moorehead, *Over the Rim*, 184.

7. Ibid.

8. Stark, *Dust in the Lion's Paw*, 63.

9. Ibid.

10. Lucy Moorehead, ed., *Freya Stark Letters*, vol. 4, *Bridge of the Levant, 1940–43* (Wilton, UK: Michael Russell, 1977), 90.

11. Stark, *Dust in the Lion's Paw*, 59.

12. Ibid., 107.

13. Ibid., 147.

14. Ibid., 160.

23. TO THE END OF THE ROAD

1. Stark, *Dust in the Lion's Paw*, 168.

2. Ibid., 172.

3. Ibid., 209.

4. Caroline Moorehead, *Freya Stark Letters*, vol. 7, *Some Talk of Alexander* (London: Michael Russell, 1982), 165.

5. Ibid., 162.

6. Ibid., 170.

7. Ibid., 14.

8. Ibid., 185.

9. Ibid., 250.

10. Lucy Moorehead, *Freya Stark Letters*, vol. 6, *The Broken Road, 1947–52* (London: Michael Russell, 1981), 162.

11. Caroline Moorehead, *Freya Stark Letters*, vol. 8, *Traveller's Epilogue, 1960–80* (Wilton: Michael Russell, 1982), 238.

12. Caroline Moorehead, *Freya Stark Letters*, 7:100.

13. Lucy Moorehead, *Freya Stark Letters*, 6:177.

14. Caroline Moorehead, *Freya Stark Letters*, 7:33.
15. Ibid., 8:168.
16. Lucy Moorehead, *Freya Stark Letters*, 6:161.
17. Caroline Moorehead, *Freya Stark Letters*, 8:245.
18. Ibid., 270.

Bibliography

This bibliography is divided into seven sections: General, Zenobia, Hester Lucy Stanhope, Jane Elizabeth Digby El Mesrab, Isabel Arundell Burton, Gertrude Margaret Lowthian Bell, and Freya Madeline Stark. The General section provides references that deal with historical and cultural contexts that apply to more than one of the improbable women.

General

Aburish, Saïd K. *Nasser: The Last Arab*. New York: St. Martin's Press, 2004.

Alsop, Susan Mary. *Lady Sackville: A Biography*. New York: Avon Books, 1978.

Anderson, Bonnie S., and Judith P. Zinsser. *A History of Their Own: Women in Europe from Prehistory to the Present*. Vol. 2. New York: HarperPerennial, 1989.

Are, Thomas L. *Israeli Peace/Palestinian Justice: Liberation Theology and the Peace Process*. Atlanta, GA: Clarity Press, 1994.

Armstrong, Karen. *Holy War: The Crusades and Their Impact on Today's World*. New York: Anchor Books, 1992.

———. *Muhammad: A Biography of the Prophet*. San Francisco: Harper-Collins, 1992.

Arnold, Matthew. *Poetical Works of Matthew Arnold*. London: Macmillan & Co., 1907.

Asher, Michael. *The Last of the Bedu: In Search of the Myth*. London: Viking, 1996.

———. *Lawrence, the Uncrowned King of Arabia*. Woodstock, NY: Overlook Press, 1999.

———. *Thesiger: A Biography*. London: Viking, 1994.

Ashrawi, Hanan. *This Side of Peace: A Personal Account*. New York: Simon & Schuster, 1995.

Barakat, Halim Isber. *The Arab World: Society, Culture, and State*. Berkeley: Univ. of California Press, 1993.

Blake, Robert. *Disraeli*. Garden City, NY: Anchor Books, Doubleday & Co., 1968.

Blumberg, Arnold. *Zion before Zionism: 1838–1880*. Syracuse, NY: Syracuse Univ. Press, 1985.

Bradford, Sarah. *Disraeli*. New York: Stein and Day, 1983.

Brent, Peter Ludwig. *Lord Byron*. London: Weidenfeld and Nicolson, 1974.

Burton, Elizabeth. *The Pageant of Early Victorian England, 1837–1861*. New York: Scribner, 1972.

Caine, Barbara. *English Feminism, 1780–1980*. Oxford, UK: Oxford Univ. Press, 1997.

Churchill, Winston. *A History of the English-Speaking Peoples*. Vols. 3 and 4. New York: Dodd, Mead, 1956–58.

Clark, Gillian. *Women in Late Antiquity: Pagan and Christian Life-Styles*. Oxford, UK: Clarendon Press, 1993.

Cramer, Richard Ben. *How Israel Lost: The Four Questions*. New York: Simon & Schuster, 2005.

Cunnington, C. Willett. *Feminine Attitudes in the Nineteenth Century*. New York: Haskell House, 1973.

Curtin, Philip D. *Death by Migration: Europe's Encounter with the Tropical World in the Nineteenth Century*. Cambridge, UK: Cambridge Univ. Press, 1995.

David, Saul. *Prince of Pleasure: The Prince of Wales and the Making of the Regency*. New York: Atlantic Monthly Press, 1998.

Davies, Norman. *The Isles: A History*. Oxford, UK: Oxford Univ. Press, 1999.

Denny, Frederick Mathewson. *Islam and the Muslim Community*. San Francisco: HarperSanFrancisco, 1987.

Disraeli, Benjamin. *Tancred; or, The New Crusade*. St. Clair Shores, MI: Scholarly Press, 1970.

Elton, Godfrey Elton. *Gordon of Khartoum: The Life of General Charles George Gordon*. New York: Alfred A. Knopf, 1955.

Erickson, Carolly. *Our Tempestuous Day: A History of Regency England*. New York: William Morrow, 1986.

Feiling, Keith. *A History of England: From the Coming of the English to 1918*. London: Book Club Associates, 1970.

Ferguson, Niall. *Empire: The Rise and Demise of the British World Order and the Lessons for Global Power*. New York: Basic Books, 2003.

Fernea, Elizabeth Warnock. *Guests of the Sheikh: An Ethnography of an Iraqi Village*. New York: Anchor Books, 1965.

———. *A Street in Marrakech: A Personal Encounter with the Lives of Moroccan Women*. New York: Anchor Books, 1980.

Finkelstein, Norman G. *Image and Reality of the Israel-Palestine Conflict*. 2nd ed. New York: Verso, 2003.

Fromkin, David. *A Peace to End All Peace: Creating the Modern Middle East, 1914–1922*. New York: H. Holt, 1989.

Frum, David, and Richard Perle. *An End to Evil: How to Win the War on Terror*. New York: Random House, 2003.

Glass, Charles. *Tribes with Flags: A Dangerous Passage through the Chaos of the Middle East*. New York: Atlantic Monthly Press, 1990.

Glubb, John Bagot. *The Story of the Arab Legion*. London: Hodder & Stoughton, 1948.

Glueck, Nelson. *The River Jordan*. New York: McGraw-Hill, 1968.

Gorham, Deborah. *The Victorian Girl and the Feminine Ideal*. Bloomington: Indiana Univ. Press, 1982.

Granqvist, Hilma Natalia. *Birth and Childhood among the Arabs; Studies in a Muhammadan Village in Palestine*. Helsinki: Söderström, 1947.

Green, Martin. *The Adventurous Male: Chapters in the History of the White Male Mind*. University Park: Pennsylvania State Univ. Press, 1993.

Harding, G. Lankester. *The Antiquities of Jordan*. London: Lutterworth Press, 1959.

Harvey, Arnold D. *Sex in Georgian England: Attitudes and Prejudices from the 1720s to the 1820s*. New York: St. Martin's Press, 1994.

Hitti, Philip K. *History of the Arabs: From the Earliest Times to the Present*. Rev. 10th ed. New York: Palgrave Macmillan, 2002.

Hogarth, David George. *Hejaz before World War I: A Handbook*. 2nd ed. Cambridge, UK: Oleander Press, 1978.

———. *The Penetration of Arabia: A Record of the Development of Western Knowledge concerning the Arabian Peninsula*. Beirut: Khayats, 1966.

Hourani, Albert. *A History of the Arab Peoples*. Cambridge, MA: Belknap Press of Harvard Univ. Press, 1991.

James, Lawrence. *The Rise and Fall of the British Empire*. New York: St. Martin's Griffin, 1994.

Johnson, Paul. *The Birth of the Modern: World Society 1815–1830*. New York: HarperPerennial, 1992.

Kaplan, Robert D. *The Arabists: The Romance of an American Elite*. New York: Free Press, 1993.

Karsh, Efraim. *Empires of the Sand: The Struggle for Mastery in the Middle East, 1789–1923*. Cambridge, MA: Harvard Univ. Press, 1999.

Keay, John. *Sowing the Wind: The Seeds of Conflict in the Middle East*. New York: W. W. Norton & Co., 2003.

Kobak, Annette. *Isabelle: The Life of Isabelle Eberhardt*. New York: Alfred A. Knopf, 1989.

Kornberg, Jacques. *Theodor Herzl: From Assimilation to Zionism*. Indianapolis: Indiana Univ. Press, 1993.

Kurzman, Dan. *Ben-Gurion: Prophet of Fire*. New York: Simon and Schuster, 1983.

Kurzman, Dan, and Yitzhak Rabin. *Genesis 1948: The First Arab-Israeli War*. New York: Da Capo Press, 1970.

La Guardia, Anton. *War without End: Israelis, Palestinians, and the Struggle for a Promised Land*. New York: St. Martin's Press, 2002.

Lamb, David. *The Arabs: Journeys beyond the Mirage*. New York: Random House, 1987.

Levine, Philippa. *Victorian Feminism, 1850–1900*. Tallahassee: Florida State Univ. Press, 1987.

Lewis, Bernard. *The Crisis of Islam: Holy War and Unholy Terror*. New York: Random House, 2004.

———. *The Middle East: A Brief History of the Last 2,000 Years*. New York: Scribner, 1995.

———. *What Went Wrong? The Clash between Islam and Modernity in the Middle East*. New York: Perennial, 2003.

Lieber, Sherman. *Mystics and Missionaries: The Jews in Palestine, 1799–1840*. Salt Lake City: Univ. of Utah Press, 1992.

Madden, Thomas F. *God Wills It!: Understanding the Crusades*. Sound recording. Prince Frederick, MD: Recorded Books, 2005.

Manchester, William. *The Last Lion: Winston Spencer Churchill; Visions of Glory: 1874–1932*. New York: Bantam Doubleday Dell Publishing Group, 1989.

Mancoff, Debra N. *David Roberts: Travels in Egypt & the Holy Land*. San Francisco: Pomegranate Communications, 1999.

Margetson, Stella. *Regency London*. New York: Praeger, 1971.

Markham, Beryl. *West with the Night*. San Francisco: North Point Press, 1983.

Masters, Anthony. *Nancy Astor, a Biography*. New York: McGraw-Hill, 1981.

Mattar, Philip. *The Mufti of Jerusalem: Al-Hajj Amin Al-Husayni and the Palestinian National Movement*. New York: Columbia Univ. Press, 1988.

McCarthy, Justin. *The Population of Palestine: Population History and Statistics of the Late Ottoman Period and the Mandate*. New York: Columbia Univ. Press, 1990.

Melchett, Sonia. *Passionate Quests: Five Modern Women Travellers*. Boston: Faber and Faber, 1992.

Melman, Billie. *Women's Orients—English Women and the Middle East, 1718–1918: Sexuality, Religion, and Work*. Ann Arbor: Univ. of Michigan Press, 1992.

Mitchell, Sally. *Daily Life in Victorian England*. Westport, CT: Greenwood Press, 1996.

Mogannam, Matiel E. T. *The Arab Woman and the Palestine Problem*. Westport, CT: Hyperion Press, 1976.

Morris, James. *Heaven's Command: An Imperial Progress*. New York: Harcourt Brace & Co., 1973.

Morris, Mary. *Maiden Voyages: Writings of Women Travelers*. New York: Vintage Books, 1993.

Muslih, Muhammad Y. *The Origins of Palestinian Nationalism*. New York: Columbia Univ. Press, 1988.

Omar Khayyam. *Rubáiyaát of Omar Khayyám/Rendered into English Verse by Edward Fitzgerald*. New York: Doubleday, 1952.

Negev, Avraham. *Nabatean Archaeology Today*. New York: New York Univ. Press, 1986.

Orni, Efraim, and Elisha Efrat. *Geography of Israel*. 3rd rev. ed. Jerusalem: Israel Universities Press, 1973.

Patai, Raphael. *The Arab Mind*. Rev. ed. New York: Scribner, 1983.

Philby, H. StJ. B. *Arabian Jubilee*. New York: John Day Co., 1953.

Phillips, Janet M. *Victorians at Home and Away*. London: Croom Helm, 1978.

Porter, Roy. *London, a Social History*. Cambridge, MA: Harvard Univ. Press, 1995.

———. *The Creation of the Modern World: The Untold Story of the British Enlightenment*. New York: Norton, 2000.

Pryce-Jones, David. *The Closed Circle: An Interpretation of the Arabs*. New York: HarperPerennial, 1991.

Rabinovich, Abraham. *The Yom Kippur War: The Epic Encounter That Transformed the Middle East*. New York: Schocken Books, 2004.

Rees, Barbara. *The Victorian Lady*. London: Gordon & Cremonesi, 1977.

Robinson, Jane. *Unsuitable for Ladies: An Anthology of Women Travellers*. Oxford, UK: Oxford Univ. Press, 1994.

Sacher, Howard M. *A History of Israel: From the Rise of Zionism to Our Time*. 2nd ed. New York: Alfred A. Knopf, 1996.

Sale, Kirkpatrick. *Rebels Against the Future: the Luddites and Their War on the Industrial Revolution: Lessons for the Computer Age*. Reading, MA: Addison-Wesley, 1995.

Schama, Simon. *A History of Britain: The Fate of Empire, 1776–2000*. New York: Miramax Books, 2002.

Sicker, Martin. *Reshaping Palestine: From Muhammad Ali to the British Mandate, 1831–1922*. Westport, CT: Praeger, 1999.

Sim, Katherine. *David Roberts R.A., 1796–1864: A Biography*. London: Quartet Books, 1984.

Simmons, James C. *Passionate Pilgrims: English Travellers to the World of the Desert Arabs*. New York: William Morrow & Co., 1987.

Stewart, Desmond. *Theodor Herzl*. Garden City, NY: Doubleday & Co., 1974.

Stewart, John David. *Gibraltar: The Keystone*. Boston: Houghton Mifflin, 1967.

Strachey, Lytton. *Queen Victoria*. New York: Harcourt, Brace & World, 1960.

Tavris, Carol. *The Mismeasure of Woman*. New York: Simon & Schuster, 1992.

Taylor, Jane. *Petra and the Lost Kingdom of the Nabateans*. London: I. B. Tauris, 2002.

Tinling, Marion. *Women into the Unknown: A Sourcebook on Women Explorers and Travelers*. New York: Greenwood Press, 1989.

Toy, Barbara. *The Highway of the Three Kings: Arabia from South to North*. London: Murray, 1968.

Turki, Fawaz. *Soul in Exile: Lives of a Palestinian Revolutionary*. New York: Monthly Review Press, 1988.

Williams, E. N. *Life in Georgian England*. New York: G. P. Putnam's Sons, 1962.

Wilson, A. N. *After the Victorians: The Decline of Britain in the World*. New York: Farrar, Straus & Giroux, 2005.

———. *The Victorians*. New York: W. W. Norton & Co., 2003.

Wilson-Smith, Timothy. *Delacroix: A Life*. London: Constable, 1992.

Withey, Lynne. *Grand Tours and Cook's Tours: A History of Leisure Travel, 1750 to 1915*. New York: William Morrow, 1997.

Wright, Beth S., ed. *The Cambridge Companion to Delacroix*. New York: Cambridge Univ. Press, 2001.

Yapp, M. E. *The Making of the Modern Near East, 1792–1923*. New York: Longman, 1987.

Zeine, Zeine N. *The Emergence of Arab Nationalism, with a Background Study of Arab-Turkish Relations in the Near East*. Rev. ed. Beirut: Khayats, 1966.

Ziegler, Philip. *Omdurman*. 1st ed. New York: Knopf, 1974.

ZENOBIA

Addison, Charles G. *Damascus and Palmyra: A Journey to the East*. Vol. 1. Philadelphia: E. L. Carey and A. Hart, 1838.

Colledge, Malcolm A. R. *The Art of Palmyra*. London: Thames and Hudson, 1976.

Fraser, Antonia. *The Warrior Queens*. New York: Knopf, 1989.

Garnsey, Peter. *Food and Society in Classical Antiquity*. Cambridge, UK: Cambridge Univ. Press, 1999.

Gibbon, Edward. *The History of the Decline and Fall of the Roman Empire*. Vol. 1. London: Allen Lane, Penguin Press, 1994.

Kazimierz, Michalowski, and Dziewanowski, Andrzej. *Palmyra*. New York: Praeger, 1968.

Macurdy, Grace Harriet. *Vassal-Queens and Some Contemporary Women in the Roman Empire*. Baltimore: Johns Hopkins Univ. Press, 1937.

Rostovtzeff, Michael I. *Caravan Cities*. Translated by D. and T. Talbot Rice. New York: AMS Press, 1971.

———. *Out of the Past of Greece and Rome*. New Haven, CT: Yale Univ. Press, 1932.

Southern, Pat. *Empress Zenobia: Palmyra's Rebel Queen*. New York: Continuum US, 2008.

Stoneman, Richard. *Palmyra and Its Empire: Zenobia's Revolt against Rome*. Ann Arbor: Univ. of Michigan Press, 1992.

Wilson, A. N. *The Victorians*. New York: W. W. Norton & Co., 2003.

Vaughan, Agnes Carr. *Zenobia of Palmyra*. Garden City, NY: Doubleday & Co., 1967.

Ware, William. *Zenobia; Or, The Fall of Palmyra*. In *Letters of L. Manlius Piso from Palmyra, to his Friend Marcus Curtius at Rome*. Vols. 1 and 2. New York: G. Munro, 1886.

HESTER LUCY STANHOPE

Bruce, Ian, ed. *The Nun of Lebanon: The Love Affair of Lady Hester Stanhope and Michael Bruce: Their Newly Discovered Letters*. London: Collins, 1951.

Childs, Virginia. *Lady Hester Stanhope: Queen of the Desert*. London: Weidenfeld & Nicolson, 1990.

Cleveland, Duchess of. *The Life and Letters of Lady Hester Stanhope*. London: John Murray, 1914.

Haslip, Joan. *Lady Hester Stanhope: A Biography*. New York: Frederick A. Stokes, 1936.

Kinglake, Alexander William. *Eothen*. London: J. M. Dent & Co., 1908.

Leslie, Doris. *The Desert Queen*. London: Heinemann, 1972.

Meryon, Charles Lewis. *Travels of Lady Hester Stanhope*. 3 vols. London: Henry Colburn, 1846.

Newman, Aubrey N. *The Stanhopes of Chevening: A Family Biography*. London: Macmillan & Co., 1969.

Stanhope, Hester Lucy. *Memoirs of the Lady Hester Stanhope.* Vol. 1. London: Henry Colburn, 1845.

———. *Memoirs of the Lady Hester Stanhope.* Vol. 2. London: Henry Colburn, 1845.

———. *Memoirs of the Lady Hester Stanhope as Related by Herself in Conversations with Her Physician; Comprising Her Opinions and Anecdotes of Some of the Most Remarkable Persons of Her Time.* Vol. 3. London: Henry Colburn, 1845.

Ure, John. *In Search of Nomads: An Anglo-American Obsession from Hester Stanhope to Bruce Chatwin.* New York: Carroll & Graf, 2004.

Vogelsberger, Hartwig A. *The Unearthly Quest—Lady Hester Stanhope's Legacy.* Salzburg: Institut Für Anglistik und Amerikanistik, Universität Salzburg, 1987.

Watney, John. *Travels in Araby: The Travels of Lady Hester Stanhope.* London: Gordon and Cremonesi, 1975.

JANE ELIZABETH DIGBY EL MESRAB

Allen, Alexandra. *Travelling Ladies.* London: Jupiter Books, 1980.

Balzac, Honoré de. *Lily of the Valley.* 2nd ed. New York: Carroll & Graf, 1997.

Blanch, Lesley. *The Wilder Shores of Love.* New York: Simon and Schuster, 1954.

Bligh, E. W. *Sir Kenelm Digby and His Venetia.* London: Sampson Low, Merston & Co., 1932.

Chirol, Sir Valentine. *Fifty Years in a Changing World.* New York: Harcourt, Brace & Co., 1928.

Digby, Kenelm, Sir. *Journal of a Voyage into the Mediterranean by Sir Kenelm Digby, A.D. 1628.* Edited, from the original autograph ms. in the possession of William Watkin E. Wynne, by John Bruce. Printed for the Camden Society, 1868. New York: AMS Press, 1968.

Digby, Kenelm. *Private Memoirs of Sir Kenelm Digby.* London: Saunders and Otley, 1827.

Fraisse, Geneviève, and Michelle Perrot, eds. *A History of Women in the West: IV. Emerging Feminism from Revolution to World War.* Cambridge MA: Belknap Press of Harvard Univ. Press, 1993.

Lovell, Mary S. *A Scandalous Life: The Biography of Jane Digby el Mezrab*. London: Fourth Estate, 1995.

Oddie, E. M. *Portrait of Ianthe: Being a Study of Jane Digby Lady Ellenborough*. London: Jonathan Cape, 1935.

Porter, J. L. *Five Years in Damascus*. London: John Murray, 1855.

Schmidt, Margaret Fox. *Passion's Child: The Extraordinary Life of Jane Digby*. New York: Harper & Row, 1976.

Simmons, James C. *Passionate Pilgrims: English Travelers to the World of the Desert Arabs*. New York: William Morrow & Co., 1987.

Wallace, Irving. *The Nympho and Other Maniacs*. New York: Simon and Schuster, 1971.

ISABEL ARUNDELL BURTON

Barks, Coleman. *The Essential Rumi*. New expanded ed. New York: HarperOne, 2004.

Brodie, Fawn M. *The Devil Drives: A Life of Sir Richard Burton*. New York: Ballantine Books, 1967.

Burton, Isabel. *Arabia Egypt India: A Narrative of Travel*. London: William Mullan and Son, 1879.

———. *The Inner Life of Syria, Palestine, and the Holy Land: From My Private Journal*. London: Kegan Paul, Trench & Co., 1884.

———. *The Life of Captain Sir Richard Francis Burton, K.C.M.G., F.R.G.S.* Vols. 1 and 2. London: Chapman and Hall, 1893.

Burton, Jean. *Sir Richard Burton's Wife*. New York: Alfred A. Knopf, 1941.

Burton, Richard. *Personal Narrative of a Pilgrimage to El Medinah and Meccah*. 2nd ed. Vols. 1 and 2. London: Longman, Brown, Green, Longmans, and Roberts, 1857.

———. *The Arabian Nights' Entertainments or The Book of a Thousand Nights and a Night*. New York: Modern Library, 1997.

Edwardes, Allen. *Death Rides a Camel: A Biography of Sir Richard Burton*. New York: Julian Press, 1963.

Farwell, Byron. *Burton: A Biography of Sir Richard Francis Burton*. London: Penguin Books, 1963.

Jutsi, Alan H., ed. *In Search of Sir Richard Burton: Papers from a Huntington Library Symposium*. San Marino, CA: Huntington Library, 1993.

Lovell, Mary S. *A Rage to Live: A Biography of Richard and Isabel Burton.* New York: W. W. Norton & Co., 1998.

Nichols, Pamela Catherine. *Force and Charm in the Desert: Manly Adventure and Gentlemanly Behaviour in the Middle Eastern Travel Writings of Richard and Isabel Burton and Wilfred Scawen and Anne Blunt.* Ann Arbor, MI: University Microfilms International, 1994.

Rice, Edward. *Captain Sir Richard Frances Burton: The Secret Agent Who Made the Pilgrimage to Mecca, Discovered the Kama Sutra, and Brought the Arabian Nights to the West.* New York: Charles Scribner's Sons, 1990.

Wilkins, W. H. *The Romance of Isabel Lady Burton: The Story of Her Life.* Vols. 1 and 2. New York: Dodd, Mead & Co., 1897.

GERTRUDE MARGARET LOWTHIAN BELL

Bell, Gertrude. *Amurath to Amurath.* London: William Heinemann, 1911.

———. *Persian Pictures.* London: Ernest Benn, 1947.

———. *Syria: The Desert and the Sown.* London: William Heinemann, 1908.

———. *The Arab of Mesopotamia.* Basrah: Government Press, 1917.

———. *The Arab War: Confidential Information for General Headquarters from Gertrude Bell Being Despatches from the Secret "Arab Bulletin."* Great Britain: Golden Cockerel Press, 1940.

———. *The Hafez Poems of Gertrude Bell.* Bethesda, MD: Iranbooks, 1995.

Bell, Lady, ed. *The Letters of Gertrude Bell.* Vols. 1 and 2. London: Ernest Benn, 1927.

Bodley, Ronald, and Lorna Hearst. *Gertrude Bell.* New York: Macmillan Co., 1940.

Burgoyne, Elizabeth. *Gertrude Bell: From Her Personal Papers, 1889–1914.* London: Ernest Benn, 1958.

Catherwood, Christopher. *Churchill's Folly: How Winston Churchill Created Modern Iraq.* New York: Carroll & Graf, 2004.

Courtney, Janet E. "Gertrude Bell." *North American Review* 223 (Dec.–Jan.–Feb. 1926–27).

Cowlin, Dorothy. *A Woman in the Desert: The Story of Gertrude Bell.* London: Frederick Muller, 1967.

Goodman, Susan. *Gertrude Bell*. Dover, NH: Berg Publishers, 1985.

Kamm, Josephine. *Daughter of the Desert*. London: Bodley Head, 1956.

Macmillan, Margaret Olwen. *Paris 1919: Six Months That Changed the World*. New York: Random House, 2001.

Richmond, Elsa, ed. *The Earlier Letters of Gertrude Bell*. New York: Liveright, 1937.

Ridley, M. R. *Gertrude Bell*. London: Blackie & Son, 1941.

Tibble, Anne. *Gertrude Bell*. London: Adam & Charles Black, 1958.

Wallach, Janet. *Desert Queen*. New York: Doubleday, 1996.

Winstone, H. V. F. *Gertrude Bell*. New York: Quartet Books, 1978.

FREYA MADELINE STARK

Geniesse, Jane Fletcher. *Passionate Nomad: The Life of Freya Stark*. New York: Random House, 1999.

Izzard, Molly. *Freya Stark: A Biography*. London: Hodder & Stoughton, 1993.

Maitland, Alexander. *Rivers of Time*. Edinburgh: William Blackwood, 1982.

Moorehead, Caroline. *Freya Stark*. New York: Viking Penguin, 1985.

———, ed. *Freya Stark Letters*. Vol. 7: *Some Talk of Alexander, 1952–59*. Wilton, UK: Michael Russell, 1982.

———, ed. *Freya Stark Letters*. Vol. 8: *Traveller's Epilogue, 1960–80*. Wilton, UK: Michael Russell, 1982.

———, ed. *Over the Rim of the World: Freya Stark Selected Letters*. London: John Murray, 1988.

Moorehead, Lucy, ed. *Freya Stark Letters*. Vol. 1: *The Furnace and the Cup, 1914–1930*. Salisbury, UK: Compton Russell, 1974.

———, ed. *Freya Stark Letters*. Vol. 2: *The Open Door, 1930–35*. Tisbury, UK: Compton Russell, 1975.

———, ed. *Freya Stark Letters*. Vol. 3: *The Growth of Danger, 1935–39*. Tisbury, Wiltshire: Compton Russell Ltd., 1976.

———, ed. *Freya Stark Letters*. Vol. 4: *Bridge of the Levant, 1940–43*. Wilton, UK: Michael Russell, 1977.

———, ed. *Freya Stark Letters*. Vol. 5: *New Worlds for Old, 1943–46*. Wilton, UK: Michael Russell, 1978.

———, ed. *Freya Stark Letters*. Vol. 6: *The Broken Road, 1947–52*. Wilton, UK: Michael Russell, 1981.

————, ed. *Freya Stark Letters*. Vol. 7. Wilton, UK: Michael Russell, 1981.

————, ed. *Freya Stark Letters*. Vol. 8. Wilton, UK: Michael Russell, 1981.

Ruthven, Malise. *Traveller Through Time: A Photographic Journey with Freya Stark*. New York: Viking Penguin, 1986.

Stark, Freya. *Alexander's Path: A Travel Memoir by Freya Stark*. Woodstock, NY: Overlook Press, Peter Mayer Publishers, 1988.

————. *The Arab Island: The Middle East, 1939–1943*. New York: Alfred A. Knopf, 1946.

————. *Baghdad Sketches*. London: John Murray, 1946.

————. *Beyond Euphrates: Autobiography, 1928–1933*. London: John Murray, 1951.

————. *The Coast of Incense: Autobiography, 1933–1939*. London: John Murray, 1953.

————. *Dust in the Lion's Paw: Autobiography, 1939–1946*. New York: Harcourt, Brace & World, 1961.

————. *East Is West*. London: John Murray, 1945.

————. *The Freya Stark Story*. New York: Coward-McCann, 1953.

————. *Ionia, a Quest*. New York: Harcourt, Brace & Co., 1954.

————. *The Journey's Echo: Selections from Freya Stark*. London: John Murray, 1963.

————. *Letters from Syria*. London: John Murray, 1942.

————. *The Lycian Shore*. London: John Murray, 1956.

————. *The Minaret of Djam: An Excursion in Afghanistan*. London: John Murray, 1970.

————. *A Peak in Darien*. London: John Murray, 1976.

————. *Perseus in the Wind*. Boston: Beacon Press, 1956.

————. *Riding to the Tigris*. London: John Murray, 1959.

————. *Rome on the Euphrates: The Story of a Frontier*. New York: Harcourt, Brace & World, 1966.

————. *The Southern Gates of Arabia: A Journey in the Hadhramaut*. London: John Murray, 1938.

————. *Traveller's Prelude*. London: John Murray, 1950.

————. *The Valleys of the Assassins and Other Persian Travels*. London: John Murray, 1936.

————. *A Winter in Arabia*. London: John Murray, 1940.

————. *The Zodiac Arch*. London: John Murray, 1968.

INDEX

Page numbers in italics refer to photographs or illustrative material.